# THE MUSTARD SEED

## by
## Cynthia Bradshaw

(Also known as Katy)

**Spiritual Teachings and Development of unusual Gifts of the Spirit**

*With best wishes*

*Cynthia*

**CON-PSY PUBLICATIONS MIDDLESEX**

This Edition 2005

© Cynthia Bradshaw

Spiritual Gifts and Life Lessons

Cynthia Bradshaw
* Upper Crossing Lodge * 83 Heol Gleien *
* Upper Cwmtwrch * Swansea SA9 2UF *
* Phone 01639 831164 *

Published by

CON-PSY PUBLICATIONS
P.O. BOX 14,
GREENFORD,
MIDDLESEX, UB6 0UF.

ISBN 1 898680 38 8

# CONTENTS

In helping individuals locate that which needs healing in themselves, clarity and insight emerges as the individual Psyche puns words and images, enabling each person to become clearer as to their own personal motives and thus be able to take personal responsibility for their own actions and rise to a new level of personal power.

THE CONCEPT being that every energy expelled mentally, emotionally, physically or spiritually comes full circle to the source. We can change ourselves and our responses. "What goes around comes around."

# INTRODUCTION

Every person is Psychic, owing to the Psyche being an aspect of the soul. The Psyche is the part of us that puns words and images symbolically but is nothing to do with being a Medium. All Mediums are Psychic but not all Psychics are Mediums - proven by their lack of contact with a loved one or Guide and drawing on their own intuition and experiences to give readings. A Medium can see, hear and feel Spirit people exactly the same as if they were in the physical body.

A Sensitive is someone who just senses the presence of the spirit world. A Medium not only sees Spirit people who no longer have a material body, either subjectively in their mindís eye or objectively out in the room which is known as Clairvoyance - clear seeing but also picks up impressions psychically as well. A Medium hears spirit people speak either in their mind subjectively, like children often describe as "talk in their mind" or loud and clear objectively as though there was someone standing right beside them on their right side and this is known as Clairaudience - clear hearing. A Medium also feels the presence of invisible spirit people like someone is right next to them the same as if there was a real person in a physical body and senses their presence - this is known as Clairsentience - clear sensing. Not every person is a Medium between the invisible realms and the material world. A true Medium develops every one of these gifts which often takes many years. Once a connection to those in spirit is made, dropped thoughts often occur giving more ideas and information. Most Mediums are born with the gifts and have experiences as a child, which denotes their chemical makeup and choice in this lifetime. No Medium has an easy life because difficult lessons are only given to the best students. The gifts of the Spirit are earned by services given to other people and situations. In fact the more we give - the more we are given to give and the stronger and more enlightening the development.

It is now accepted that radio waves are buzzing through the atmosphere around us invisible to human eyes. Pictures are also beamed in to our living rooms as well as a multitude of telephone messages. This has given credence to the fact that we can also hear "Voices" from Spiritual realms, "See" People who no longer have a physical body and "Feel" their presence. The multiple facets of our innermost being are connected to the whole Universe as well as our own "intuition" our Inner Tutor and our Psyche, which communicates, messages to us in dreams by punning words and images. There are various ways we communicate with both our inner unconscious levels, by using the psyche, consciously with logical reasoning and with our Spiritual facets with other realms.

Many of us have already linked with other people, telepathically as well as with body language, whether unconsciously or deliberately. When communicating within the spiritual realms in the Universal Consciousness, from a finer more aware state of consciousness, directly to the Source of all things, we find a host of many other ways of communication are heightened with access to the Akashic records, Masters and wise beings with true knowledge and information.

Therefore, in order to clarify the differences please remember that each one of us is on a pathway of varying degrees of development and each has an innate knowledge of where they are personally. The following examples from my own experiences may help you to recognise a few details in yourself and those you come in contact with.

In Spiritualism the training and development of Spiritual gifts of Communication with the Spiritual realms is primarily used to prove the survival of loved ones, who have died and shed their physical overcoat, proving that what all religions say, about life everlasting, is true. They demonstrate that man is not just a physical being and that the true purpose of life is a spiritual one. There is no death to the spiritual personality part of us and many prove this daily, when they go to sleep at night and pop out of the body in to the spirit realms where they actually visit loved ones guides and helpers. Sometimes we remember a dream where we saw a loved one younger than when they actually died and spoke with them. Sometimes it is only a memory of something happening that we cannot put our finger on. The guidance we receive either just before going to sleep or just before waking up is either done by our own higher self - the non-judgemental wiser inner tutor - intuition - or by a guide who has chosen to walk this pathway with us and help us to attain that which we chose to do in service to mankind. As we listen, take notes and remember so we learn.

The more advanced Mediums go beyond communicating with those who have recently died and raise their consciousness to much higher and finer vibrations to realms where they communicate with Masters, Light Beings and Angels passing on knowledge and wisdom of the Sages, Seers, Teachers and Prophets from long ago as recorded throughout the ages.

My story began before I knew any of these things and I thought everyone could see, hear and sense Spirit until I realised that many have closed this ultra sensitive side of themselves down usually with an emotional mind block which needs to be cleared in order for a continuing development of these gifts to flow. Others open up quite a bit later in life and are then developed by our loved ones and helpers. Some are born this way and then led astray within their earthly life or to finish a previous debt they owe to someone before opening up to the realms of Spirit. All are on a Spiritual pathway and are aiming for the re-union with the divine their own way and

5

through life's obstacles, exams and tests.

The following excerpts are from my own experiences as I was trained and developed further. Also recorded readings from some well known Mediums guiding and confirming the things I learned as part of the long journey that has happened to me and is still happening as I go with the flow finding myself in the right place at the right time for these unusual happenings. I believe all people experience such events as and when they are ready for soul development.

# CHAPTER 1

## Facing Fear

My earliest recollection was at about two years old when I was in a pram in the sun. My baby brother was so tiny and he was only almost two years younger than me. He had been put in a pram, in the shade, underneath a tree. The feeling I had was of anger at being left in the sun, which caused me to address a tremendous energy at an early age. Learning to use anger in a positive constructive manner seemed part of my life lesson.

As a child, like many others, I had dreams. One recurring dream, which was pretty scary, involved me running along a high wire through the rooms of my Parent's bungalow. At each pole in each room, there were angry Native Americans and nasty looking Africans, pirates and many other people waving tomahawks, knives and hatchets at me. They scrambled up the poles in an effort to knock me off the high wire. I just kept running and when I reached the end of the wire the dream finished. After weeks of running, and recognising being in the same position, I realised I hadn't been caught yet. This caused me to stop in my tracks, whilst still in the dream, and turn round to see what was happening behind me. I had to fathom out why I had still not been caught. I saw the Native people angrily trying to clamber on to the high wire but they were unable to walk the tight rope like I did and fell off - I was safe. Once the fear was faced the dream never returned and I realised an early lesson of facing my fears and looking at them, rather than running away or denying them.

In later years I found people telling me I was talking above their heads and there was a constant 'putting down' effort from people who did not like being put in a position of facing their own weaknesses. I seemed to be a mirror effect - reflecting parts of themselves back to themselves. As people looked at me they saw an aspect of themselves, which they didn't like, and as a result they tried to eliminate me from their world, little realising that if they questioned themselves about which part of them was re-acting this way and asked themselves why, they would be dealing with a problem within themselves and be half way to achieving a tremendous inner spiritual growth. Avoiding the issue within themselves and putting blame outside of themselves seems to be a major problem in the world today.

There is a well-known story about spiritual attainment, where a man was walking a tight rope, when a black bird flew to the side of him. He ducked to avoid the colour of the bird. Subsequently, he lost his footing and fell. The next time he managed to walk the tightrope, a white bird flew at his side and he reached out for it and lost his balance thus falling off again. Falling had never happened to me, as I was always aware of where my feet went. Balancing the Material and the Spiritual is important. There must be a moral in both stories to do with dangers of being knocked off balance from the tests and trials in life, living in the clouds and our thought patterns. Attacks from beneath us could come from unconscious fears or our own reaction to events either side of us, in life situations, which could knock us off balance. Facing these fears causes them to be put in the light of day and then they no longer trouble us.

In another dream I found myself flying behind an old pram whilst running down the field at the back of the house. A few days later I found myself actually running down the field pushing an old pram. Remembering the dream and flying, I tried to get my feet off the ground. For a few seconds I achieved the uplift and flew. This was, I learned later, levitation. I was so excited I told my Mother who was disbelieving and told me not to tell stories; I never talked about these things again. There were many dreams of flying and jumping over the house. It was a wonderful sense of complete freedom, which I seemed to lose once I started school. The memory of flying has remained with me and I know levitation is possible if only we could let go enough and just let it happen.

At eight years old I changed schools and journeyed by train. This meant it was after five at night, which was dark, when we came home. My cousin lived next door, was a year older than me and caught the same train, but often stayed talking to her friends and I walked home alone. We had a long dark drive down to both of our houses. Each time, I reached the end of the drive; I took a deep breath and ran down the dark drive to get home quickly.

One day as I was about to take a deep breath and run when a 'Voice' spoke over my right shoulder:

"What are you running for?"

I looked all around, but there was no one there.

"Something might get me. I answered surprised that I was not afraid.

"What might get you?"

"Well someone might be hiding in the bushes waiting."

"So you are so important that someone is going to wait especially for you?"

"No, but they might be."

"What would happen if they were?"

"Well they might hurt me.

"So really, you want your picture and name in the newspapers for being hurt or something."

"No, I don't."

"Well how about walking and finding out what is there". With my heart pounding like mad, I walked but pretty quickly, looking both left and right. As I reached the safety of home and breathed a huge sigh of relief thinking to myself that I had actually made it, the "Voice" spoke again and almost made me jump: "That wasn't so bad was it?"

"No. But I was still a little frightened.

"See what you can see tomorrow."

Everyday I walked and looked. I had no more fear of the dark, now I could see what was there. Plants glowed in the dark. I wondered about the voice that had spoken and how to get it to come again but I never heard from it until later when I was in my teens. I was flirting with the boys and leading them on when, suddenly the 'Voice' spoke and said: "You have done that before and you know the consequences." I then received picture after picture of incidences of leading boys on and the after effects, which seemed to be of me in various other guises in previous lifetimes. I stopped flirting and didn't do it again as I knew it was not fair to them and I couldn't hurt people.

I thought everyone could hear my visiting "Voice," and that they had the same sort of information given to them too. It was so natural and normal to me. The voice was outside of myself and completely different to the voice of conscience. My conscience seemed to be an inner conflict between what was right and what was selfish or not very nice and was there all of the time, whereas my voice appeared like a long lost friend outside of myself. The 'voice' did not come to order but only at important lesson times and I didn't always listen to it either and then learnt lessons the hard way!

At school I found certain people liked me automatically and they were easy to be with. There was one person who had a crush on me and adored my every move. She used to bring me presents and in the background I noticed a friend of hers who looked at me with daggers drawn. She was jealous of the contact and made it known to me in subtle ways. I didn't want this sort of behaviour from either one of them and thought up ways of how to become a friend to the one who was jealous. I talked about things that interested her and went out of my way to always be on her wavelength without looking for any response from her. This brought about a much deeper relationship and friendship, which lasted a lot longer than the other one. Without realising it I had learnt another tool in my everyday life as well as for the sales business, which was to become a part of my life too.

When I left school, I worked in Scotland, trained in Cambridge, worked in London then spent two years in Switzerland, before coming back to England and working for my Father. I had a boyfriend who was taking his articles to become a solicitor. I really liked him but when he proposed marriage I thought about it and wondered if I could really live with a 9 - 5 man entertaining his friends. Then a major decision came up in my life when I applied to do Nursing and also saw an advertisement for a job in America, which sounded wonderful. I applied, little thinking I would get the job. On the same day that I received acceptance for Nursing I also had a telegram asking me to phone about the job in America. Did I really want to go back to school and take up Nursing or was I ready for an adventure in to the unknown? I decided to go for the adventure to America as a Governess. This meant I couldn't get married and I broke off our relationship saying we would remain friends. I was to begin learning tough lessons all the way through my life, as well as have a lot of joy and fun.

Now, as you prepare to develop your own gifts of the Spirit, go back in time to the unusual occurrences that have happened to you. Highlight the co-incidences where you met like-minded people and started your own search.

The family, I lived with and worked for, were staying in Palm Beach. We were more like sisters and took turns with the four children. I had many dates and experiences plus two more proposals of marriage. With both of these relationships we did not part - we drifted and did our own thing. In looking back I now see that I gave people freedom to get on with their own lives whilst I gained freedom to live my own life and in so doing we never ever fell out or broke up. If we were to meet again it would be exactly as it was when we were together. One did come back in to my life twice before I left America and wrote to me afterwards.

.        In my second position as a Governess, I met a middle-aged lady who looked after newborn babies. To this day I cannot remember how we met. I mixed with people in my age group who also worked with 6 and 8 year olds. Rose was Scottish. She pushed some keys into my hand saying

"Take them and use them when you need to."

"I don't want your keys. I gave the keys back.

"Take them they are to my apartment in New York. Use it when you need to." She pushed the keys back into my hand, with the address I argued but ended up taking her keys.

When I met my daughter's Father, Frank, a year or so later, my "Voice" spoke or rather shouted in my ear "NO"

"Who tells me no." I replied and carried on. I didn't always listen and now I learnt the hard way. Life could have been different if I had listened. We travelled from Coast to Coast and Border to Border. I saw life at it's roughest and met some wonderful people too.

Whilst in Washington D.C., I wanted to cross a six lane road. The lights were red and the cars had stopped but I thought I'd be too late getting to the crossing. I walked between two lanes of cars that had come to a standstill, in order to cross the road. Looking left and right and seeing the cars standing still at the lights I stepped off the curb and went to run across the road. I was instantly knocked back onto the car I was standing next to. The next thing I heard was; "She's dead, she's a goner!" I thought to myself; 'How can I be dead, standing here.' The Ambulance arrived in next to no time. A man's voice said; "Be careful of that leg, don't stand on it."

I looked down and saw blood down my front, which was pouring from my mouth and chin. We arrived at the hospital and I was X-rayed from top to toe. No bones were broken but I screamed in pain as I was manoeuvred on the table for the X-ray photographs. My chin was stitched. I had knocked a front tooth out but the roots remained. The Dentist explained that he couldn't give me anything for the pain whilst he was extracting the roots of my tooth.

"My knee is hurting so much, I cannot feel anything else." I exclaimed. He removed the roots of the tooth and I never felt anything. My body only registered the extreme pain in my knee, which covered all other pain. Our bodies have an inbuilt system to deal with pain. When our endurance level is reached we become unconscious. My leg was agony as I was put in a plaster from my ankle to my thigh. I was then sick with the blood I had swallowed. Once back at the Hotel I couldn't sleep and when I turned over something moved in my knee causing me to scream in pain. Frank came in and yanked my leg until it clicked back into position. I went back to the original Doctor and asked him to cut the plaster off. There are no bones broken and I am in agony." We argued as he refused to cut the plaster off saying; "You are out of my hands if I cut the plaster away."

"So be it, I'll find someone else. I cannot sleep with the pain and I want to know what is wrong with my knee." I explained. He cut the plaster off and I visited another Doctor who said that I needed whirlpool treatment to get the swelling down.

We decided to head for a warmer area and headed down to Miami, Florida. I screamed with the pain of every movement in the car but to no avail. I was exhausted. Once we arrived, I slept like a log. There was a pool at the Hotel and the sun shone. I could swim and exercise in the pool and try to get the swelling down. The plastering of my leg had left it very stiff and swollen. I was hobbling around on crutches.

I decided to see another Doctor and sort out my problem knee. He took a look and said there was no way the swelling would subside until I had had an operation. You have a torn cartilage and some ligament damage, which will need an operation. He diagnosed.

"Go and pack your things up and get to the hospital by 4pm, then I will operate in the morning." He phoned the hospital and arranged for a bed. I went back to the Hotel and packed my bag arriving at the hospital just before 4pm.

The operation was performed in the morning and left me with a big scar. The Surgeon had to fish around for the torn ligaments. I found myself in the recovery room howling and crying for no reason. The nurse in charge tried to console me without success. All my frustrations and inner blocks seemed to be released at this time. What had I been doing to myself to cause my body to react with an accident? Obviously I was not going with the natural flow of life and needed to re-adjust my way of life before something else happened. Within a few minutes of returning to my hospital bed, the surgeon arrived.

Sit on the edge of the bed please."

I did this with my leg stuck out in front of me.

"Bend it," he said as he reached over to help me bend my knee.

"I cannot, it hurts." I exclaimed.

"You can and will! If you don't bend it now you never will." He said as he helped me bend it. The tears were rolling down my face as I bent my knee.

"O.K. I want you to bend it every hour and then hang your handbag on your foot with more and more things in it and lift it up and down. This will strengthen the wasted muscles."

"Will I ever walk on it properly again and be able to sit on my heels?" I questioned.

"If you do as I tell you and you work at it now, before it gets set in position, you will be as good as new. "He laughed, smiling at my concern. When you leave the hospital after a week, I want to see you in my surgery the following Friday."

I was determined not to be a cripple and worked hard lifting weights with my foot and exercised regularly. I was still on crutches but I could swim and bend my knee and exercised it in the water. The Doctor refused to say I was fit to travel unless I could walk into his surgery without my crutches, Frank had taken off for Chicago and wanted me to follow in the other car with the group of people we were now working with. I walked into the Surgery propping my crutches at the door. The Doctor laughed and said; you are determined to go aren't you? I would rather you gave it another week or two before travelling to allow the ligaments to mend." He requested I take care.

What was happening inside me to cause my physical body to react with left leg damage to ligaments and the cartilage? The left side responds to our inner, feminine intuitive side and stress causes us to crumble.

Light stages of stress result in minor accidents, but soft tissue injuries are related to a deeper level of inner stress. The extreme level of stress would result in broken bones and could lead to eventual suicide or death. The right side relates to our extrovert, active, doing masculine side, which, for me, was still all right.

The man, who was to drive us to Chicago, had been drinking and gave us a hair-raising ride nearly missing cars and lorries.

"Let me drive" I exclaimed after we all sucked our breath in again. "It's an automatic and I don't need to use my damaged leg." He changed seats and promptly fell asleep. My leg swelled with the long journey. I ripped my trouser leg open to free the swelling. Eventually we arrived and I was able to lie down and get my leg back to normal. This extended the period of using crutches but eventually I could walk more easily.

Within months, I found myself pregnant. Frank was already married. His wife had gone back to Sweden. I would only be allowed to leave on a marble slab, he had stated. He showed a nasty jealous side when he had been drinking and I was afraid he would hurt someone else or even myself. I tried to leave but didn't have any money or anywhere to go. Maybe things would change after I had the baby.

My daughter was born in San Francisco. I really believed our lives would change once she was born. That was a tough lesson, which I soon learnt. We can only change our response to life and no outside forces would change either one of us. Change is an individual personal responsibility. I was becoming trapped and cried a lot. Frank suggested we got married once his divorce was through. I said that wouldn't change anything, I was just not very happy. I decided to leave and actually left 6 times but as I had nowhere to go, I went back. I knew I would have to plan my escape. We travelled extensively. Then I found I was pregnant again. I just knew I had to get back to England.

Another car accident helped me to make my decision. This time I was driving our new 9-passenger station wagon and as I drew up to some traffic lights behind a row of other cars I was looking in my driving mirror to see someone coming very fast at the back of me. He is not going to stop. I thought to myself as I looked for an escape route. There was a brick wall at my side and traffic flowing non-stop the other side. I braced myself for the inevitable crash. He ran into the back of me. I ran in to the cars in front and about six cars were all jammed together. I couldn't believe he hadn't seen the row of cars. I had plenty of time to brace myself, after looking all around for an escape route and just suffered shock! When I returned to the

Hotel with a damaged car I explained what had happened and instead of asking me if I was all right Frank jumped up and tore outside to look at the car. That did it - the straw that broke the Camel's back. The lack of attention to my pregnancy, caused me to realise how selfish and materialistic this man was.

Within days, I thought things out and suggested it was cheaper to have a baby in England than in the U.S.A. I knew I had to be careful how I phrased my request. Frank eventually agreed to my going back to England, saying that I was to leave Kerri with him in lieu of my coming back. I readily agreed and suggested I could be dropped off in New York at the apartment to which the keys I was given belonged to. There was no way I was going without Kerri but I had gained one step. The following week I teased him about being very restricted with a toddler around him all day, whilst I was away. He, obviously thought about it and was surprised that I hadn't said I was taking her. I knew that in order to take her, he would have to completely let me go. After a while I did say that my parents hadn't seen her and if he liked and wanted freedom of movement I could take her on holiday with me. He eventually agreed. I wonder whether he realised his mistake, as, when we arrived in New York I was just dropped off on the pavement with no help. After using the Elevator and knocking on the door to make sure it was all right for me to stay, finding no one home, I wondered how to manage looking after my daughter and fetch the luggage at the same time. I reluctantly left my daughter alone in the apartment, praying she wouldn't get into mischief, whilst I fetched the entire luggage up. I was on tenterhooks the whole time as it took two journeys.

Once this was accomplished, I sat down and burst out crying at the position I had put myself in. I was alone in a huge city without anyone to call on for help. And the baby was due any day. What would happen if the baby came early? It was already in preparation for the birth, the doctor had told me when I visited a hospital in Fort Lauderdale. The doctor had suggested I booked a place at the hospital there and then.

The door opened and in walked Rose, the lady who had given me the keys.

"I knew you would be here, you need some milk, orange juice and food. I'll just go and do some shopping."

I was stunned. How did she know I was there? She returned with food, juice and milk and then showed me how to operate everything.

"Stay as long as you like and use anything you want." She was an angel in disguise.

"I need to use the phone to phone England and I don't have any money."

14

"Use what you need to and don't worry about the money." She reassured me.

"Stay as long as you need to, I already have a job with a new baby and only stay here in between jobs." With that she left and that was the last time I ever saw her.

As I had no push chair/buggy or means of carrying Kerri I used the shopping trolley to carry her. We must have been a pretty sight as we travelled on the trains to the Embassy. I had to write away for a birth certificate before I sorted our passports and organised the luggage. This took another 2 weeks. The money I had requested from England did not turn up and I worried about the baby arriving. I then decided to phone my former employer who asked why I hadn't told her about my situation earlier. Luckily she was now married to someone in charge of an airline, who could get me a plane ticket. It was arranged for me to collect it at the airport and I could pay her back when the money arrived or when I got back to England. Things began to slot in to place and the flight was a relief from all the hassle and stress.

The air stewardess moved me from a seat in between people to a front seat and provided me with a carrycot for my young toddler and eventually we managed to return to England. I had wired my parents to collect me but there wasn't anyone there when I arrived at 10.30 pm. I could not get any English money as the banks were closed. I needed to phone home but there wasn't anyone around to help. I turned out all the change I had and proceeded to feed the telephone with it. Some came straight out and enough was accepted but there wasn't anyone at my Parents house. Maybe they were on their way. I waited and waited. Then I thought I would phone my Aunt and Uncle who lived next door. "Oh Cynthia are you phoning us from America?" They were excited to hear from me and explained that my Parents were out for the evening and had no idea I was coming home. They agreed to wait up for them and tell them I was waiting at Heathrow. Luckily Kerri slept throughout, as I waited until they arrived at 3.30 am. I was shattered, relieved to be back in England and was very glad to eventually get to bed.

## An Exercise for Fears

In the beginning, each person chose to be born for individual soul progress. In order to overcome their own individual blocks they come with certain traits, gifts of the spirit and previous karma, into the families they chose for their cutting edges. The parents were chosen for the genes that would create the perfect vehicle for the soul in this lifetime.

Have you noticed how the biggest obstacles to progress lie in family matters? This is where many of our lessons are taught by experience, both positively - what we want more of, and negatively - what we want less of. Fear is the biggest obstacle to all soul progress, therefore the biggest training is always in matters of fear."

Fear of the unknown.

Fear of failure.

Fear of being shamed.

Fear of being blamed.

Fear of what another person may do.

And the list is endless. Taking a risk into the unforeseeable future - alone and isolated, is a frightening step for many people. Yet we took that step alone when we decided we needed to polish a few things and learn more. We have forgotten our major purpose and remain a little fearful of the consequences. Becoming childlike again free, full of joy, upliftment and excitement can be transformational. There is an opposite positive pole for every negative aspect, which happens in our lives. It is up to us to look for the opposite of every fear and seek the tools to transform our lives for ourselves. No one can do it for us. We are captain of our own souls and therefore quite able to go within to the stillness of nothing - the connecting link to the source of all things. Real progress involves growing and developing. Changing inside. Fear is the biggest obstacle to progress. Fear is ignorance; a lack of knowledge therefore learning about the things we fear brings knowledge and understanding.

Start with a clean sheet of paper and pen.

Close your eyes and empty your lungs.

Then take a deep breath filling the whole of your chest and abdomen.

Again empty your lungs and squeeze your tummy onto your backbone.

Now breathe in again.

Do this twice more and then allow your breathing to regulate itself.

Imagine a teacher that resides in your heart, is coming to help you.

Think about all the things that are going on in your life at the moment.

Open your eyes and write them all down. Spend a few minutes writing.

Now put a number against each in order of priority.

Start with the one that has been bothering you the most and describe it.

Next - go on to the one that it not quite as important.

Empty your lungs, once again, squeezing the air right out until you feel your tummy pressing towards your backbone and breathe in deeply counting up to five and holding your breath to the count of five. Now release your breath to the count of eight and hold it out for five. Repeat this twice.

The fact that you are now using your lungs to their full capacity will enable the life force energy to flow in to your blood stream and reach all the parts of your body that contain the blocks. This will help you to release these blocks without pain.

Now you are ready to ask your inner tutor *(intuition)* to help you to write a solution to each of the situations you have written down.

Write whatever comes to mind instantly without thinking about the consequences or pausing.

Once you have written everything; that came to mind, down on to the paper, examine it with your logical thinking and decide whether there is an unconscious fear attached to what you have written.

Now write down the worst thing that could possibly happen to you if you were to follow up some of these things.

Empty your lungs and breathe deeply, as you close your eyes and become still.

Now imagine actors preparing to play out the worst scene you could imagine happening, whilst you watch what happens.

Once you have seen the worst - open your eyes and think about how you could direct the actor/actress, that plays yourself, to become a star performer and take the leading role in the scene

Try different ways of playing your own scene and see what happens with the other characters in the play.

One sequence may give you some ideas of how to play the scene in real life without any fear or misgiving.

Close your eyes and ask for help and guidance to do what you decide without fear of any kind. Now write it down and try to follow your heart.

Through my ordinary physical life another test of endurance, stamina and overcoming fears became apparent. After playing in a Badminton Match, I arrived home at about 2 am. To walk Tara, the dog, at this late time never bothered me as the streets were well lit. This time I heard footsteps following me. As I stopped for Tara so the footsteps stopped. Someone was following me. I listened again and the footsteps stopped a second time. The next time Tara stopped, I turned around to see a man coming along the street behind me. I thought about protection from Tara, realising that she would probably hide between my legs! That was no good - it was up to me to take control of the situation. I turned around and walked up to the man: "Excuse me, are you lost?"

"No." He replied; "I know where I'm going."

He quickly crossed the road and headed in another direction. I had taken him by surprise and put him on the spot. I remembered previous situations in America. One man had told me, that I put myself in control of the situation, therefore preventing anyone from taking advantage of my feminine weaknesses.

Another time, I watched as people crossed the road to avoid walking past a group of boys with knuckle-dusters and bikes. I, personally, didn't see why they should have that form of control over the road. Therefore, with my heart pounding in my mouth, I walked slowly up to them and said: "Excuse me lads, could I come through please?" They looked at me with surprise, stood aside open mouthed, as I walked past them, without crossing the road. After that I realised that fear of what might happen was the biggest obstacle and my lessons in life involved using my head to sort out what the other person would do if I carried on without showing fear. I then looked at the worst thing that could possibly happen to me and accepted it. It never happened.

**Another exercise with coins buttons or objects.**

Pick an object, button or coin for each of the people in your life. Place them on the table in front of you as they are in your life at the present moment, including one for yourself.

Now put your feelings in to the marker of yourself, as you move this away from the others and see how you feel about the situation. Then look at the reaction of the other markers and see how they would move after you have moved. Does this feel better or worse? Practice moves until you feel comfortable with the changes then you are ready to start moving in real life according to these initial changes. We cannot change another person but we can act according to our higher purpose and plan and feel comfortable with our own choices.

'Were a man's sorrows and disquietude's summed up at the end of his life, it would generally be found that he had suffered more from the apprehension of evil than from the evils which had befallen him.' Addison

# CHAPTER 2

## A PREMONITION

Arriving in England expecting a baby meant I would have the baby at my Parent's home with a mid wife. The baby arrived quickly, easily and early but what a relief, I had made it back to England. The same night I had a dream. In the dream my baby died in a cot at the side of my bed. The dream was detailed and disturbing. I woke up and jumped out of bed running across the room to where the baby slept. Whew, she's breathing, it was only a dream. I must have eaten something. I talked about the dream and then it completely left my memory bank.

Over the coming months I enjoyed the children and watched my baby, realising how intelligent she seemed to be, for one so tiny. She would lie on her tummy and raise her head over the side of the pram, laughing at her sister. I could just imagine pince nez on the end of her nose. She reminded me of a schoolteacher.

Five and a half months later, she hadn't been very hungry and was awake when I went to bed. I picked her up and put her in my bed on the pillow in front of me. She stroked my hair and her mind spoke to my mind. I'll see you again soon."

"Of course you will, in the morning." I mentally replied, thinking, "You are so beautiful." I wanted to keep her in bed with me but a 'voice' said: "You will never forgive yourself if you do."

I then imagined myself rolling over on to the baby and reluctantly put her back in her cot at the side of my bed.

In the morning my lively girl jumped on my bed and looked at the baby. She looked as though she was still sound asleep. Shush, you'll wake her up." I admonished, seeing how peaceful she was. I looked at my watch, realising it was time to get the pair of them up and dressed. I picked the baby up and found a blue mark on her cheek where she had lain on her hand. She was cold. She was dead. I carefully put her back in her cot and went down to the kitchen.

"Where is the baby?" My Mother questioned.

"She's dead." I replied.

My Mother screamed and ran to the bedroom to fetch the baby. She tried mouth-to-mouth resuscitation.

"It's no good, she's dead" I emphasised.

"Phone the Doctor."

I remained calm and phoned the Doctor, explaining what had happened. He arrived very quickly, confirming her death and explaining that she would have to be taken away for a post mortem.

I suddenly remembered that I had been warned. The dream came back. Now why hadn't I remembered the dream when I was moved back into my old bedroom and put the cot at the side of my bed? What could possibly have been the reason for such a short life?

In my reasoning I felt I had gone off track when I met my daughter's Father. My "Voice" had said "No" loud and clearly. I had ignored the emphasis and gone ahead, making quite a mess of my life, with accidents. Boy, was I learning my lessons the hard way. Surely there was an easier way than this. But then I seemed to have an awful lot of guidance and helpers along the way. There was much more to life than met the eye. The strange co-incidence of Rose and the keys to her apartment seemed to have been in advance of what I was going to do. I had not even met Frank at that stage. The Powers that be had tremendous fore knowledge and there must be another more spiritual purpose to my life for such protection and guidance. Could it be possible for this soul that took a baby's body, to have chosen a brief life in order to get me away from America without leaving dead on a marble slab? This seemed to make sense, especially when I had a dream the day she was born; telling me what was going to happen so specifically - a warning. Of course, I could not remember the dream, otherwise I would have changed the events and that was not intended. I was only to be prepared and aware of what was going on - not to change the end result.

It was three days later when I howled and howled at the loss, not only of my baby but all the previous events. My Father sat near by and was obviously concerned; "Cynthia don't". I knew it had to come out and I couldn't stop until the depths had been reached and cleared.

The resulting enquiry gave a result of 'death by misadventure.' She had been well cared for. I became interested in other cot deaths and felt for those parents especially Val Doonican. I realised that there were multiple causes and effects involved for both the individual souls and the Parents. Some of these children could have shortened a previous life, as in taking their own life in a previous one. This would mean coming back to finish their time span in this life as a baby. Others were acting out a service as a difficult lesson to Parent's who had difficulty learning compassion for other people. There were many reasons and many stories but each parent 'knew' their own story deep inside themselves where the truth is strongly embedded. Denial of the truth about us causes many other problems to be effected until the truth is recognised and dealt with.

The funeral was sad and I was distraught. I could not even scatter soil on the coffin. Afterwards I tried to talk to the Rector about the dream and events. He physically took 3 steps backwards and I realised he knew nothing of the spiritual truths and divine interventions. He was only doing a job he had learned at College and was now employed to do. How could a spiritual leader and a calling by the Divine be a job learned at a Theosophical College? I needed to find out more about premonitions and where the information came from. My search for the truth of life had begun.

This was the beginning of my spiritual growth and ascension from the 3rd dimension of materialism to the 4th dimension of 'going with the flow.' I could so easily have completely broken down but had somehow broken through. I lived for Kerri. I had let go of material possessions, people and howled away everything. I was completely empty and ready to be filled with new energies and enlightenment.

The following years I lived for my daughter re building my life back brick by brick. I went to work at Fenwick's in Leicester whilst my mother had Kerri all day but I was not happy about leaving Kerri and decided to get a live in job where she could be with me all the time. I advertised myself and had over 150 letters in reply. The majority would provide living conditions but no money for the work. I needed a certain life style with some money, a car to drive and decided I needed to word my advert to this effect but needed more time to think it out. A couple of weeks after my advertisement came out, I received a letter from a Dentist offering exactly what I had set myself. This seemed a co-incidence and I replied, went for an interview and got the job. From then on I worked as a Cook, Housekeeper looking after other people's children where Kerri had other siblings to play with and be a part of a greater family. All my energies were used in creating a happy atmosphere, in various households, including a Dentist, a Pilot, a Teacher, a Lord and a Pop Star. At one of my positions as a Housekeeper with older children, I received another proposal and we lost touch when I moved.

The more I did for others the less painful my own wounds became. I had sort of shut down emotionally. Doing for others was like a healing balm to my wounds, as I shared the happiness and security I gave to everyone else. In doing for other people what I would have appreciated other people doing for me, I thoroughly enjoyed the challenges life brought. My attention was taken up thinking of what to do and where to go, which the busy schedule running and organising a busy home for other people normally brings. I had no thoughts for myself and, before I knew it, all the pain of my previous experiences had been worked through. Time heals, but normal everyday living for another person helps the process and gives a new purpose and direction to life.

My moral values and issues of truth were not the same as every one else's and I refused to be squashed or controlled. A few jobs lasted a year each. Every year I seemed to be moving my home with changing live in jobs. My emotions were being tested to the hilt. I cried every time I left the children I had been working with. I cried for them and with them over the injustices of life.

At the same time arguments with my Mother seemed to also be a form of control and a power struggle. One weekend my 'voice' suggested I bit my tongue and allowed my Mother free reign, without my retaliating in any way. This was going to be very difficult I argued. I arrived and my mother started on about my life and how I should bring Kerri up, whilst I held my tongue. My Mother then accused me of not listening. "I heard every word." I replied calmly. Again and again I was being drawn to retaliate. What did she get from me when I had previously retaliated? Negative energy? I bit my tongue time and time again. In fact my tongue became quite sore from holding on to my peaceful calmness and not allowing one word to disturb me.

As I drove away I was overjoyed at succeeding in a very difficult situation and felt a sense of achievement. I had gone two steps up the ladder of progress. After that it became much easier in every area of my life and no one could disturb me, as I remained in my Centre of peace. I felt that I had accomplished a major break through. I then only gave positive responses and energies affirming what I enjoyed about people although a part of me was not happy with a lack of the very best in people remaining hidden and the truth of the matter being suppressed by some form of control. I understood why the Angel of Truth was the one that no one liked. Everyone knew the truth but did not like other people to know it - hence their control mechanisms.

In the following jobs I was to remain much longer. I worked for a Lord for three years, receiving yet another proposal of marriage whilst going out with a friend who visited regularly and then I worked for a Pop star before moving on again to a tied Elizabethan cottage.

At 33 years old I was still searching for the truth of life. I had spoken to many so-called Spiritual Leaders in many faiths but they had no enlightenment to offer me. I was now in a position where everything I did was not right for my Employer. However hard I tried I was wrong. Eventually her husband told me he didn't know what was wrong as I was working correctly and satisfactorily. He sent his wife on a cruise. At this time I received a knock on the door and made friends with a local Mother of two children called Pat. She explained that the local Spiritualist Church had helped her, in times of need and through her divorce. Maybe the people there could help me. Was this person moved by the Powers that be to line me up again? I decided I had nothing to lose by exploring her suggestion. To keep the Circles of Light moving, each Light worker commits to bring in one new member while in the 4th dimension of flow was I being brought in to become a 'giver.'

We went to an afternoon service in Windsor together. Where the Medium sort of pounced on me as the first person she spoke to in the Clairvoyant part of the service. Who had told her that I was there?

"They are telling me you are going through a very difficult time and they are saying they are taking you away from all of this and putting you somewhere else."

This would be something new. Who were they? I had always done everything myself so allowing someone else to do it for me would be a new experience.

My Employer returned and was even worse than before. We eventually agreed I would leave. I rented a bed-sit and decided to try out what the Medium said and let "Them" do it for me. This would be a new experience because I always believed that we had to make the first move to help ourselves. Nothing happened so where were 'they?' I returned to another Church and the Medium again came to me saying: "I have a Grandfather figure here rolling up his sleeves about to do a job of work, and he's looking at you and saying 'What about you my girl?" This hit home and I blushed. I always knew I would have to do it myself and no one was going to do it for me. I wondered why the first Medium had stated such an obvious mistake the first time and wondered about her training and development. I received what I called inspiration but never had any actual physical help - just guidance. I proceeded to search for a position in the area where I had lived before, for several years, in order that I could get on a council list and eventually not have to change my daughter's school every time I changed jobs.

My search for another job was successful and enabled me to move back into the area I had lived in before. My daughter went to the local school again. We lived in a tied cottage joined to the main house. I bought a tape recorder to test and try the Mediums. I found some were good but others were rubbish and I wondered why. It was lovely when Spirit moved the person choosing the hymns and the separate person who gave a reading, to the same point that the Medium reached and tied in with their Address. I thought that part was of more proof than some of the Clairvoyance, which did not have quite the same feeling. Many were psychics and had no contact with the Spirit world. They seemed to just reach out in to someone's energy field and talk about their health or feelings.

Regular visits to various Churches, where I met some lovely

people, became a Sunday ritual. A nurse friend, I had introduced to the Church, asked me to go with her to a demonstration of Healing by Harry Edwards, who was opening a Sanctuary in Amersham. This proved to be the most moving experience to date as well as my opportunity to experience his healing, when he asked if anyone was deaf in one ear. I was aware of the Power of Spiritual love entering the hall when Harry Edwards entered and this caused many to weep with joy. The amazing energy field of love really interested me in how he had developed as this was, by far, more spiritual than any of the "messages" in the Churches. I watched as Harry healed rheumatoid arthritis. This was amazing because arthritis is like concrete. He moved each joint, which seemed to melt under his fingers and became flexible without any pain. I watched the lady afterwards as she spent the rest of the time wiggling her fingers in disbelief. Another, in a spinal jacket, knelt on the floor unable to move through the crowds back to her seat. At the end someone asked her if her knees were sore.

"But I haven't been able to kneel since I was 12 and I did it without thinking!" She exclaimed.

Harry was a normal natural comfortable person with a presence of peace and love, which filled the room. As he gave me Healing he explained that dead nerves could not be repaired but good music would encourage my ear to work. How did he know the Doctors had said the nerve was dead in my ear and there was nothing they could do. *(Years later, when I retired, I asked to be tested for hearing in that ear. Yes, there was hearing although very low and a hearing aid sounded like something from out of space.)* I was on cloud nine for two weeks after the healing and felt that Harry Edwards had triggered something else that was much more spiritual, within me.

A Medium in an upstairs church room, in Windsor, said: "Although it is very nice to hear from loved ones and know about them, that is not the reason you have come in to this movement. You will be moved some distance away and the work will formulate itself. It is for the younger people of today, who need to know of these things - to learn of these truths."

He was more in tune with the reason I was interested in this work. I wondered about the move. But three years were to go by before I moved again.

# CHAPTER 3

## MEDIUMSHIP DEVELOPMENT

For five years I explored and tested Mediumship in several Churches, read books and learned a lot. I taped all the messages and tore them apart, finding very few gems from the majority of Mediums. There was definitely something in some of it. I enjoyed the Address and Teachings as well as being privileged to be given books to read by the president of the Slough Church. When names were given to me I often had to ask in the family. My father walked out and slammed the door. Typical of anyone who is frightened of the unknown? Mary and Martha were mentioned several times. I knew of great Aunt Mary but had never heard of a Martha. I asked my Mother if she knew who it could be.

"That was Auntie Patty, why don't you leave those dead people alone?"

"Me leave them alone! I don't even know who they are. They are bothering me. That is why I am asking you. How was I to know that Martha meant Auntie Patty?" I quickly retorted.

Another Medium told me quite a few personal facts then said Spirit wanted me to get hold of a book "Way of Life" by Arthur Findlay as this was my way of life. No one had a copy. It was several years later when I actually found a copy.

After my Parents, brothers and sister tried to stop me from finding out more, another Medium came to me one Sunday and said:

"People around you have been trying to tempt you out of it, not out of spiritualism itself but out of your beliefs. You've got that glow around you because you're good and you throw goodness out. You attract goodness to yourself and evil cannot penetrate. Because of this, it gets to the people around you, who are not as high as you and that is the way they get through to you. Not with deeds with words. Words can hurt more. Your life has been very difficult like most people here tonight. You are in the well and they are still trying to knock you back down and that is what your hardest test will be, is to keep forgiving. If you keep forgiving them, they will soon vanish completely and that is why they are doing it."

This seemed similar to my recurring dream as a child where the nasty people were trying to knock me off the high wire. I was obviously above most people's heads. What a tough life I had taken on. I only hope it is worth it because forgiving and forgiving is so very hard to do, but this was obviously part of my pathway! It was certainly true that 'something got into people around me' to have a go at destroying my spirit. I wondered if they ever thought about it themselves. Some do acknowledge they have been unreasonable and say; "I just don't know what got in to me."

Many Mediums emphasised that I should sit in a developing circle. There were circles around but most were very secretive. I knew that the day I committed myself to a circle, I would dedicate my life to 'God' or 'Spirit' and never miss. I was not prepared to do that, yet as I enjoyed a very full life, including my Badminton. I was playing for two clubs, several matches and league games, involving quite a few nights a week and I was working full time to provide a roof over our heads. I thrashed out all my frustrations on the shuttlecock. I was also an achiever and loved the game. I stuck to going to different churches on Sundays, reading books and marking time.

Eventually another test of endurance, stamina and going with the flow of my inner truth resulted in being evicted from the tied cottage where I had lived for three years and gaining a Council flat. I was moved some distance away. The first message I received, at the new local church, related to moving house. I agreed and said that I had just moved. She emphasised another move yet to come.

When I moved, I joined a different local Badminton Club and dropped one of the other Clubs. A conflict happened one Saturday when I received a phone call about my not being at the venue to play in a Badminton match, for which I had not been asked to play but a misunderstanding caused an expectation for me to be there this very minute. When I was told to get there immediately or did I really want to be a member of the Club, I resigned as of that moment.

As co-incidences go, the next day was Sunday and I went to church. The President announced there was an Open Circle on the Tuesday, which I now had free. I joined the open Circle, committing my life to God or the Divine Spirit for this work. In the very first session I 'saw' a stained glass Church window and 'heard' music playing. I dismissed this because we were sitting in a Church. As every one else gave off what they got and I heard a man stating that he had got exactly the same as I had, I realised that this was very clever and that there was another source working with me, that had given both myself and him exactly the same information slightly differently. I became quite upset when the Circle closed two weeks later. After all, it had taken me 5 years to commit myself and the President just closed the Circle down willy nilly, without a thought to any of the Church members who benefited from these sessions. Where was the Spirituality? I was about to learn that not all people in the movement were Spiritual.

Eventually Sylvia a friend, I had made in that Circle, found another home circle. We both went to meet the Leader. When she opened her door, I felt very disheartened as I picked up that she only wanted contact with her dead daughter and I was not interested in that at all, but as there was nothing else on offer and I had committed myself to learning what I could therefore we both joined. I was about to learn all the things not to have in a Circle!" The Circle was started by two highly acclaimed Mediums. There were two dogs in the house, which were very distracting but I managed to calm them down each week and often sat with both of them on my knees. It was here I had met another lovely lady called Noreen, who had trained as a healer in Twickenham under Jesse Nason, a famous Medium.

Then, during my first session of meditation, I clearly saw a nest of snakes and was impressed to put my hand in amongst the snakes. Who in their right mind wanted to put their hand in the middle of a nest of snakes? I felt myself recoil and pull back. What did it mean?

As I recoiled at the sight of the snakes, I felt the most wonderful loving, presence, come at the back of me behind my right shoulder, just as I resisted putting my hand in the nest of snakes. "Oh, if you are there I can do anything!" I mentally said, feeling that this was Jesus emanating the most wonderful strength and love to empower me to put my hand in the middle of the nest of snakes. I felt it had something to do with healing. The picture went away.

Who was this presence? Was it Jesus? Why had he come? What did I know about snakes? It was something to do with Healing, as the symbol of the medical profession was a staff with two snakes entwined around it. Putting my hand in the nest obviously meant I was to be instrumental with healing. The presence, at my back, was a wonderful support, just like the "Voice" I loved and was learning from. I was aware that I was already being guided, owing to the co-incidences around my coming into Spiritualism and the links I was making.

The circle was closed after 18 months when Sylvia did some peculiar actions, in a so-called Trance state, which caused quite a disruption. The two Mediums who had started us were called back and disbanded the Circle. Sylvia had spoken of some nasty experiences at home. Then every time I phoned her she said I didn't want to speak to her and brought this man voice on the phone, which I certainly didn't like or think much of. I was learning what I didn't like and the lack of commitment to the Divine, from other people. Also the sort of peculiar actions, which caused negativity and attracted the negative forces. I stopped all contact with her when I heard how she had caused someone agony when she said she was giving them healing. I suppose this was all part of my training too, as there are dangers involved which I needed to know about. Noreen, who was already a trained healer with some years experience behind her, was the only one I related to. She was the only one I was interested in. I asked her if she would be willing to open her home for us to sit quietly.

"But I cannot lead a circle."

"Of course you can, you have more knowledge and experience than this circle."

Having dealt with my own responses to control situations and the way people attract lower forces to themselves by enforcing their will over the divine order of 'Flow', I began to realise the saying; 'Like attracts like' and send healing thoughts out to those entrapped in a misuse of energy. Was this part of my role of putting my hand in amongst snakes? If so, these were the small ones.

A new housing development was being built nearby and as the houses went up I walked around and decided to apply for one of these as an application for an exchange had fallen through. With walking Tara the dog and having no garden, life was restrained. It would be much easier to have a garden. After three attempts I was offered a house and moved again.

Eventually Noreen agreed to invite friends of hers to see if any would like to join her Circle. When I turned up and looked around the room, I thought to myself that if any of those came, I could not join. Not one was of the calibre I was looking for. It was out of my hands, I let go and was quite surprised when none of those joined! Instead a friend of Noreen's, Noreen and I started a lovely Circle. We three went to London and visited Coral Polge in the SAGB in Belgrave Square. Coral drew a picture of my baby grown up in Spirit. As she drew the hair I shuddered as it had exactly the same kink as her father's and although I said I couldn't prove it, Coral said there must be a photo of her as a baby where her ear had a mark on it like the one she had drawn. I did find one later on and there is a sort of family likeness.

With Noreen, Coral asked for the lady with a red cardigan and as we looked around the room for this lady, I noted that no one was wearing a red cardigan. Noreen then picked up her shopping bag and pulled out a red cardigan saying: "Oh, it's me." That was clever proving that spirit people were aware of more than meets the eye. Coral drew her mother and Noreen commented on never seeing her hair done that way before. At a later date her mother spoke to her in trance and said that she could now do her hair anyway she wanted!

Every Sunday I collected Noreen and took her to Church. We met new people and chatted after church in Noreen's home. Which relaxed everyone and we became good friends. One by one they were invited to join the Circle. We sat together week after week with humour, lovely meditations and we all became better in our daily life situations. Some lasted a few months and some only one or two visits but eventually we had a good group who seemed more reliable.

At Church one evening Noreen was told that there was Direct Voice in her Circle. Noreen thought Direct Voice was a trance voice and thought it might be to do with Gill the one showing signs of trance and took no notice.

On the Circle evening I arrived early in order to be relaxed and at ease. Noreen would open with a prayer. We then sent out thoughts of healing to the people we knew, who were ill. We would then sit in silent meditation. Noreen also meditated then came back to watch. She brought us back and asked each to talk about what they received; starting on her left and going around the room. We then concentrated on a different person each week, again clockwise round the circle. I enjoyed the energy we created from the Meditation but was only interested in encouraging everyone else and pouring out this lovely power to help others. Nothing much came out of the concentration except a feeling, to me, that the ego was being given full play and people began to feel they were important. I would never be a Medium giving messages and found that part pretty boring and lifeless except for the amount of power that poured out of me supporting the others. I also felt that people tried to do it and give something to each member in the room, rather than allow it to come naturally.

Every week I went to the circle. I would race home from work and jump into a bath, to clean away the outside world. Many times I fell asleep in the bath for about 10 minutes. This seemed to be my preparation before going. One day I was at a business meeting and was held up afterwards to sort some business out. I mentally said; "If I am meant to be there tonight, please turn every traffic light to green and let me speed without getting caught and I will be there."

Every light turned green and I drove as fast as I could, to get there on time. I made it to the minute and sat down with a sigh. "Phew, I made it." No one knew the test of my commitment this day and the sense of achievement at arriving on time against all the obstacles that this experience gave me.

It would have been so much easier to phone and say I couldn't make it. I was always surprised at the lack of commitment from other people but that was their business. The slightest obstacle or family matter caused them to cancel.

The lovely feeling of power and energy replenished and balanced me. I found the more I gave to everyone else, the more I was given to give away and spiralled in to lovely states of being. I would never be a medium as I didn't do the instant pictures and 'get' things. In fact, my technicolour pictures only came in meditation, at important times, such as at the same time Noreen invited Janet, Bob's Fiancée to join us. That same night I had a clear picture, whilst in meditation, of her walking across the room and taking him away. I didn't like to say this to everyone in the room, so waited until I got home and phoned Noreen. We carried on year after year.

Noreen said I was to give what I got in the circle and that what I did get wouldn't happen anyway. I just knew it would and it did. There was another time, some years later when I was shown a picture of Noreen ill in bed with a stack of white pillows behind her and white sheets. I knew this was a hospital condition and that she was ill. How do I give this off?" I mentally questioned. "Just describe the picture". Came the reply. I didn't want to frighten Noreen and very tentatively described the picture.

"Oh you have described my bed, you must come and see it after we have finished. Even the stack of pillows, they are all white." She showed me her bedroom and it was similar but I knew what I had been given was a warning. I was happy she had taken the description and not asked for more.

The two lovers were getting married and asked Noreen for the reception to be held in her home. She agreed and I warned her about them. There was an uncomfortable feeling, as none of the circle members had been invited. Noreen mentioned this fact to them both, which resulted in a phone call on the evening the day before the wedding. I needed time to book a day off and was therefore unable to go. It was at a later date that Noreen mentioned that they wanted to wash her walls down and disinfect her home, which was already very clean and newly decorated! I was shocked but I 'knew' and had tried to warn her. The result taught me that I was often aware of more than meets the eye and could warn people but I was to accept that free will choices remain with the individual. 'You can lead a horse to water but cannot make it drink.'

Every month Noreen visited a trance medium called Muriel in Twickenham and one day she visited our Circle. This I taped:-

'I want to say this gives me great pleasure returning - and, well I know I am speaking to a younger generation - with this younger generation they remember not the first world war and the second. But One can always read the books and One can always read; to get that knowledge - but I know there is one here that I too, can say - understands the 1914 war and I am speaking to the elderly gentleman and I want to say; I want you to know that at the ending of my life I was shot by the Germans and I thought about my boys - but passing through the higher life I realised I could still continue my work, so I want you each to know that in such a circle as this, the love is here, the power is here. I, too, will bring the lads who are fighting at the present day in another country. I can bring them through and they touch this path - to lift them into the light - so this is a thought my friends - never feel you are just sitting in a circle - just developing your gifts - but it is an extension of love to the world for peace to know that you are creating the love of God - the power of God. Many nurses, many Doctors and the ones less fortunate than you - never feel it is wasted time but know that - so God bless you. May we ask the blessing on each one that is here to guide them - that each one will be a channel - to know Thy will be done on earth, as it is in heaven - in humbleness and love we leave each one of you right now - Amen.

A few months later, in the January, Noreen became ill with a nosebleed, which would not stop. She went to hospital and her nose was packed for a week. She was told that she was lucky to have had a nosebleed as this released the pressure, which could have caused a stroke. On the Friday I finished work early and decided to visit her. I phoned a friend Gill who was also in the Circle, and asked if she would like to join me. We arrived to find Noreen sitting on her bed, in her overcoat, with her suitcase packed. She greeted us with; "I have ordered a cab and I am going home." What a co-incidence arriving at that time.

"That must be why we are here. I'll drive you home and we can help you." I stated as I took her suitcase and asked the nurse to cancel the cab. It was a cold day. We were able to help with the heating and buy in some food as well as be there to talk and welcome her home. It is always sad to come out of hospital to an empty house when you live alone. Was this a co-incidence or some form of guidance that enabled me to finish work early and get to the hospital in order to bring her home? Of course there is no such thing as a co-incidence only a right time and right places when going with the flow of life.

During the following months I became aware that Noreen's health was not too good. My realisation caused me to write to Mediums and invite them to see Noreen at home when she couldn't go out far. My 'Voice' said I needed the best teachers. The Trance Medium, Muriel, who Noreen saw regularly, every month, had been cancelled, owing to her health, and she missed her visits. I suggested I brought her down, from Twickenham to see Noreen at home. I also suggested I took a week off for her benefit and we could go away.

"I'm not flying." Noreen retorted.

"There are many places in England where we don't need to fly." We agreed and I booked a week off.

The circle continued but I couldn't meditate anymore. I found I couldn't close my eyes but was impressed to watch what was going on and wasn't happy with the ones on either side of me. There was a selfish need to show off and I didn't consider that to be necessary or part of development. I just enjoyed being part of the flow of power and always felt uplifted and energised from sitting. I 'saw' colours around people as they spoke and instantly 'knew' what they were going to say and when a spirit person was with them.

Noreen said she had had her heart tied up with string when she was 38 years old, owing to having rheumatic fever as a child. This meant she had a check up every year. She had retired at 60 years old and asked God for five years retirement. She seemed worried about another operation and said she didn't want to have 'the knife' again.

In the summer she was rushed into hospital and I began to wonder about the week I had booked for her benefit. Oh well I could do some decorating or something. Then during a visit, whilst she was still in hospital, two weeks later, just before the week I was taking off, she commented. "They're letting me out on Tuesday."

"You are not fit to be at home on your own. What are they doing for you?"

"I can have meals on wheels and a Home help." She answered.

Without thinking I just said; "I'm moving in. It is our week that I booked for us."

"Oh would you?" She enquired smiling with relief.

"Yes, I booked the week for your benefit." I explained.

I picked her up at the hospital and moved in for the week. I arranged for my daughter to have a friend stay and told her I would be home every day to walk the dog. Whilst I walked the dog I received lines of hymns in my mind that seemed to be telling me things and giving me advice.

When staying at Noreen's house we stayed up late discussing all manner of spiritual things. Noreen always fell asleep in her armchair before ever going to bed. One night as I lay dozing on the sofa and Noreen slept in her chair; the whole room began to fill with gold. It was absolutely out of this world. This caused me to wonder whom it was that could come in to the room and emanate pure gold. This must be a beautiful soul similar to the presence of Jesus at my back in the previous Circle. Tears began to flow as the feeling from the presence touched my soul. What a shame Noreen was asleep and couldn't experience it too.

Kerri had a friend staying and was quite happy to have some space. Noreen fell down at the Fridge and began to cough blood day and night. This worried me as I stood at the back of her with my hands on her back and shoulders, at the basin, rubbing her back, as my hands became quite hot, in an effort to calm and ease her fears. I got very little sleep whilst this was going on.

"Ooh, if it wasn't for your hot hands I would be a goner. They are better than a hot water bottle." She commented. My hands began to itch to help whenever I could and Noreen was very receptive to the heat that flowed.

A local medium phoned me to tell me Noreen would die in a pool of blood.

"Not if I can help it." I replied. I then heard that a sitter's wife had been told the same thing from the same medium, but instead of allaying her fears, she told Noreen the same thing and when I arrived, Noreen was extremely upset. I stormed into the Church at the weekend to have this out with the medium concerned. I was disgusted at this behaviour and could see no point in telling people such nasty worrying things. Especially as Noreen did not want people clearing up such a mess when she died.

Where was the personal moral responsibility to 'Being of Service' and helping people rather than causing more stress and worry by saying such things. Noreen did not die in a pool of blood and the worry she had of leaving such a mess, really had worried her and did not help her health in any way. I personally believe in the Powers that be and prayer being beneficial. Whilst I was there, Noreen stopped coughing up blood and never did again. I was able to persuade her to contact her sister Margery in Ireland for help, especially as I was due back at work on the following Monday. Margery had already booked a trip to England to visit her other sister. I went back to work feeling a little happier.

I had a letter from Coral Polge booking a date in January. Noreen said that would be too late but I said I would keep it anyway for the others. I knew it would be too late for Noreen, but also knew I could easily change the venue for the other members of our circle.

Before too long Noreen was back in hospital but her sister was now in England. She was coming to help and moved in. I was able to visit and stay at weekends, as Kerri had a friend living at our house to keep her company.

Noreen gradually became weaker and although she still wanted to write some letters, she didn't write them although Margery and I had suggested that either one of us could write the letters for her or she could sign them. She was adamant that she could do it. She never did write these letters.

I began to take her washing home with me, rather than disturb her with her own washing machine. One day I found she had left a brooch on her favourite red dress. I decided that if I held her brooch at night, it would be a good contact for sending healing. From then on I went to bed with the brooch in my hand and woke up with it still in my hand.

After a request, from Noreen, for me to stay the night and the problem I had about feeling that her sister didn't want me there; I agreed to come later in the evening, after my Badminton. I arrived and heard Noreen calling for me but there was no room for me whilst a neighbour and her sister were helping to put her to bed. I went in after she had been put to bed. I had promised her she need never go back to hospital as we could manage at home. Now I suggested her bed was moved into the living room, owing to her lack of movement around the house. We all agreed to think about it. I went to bed upstairs and was woken up in the night hearing a voice I listened and realised Noreen was talking to herself. I went to her room and found her on the floor whispering; "Please help me." There was a strong smell, which I recognised as fear and of death.

It was the first time that I had smelt such fear. She was terrified. She had fallen out of bed. I helped her back to bed. She kicked all the clothes off. Eventually she became calm and I returned to bed. I couldn't sleep as I heard her muttering and moving about. I decided to take my quilt and pillow to sleep in her room. I didn't get much sleep. Then, when straightening her pillows for the third time, I accidentally knocked and rang the bell we had erected on a tea towel for her to ring if she needed help. This woke her sister who came running in saying; "what's going on here." I explained that she had fallen out of bed and then suggested that as she was now up maybe I could have a few hours sleep. I went back to bed to sleep.

In the morning when I woke, I dressed, made a cup of coffee and joined Noreen in the Lounge where she gave me a very wet kiss on the cheek saying "Thank you for what you did last night. You will stay today won't you?" I replied, after seeing Margery's glance of disapproval, saying; "I will take the washing home and come back later on."

"We don't need you, our nephew is coming." Margery retaliated.

"But he cannot help dress and undress her, I can come back to help." I emphasised but an insistent; "We don't need you" followed me home.

At noon I received a phone call from Margery saying that Noreen had been taken back into hospital. I was angry; "But I promised her she would never go back because we could manage." Noreen had categorically stated that she never wanted to go back to hospital. I then calmed down and asked if it would be all right for me to visit her, agreeing with Margery to let her and the nephew visit first and I would go at a later time when the family wouldn't be there. This would mean I could talk to her alone. We agreed a time after the family had been in to visit. Therefore, when I arrived at the hospital just as all the family were arriving, I wondered what was going on. It was blatantly obvious that they did not wish for me to see Noreen alone. What had happened that morning? What had they told Noreen? The same thing happened the next day when I tried to arrange a time that suited the family, so I phoned the friend who was taking Margery to the hospital on the Monday and asked what time she was going and explained what was going on.

"After six, because I'm working." She replied.

"All right, I will go at a different time." I told her, determined that no one could stop a private visit on my own.

That day whilst I was working, I was driving along the road, with a conversation about Noreen, going through my mind. When, as I pulled up at traffic lights, the conversation stopped in mid sentence and I couldn't finish the sentence. "How come I cannot think of the end of the sentence? It's not me thinking, I am being inspired." I thought to myself as I drove around the corner. Suddenly the sentence was completed from where it left off and I paid more attention to my thoughts. I must tell Noreen these things. I then realised that I was getting dropped thoughts from a Spirit source. I finished work early and amazed myself at how quickly I had done so much. I drove home to change and phoned to ask Gill if she would like to go to the hospital with me.

We arrived and there was no one there, but us, this time. Noreen turned away from me and wouldn't take my hand. Was she remembering my promise? I stood up and leaned over her as I said everything I had received that morning. She then turned to me and reached for my hand saying: "You are nice" with a look that said it all. We held hands either side of her and I realised all the panic and fear was being released as we were helping her, with the power of healing, to pass peacefully. I was pleased she was happy even though a niggle at the back of my mind puzzled over what Margery had said for Noreen to turn her face away from me; as well as never allowing me time alone with her over the weekend, in spite of my trying to fit in with the family. Never mind all was well now and she seemed strangely very happy, peaceful and sleepy as we said goodbye.

In the middle of that night I felt a hand going through my hand twice, trying to take the brooch. I became more alert and aware realising it was Noreen. "But you cannot take it where you are going." I mentally responded as I let go of the brooch.

"Give it to Margery". She replied. I agreed and I dropped off to sleep again. At about 4 am I awoke remembering that Noreen had died and come to me. She had tried to take the Brooch. It wasn't in my hand. I had let go of it, so where was it now. I couldn't feel it or see it. Where was it? She couldn't take it with her. I turned the bed upside down until I found it on the other side of the bed. She had moved it some distance and really had tried to take it with her! A phone call at 7.30pm, from a mutual friend confirmed that she had died during that Monday night in the early hours.

35

Whilst I was watching television that night Noreen showed herself, to one side of the television, as a clear live Technicolor picture. She was grinning all over her face and looked really happy. That picture has always remained with me as a remarkable fact that she was quite an amazing medium and healer with strength of purpose and knowledge as to true communication from the Spirit world.

As soon as I found out when the funeral would be, I contacted everyone. On the Friday I phoned the Trance Medium, Muriel Miller, who Noreen had visited for years and asked if she would like to go to the funeral.

"Just a minute. Hold on while I find my diary and see what I am doing. I am fully booked up these days." She returned to the phone with her diary saying: "Well I never! Well I never!" With some disbelief.

"Well I never what?" I enquired.

"You know Noreen always made bookings for a whole year in advance and I crossed them all off when she became ill?"

"Yes, I know you did."

"This one hasn't been crossed off."

"You mean to say Noreen has an appointment already for Monday?"

I enquired. "Is it for the morning or afternoon?"

It's for 11 am in the morning.

"How would you feel if I took that booking and then we go out for lunch before attending the funeral?"

"I don't know about that. "Come up in the morning for coffee and we will see what happens." We agreed I would arrive at 10.30 am.

The following day, on the Saturday, I was attending the Church Fete and booked a Reading. The Medium began to talk about a lady that hadn't passed over very long.

"She tried to do something the night she died and it didn't quite come off."

How accurate this was and it confirmed my own thoughts of her really trying to take the brooch with her. I gave the brooch to her sister Margery, the day after Noreen died. Life was pulling on me from all directions.

The growth in my own development was going ahead without me trying to do anything. The more I let go of trying to do anything and just went with the flow of life - the more guidance and happenings occurred. Owing to not being able to set a time each day, I gave God 10 minutes a night before I went to sleep and also received inspirational writings.

What a strange co-incidence; Noreen already had an appointment booked on the day of her funeral. But then so many strange things had already happened and nothing would surprise me now.

Monday 15th November 1982 arrived and I was excited at the prospect of a possibility of a communication from Noreen herself on the day of her Funeral. This would be quite an achievement if it happened. Noreen was a Medium and Healer; therefore with her knowledge of communication and the power of her guides, all things could be possible.

I arrived in good time. We enjoyed a cup of coffee and discussed the recent events and happenings. Muriel suddenly said "I will sit," As Muriel prepared for trance, a beautiful atmosphere enveloped us both in a peace and around Muriel appeared an aura of apricot shades. She began to speak:

"In all humbleness, dear Father God, we are now linking together on this memorable day. Firstly to say thank you for all thy powers, for all thy peace. Loving Father God thou knowest the daughter that comest before thee, the walks of her life, the sincerity within her heart, it is to serve. Father God open the doors, that others may continually see thy light within her. Bless her loved ones and the helpers that have gathered. Father God, let us remember, in this quiet hour, the dear sister that has departed to the higher life, for we know thy will be done, and all that love that was created on this earth - to know, Father God, there has been a wonderful worker. Father, we leave these thoughts to thee, to ask a blessing upon those in Spirit and those of earth, that on this memorable day, Oh Father God, let each one link together in harmony and love. Father, we ask a blessing upon this earth, to bring peace to all nations and understanding. To remember even the animal world, for these are thine. Father, we ask a blessing that all that is said and done may be acceptable to thy will, and in thy name I ask this Amen."

On regaining her normal consciousness, at this stage, whispering that the Shepherd of the Hills was the speaker, then with a sigh she closed her eyes again and her control Topsy came through saying:

"Now I do come again and dat Topsy girl come and talk to you yes please? Yes and I can come and talk to you because I don't know whether you know lady but as I did come, I don't know whether you heared of Tony. Did you ever heared of Tony? Tony, well Tony is right by the side of you and he's been standing looking at you. *(Tony was Noreen's helper.)* 'Cause there has been, what you call that word a b'reavement of a dear soul that has passed into the life. Yes you understand me? But all these thoughts and all the love that has been extended to her, I want to say she has been definitely received in the Spirit world. She was greeted by a lovely love, understand, with all the peoples, with the manses and the Daddy. They were all welcoding her home with lovely flowers, waiting for her. So this is where, lady I want to say she has been very close to earth, *(oh yes)* I want to say to you there is nowhere the spirit is leaving the earth and going to -

37

yea wait a minute, and is going to rest, you understand lady when I say to you....all right...you don't mind if I talk about this lady for a little while do you lady? Because there is a Mummy and a Daddy, understand? Their wish was answered *(I believe they wanted all three daughters to meet and this actually happened just before she died)* and this has made a great happiness of the reunion. This is where they've worked very hard behind the scenery but it is, I've got to be truthful, I want to say, when this lady's spirit left her body, there were things that she didn't do that she wanted to do. Now would you understand? *(yes I do)* I don't know what I mean now. She left something undone. I want to say pen to paper. She wanted to do something in writing but I cannot see what it was. I don't know what she wants but she left it too late and this where there was a frustistration, when she wented over, because she was trying to get back to still dood it huh! *(I actually picked this up and had warned Circle sitters not to write what she wanted to do)*. But it doesn't matter lady, things, the impression has been there. She's here, the impression was there and this is where ahuhum....she....

*(Coughing)* I'm picking up her condition yes. I was there kept coughding, something in her throat. All right bless you, because I want to say spirit....Look! She is clinging to earth lady, and well lady, I don't know what I'm gonna do now because I feel so full. *(Is she able to come through?)* I feel lady; she is just here now. Don't, please expect too much, understand, but she is definitely.... she will not - er all right... Someone tells me she wants to keep the appointment. Do you understand? All right lady, I'll goad but just with all love with all healing. She's just around. We are not going to talk about material things lady, but I am not going to bring anything of the material 'cause it's not there. I want to leave it right up there, you see, so I'll go and try....I'm just getting another condition but they are taking that away. She's going to try lady because the appointment was made."

*(Very weak and faint but exactly as she was before she died)* Hello...hello..... I'm all right now...yes...I'm all right ... *(Difficulty breathing)*

"Give ...... my love to all. *(Yes I will)* Thank you.... for all your love.............and I will be in a circle with you helping.....ooothers don't understand but you do....God bless you, God bless all in my circle. God bless Muriel for holding this memorable day but I've met all my loved ones. Thank you dear...thank you..... Thank you... thank you... God bless you... bless you."

Topsy returned, "Ooh lady that was a big power. You know lady there is so much love that came. All her guides were there. The loved ones were there but now, I want to say, she will rest, she will go and have a resting period, then, until she is ready to awaken. 'Cause I feel the body was very bad, very distorted, you understand and this is where it's been a great effort because this has been her wish from spirit, to keep the appointment in this sanctuary. But to know she is so happy to come back to you and to give love to the others. Lady there is so much more but apart from that, therefore don't have any worry because I feel a re-opening of a circle as time goes on. But it's just that things have got to be reorgdanised and everything has got to be replaced but at the same time, lady, I want to say that her guides, her helpers, will not leave the circle. They will still be a help, love, understanding to do the part, understand to help. So lady there is everything going to be...nothing all right thank you, somebody says here nothing has broken, the reunion is still there, the reunion will be there but the love is so strong that wherefore that where, I want to say to you. I'd better be honest, I want to come over there, I could see somebody else could sever. No one could ever sever that which has been created from the world of spirit, definitely no. So if that door were shut lady there is a spirit door yet to open. *(When I typed this out I realised that the Spirit world already knew of the troubles I was to face with the Circle when someone tried to break the links.)*

Her Nun is here and her guides are just showing me that wherefore they are all going to re-joined, eventually, another circle, so they are all going to be servers, all going to be workers. But the link it is going to be there and she will be there too. Coughing. I mustn't pick that up again, take it away...that condition. "Which house will we be using for the circle?" I questioned. That I cannot say lady. Would you ever likeded it in yours? *(Yes but my daughter is there at the moment)* Right lady would she objected? She wouldn't like it? No. *(Would she be able to go off to America?)*

This is where she's planning. Something is opening, a door is opening and I feel that if she could go..... But she doesn't like the thoughts of spirit and she will create an upheaval, so be patient lady, 'cause I feel there has been talkie talkies about her packing her bags. So this is where, if she packs her bags lady that would be in order by spirit. This is where you would like that would you? *(For her happiness if that is what she wants.)* But how old is she lady? She is only young isn't she? Has she got somebody out there, has she got work out there? *(Not yet)* She's wanting work because I feel this is good but Americada. So we've got to leave it now in the hands of Spirit. Don't get disheartened, don't let the threads go because to be truthful, I feel just linked with you. *(Yes)* But I cannot get it happening anywhere else. Has anybody suggested anything lady? *(No).* This is where, all right, you'll find things will go according to plan. Don't get frusterstrated. We've got to leave that now in the hands of spirit but at the same time if there is one obstacle in the way, you understand? You don't want that, I want peace. Whatever she does, that girlie of yours, whatever she wants to do. She's going to do it of her own free will. 'Cause you cannot tell her. *(Oh no you can't)*. She's going to have her own way lady. And the mistakes of life, she'll make, is to be her teachings, understand? But just leave her now because your Nun and your Sister of Mercy and your loved ones are all around her to try and help her. But she's got a very hardness within her and you can't take that hardness out lady. You've tried huh? Sometimes I feel close, sometimes I don't but you can't alter the facts can you lady? Apart from that lady, just have all faith now because it's early days now isn't it? A lot of sorting out, a lot of sifting out, a lot of things got to be re-organised. But from the power in the Spirit World, they don't want anything to sever but otherwise to make a re-link, re-joining. So lady, it's going to come, but a funny thing - I feel your house. I do lady; all I can go is to you. This is where the spirit world is going to work, but there is the obstacle yet to be removed. Hold on with faith will you lady? Apart from that you is not worried is you lady? *(With my daughter - she is out of work this week. Will she be out of work a long time?)* Don't know lady. Your earth is rather difficult isn't it? But this is where the Spirit world are trying. I feel she is quite a good worker, she is a conscientious worker, but it's the material problems of earth that is very difficult. Has the door shut up against her at work? *(She shut the door)* She shut the door! What she shut the door for? *(She couldn't take the aggravation at work)* Well she should have plugged in first and shut the door afterwards. But she shut the door first didn't she? *(Exactly what I told her the day before she handed in her notice.)* You see this is where she has put a barrier up to new work. She should have done it different to that, but you see you couldn't tell her. She'll have her own way. Now she is a little regretting to what she has done. She could be difficult and yet she's a worker. All right we've got to leave it there. Still the bags will be packed, so hold on with all faith. They are not giving me time - well there is no time. You'll see the things'll just slot in the jigsaw puzzle. There is not much in your life is there? Only Spirit. So this is where you've had it in there and you've had to bury it. At the same time you have been lifted up. Definitely yes lady. Well leave everything now, taken in thought, taken in prayer, all the faith in the world. The reunion; the rejoining. I still want to say, the Spirit world want it in your house, so it's a thought isn't it? So you holded on will you lady? You've got your guides coming in. We'll let your guides come....."

"And in all humbleness daughter in all understanding of this memorable day to say, well, we already know the spirit has departed to the higher life and where that spirit is, we know there is a radiation out of love. There is a radiation out of spirituality and also, therefore, her work will continue. Daughter, as she suffered, there will be a resting period, a resting time for the spirit is now designing that rest now. At the same time there has been a fulfilment of a wish, that thought of returning, but now that has finished. She has done what she wanted to do and now. That will be the closing door of earth to depart for the resting time. Now there hold on with all love, to say Chang will work behind the scenery, yes please? Where your hearts are, where the desire is, where the faith is, to rejoin and link with a circle. For no one has broken it. No one will ever break it, but there must be a link of the material, therefore daughter, leave it there. We do our part to help you. So God bless the one who has departed to the higher life."

"Greetings to you daughter, me say yes there will be all the guides, all the helpers this memorable day, to keep the appointment of the passing of that dear soul into the higher life, but we know the door is going to shut but this is where she will re-link, rejoin and therefore, she has her wish granted, daughter, to help you. Have no fear, have faith, but One cannot take away the human element, of the one that you have loved, away because that is where so much more. But the spirit has been brought back here because that's the appointment been kept. And to know she was happy to do this and that, this was her final wish. So God Bless you and the peace I leave with you. God bless you and remember daughter - the healing hands. Bless you."

"And God bless you too" Yes I have held those hands so many times but I want to say, my child, everyone of the helpers of the circle were there and naturally her own guides. She is, bless her, she is so happy, she is radiant now, you know? She has her wish. At the same time it was a little difficult because she so wanted to come back for this appointment. Just to say what she did. What she said I do not know. What she said I cannot tell you. Only, we say, yes the love is here, thanks are there that memories will never die. So may God bless you with my heart Be strong my child to know that Sister Marguerite and all the guides will be also with this Medium, you understand, today. There is a meeting of all the guides, from the circle and this Medium, to you, to the others in the circle. They will all be there at the farewell. So God bless you child, be strong child. And now divine Father God as I've held those hands, to bless them, we know Father God, there's been other hands here too to bless her Father, to uplift. To know Father it was the greatest wish for her to have returned into this little Sanctuary. So Father God, we pray to give each one today, thy strength, thy powers, thy love at this farewell. We know it's the material body Father, but we know that material body has been loved, has been of service to many. So Father God with all these thoughts now, we leave them into thy care, thy will be done. Father open the doors of spirit for each one has a heart ready to serve

41

So Father with these thoughts, we know thou art the giver. So Father God hear our prayer, and in thy name we also say thank you for the return of the dear soul, that was loved so much, in thy name AMEN."

I was overjoyed with Noreen's achievement What determination and strength of purpose, as well as proof of survival beyond the normal. The succession of communication left me in no doubt that survival of the mental faculties, and soul continued and grew in knowledge and wisdom spiritually. Eternal life is a fact.

The day continued with lunch at a Little Chef, where we could discuss the amazing co-incidences of the 'Appointment' and subsequent message. After the service at the Crematorium, we returned to my home. I had invited all Noreen's spiritual friends to come back, owing to the family having no interest in this side of Noreen's life and not even inviting us to Noreen's home after the funeral. We were able to listen to the tape and each person verified the tape was definitely her voice and communication with absolute certainty. The circle members confirmed her strength of will and the determination she had shown.

Suddenly Muriel commented; "It's this room where your circle will be." We looked at each other and I stated; but it can't happen until I have spoken to my daughter and found someone to lead it. Maybe the ones who helped the previous two circles could help. I will phone them and see if we can all visit and talk to them."

After tea and cakes, I drove Muriel and her friend home commenting on a wonderful day and what more beautiful farewell could anyone have had.

# CHAPTER 4

## DEVELOPMENT IN MY HOME

The week after Noreen's funeral, I arranged for some of the circle members to visit the two Mediums, who had helped start the original circle, in which Noreen and I had met and who also helped Noreen to start her circle.

It was good to meet up again after five years. They were surprised that I was still involved in Circles. They said they knew the tests and trials of my daily life and material world was going to be extremely difficult and thought I would have given up ages ago. They told us that the circle should be in my home. I explained that the circle had given me the spiritual growth, strength and support to carry on but I was not a Medium, and I couldn't give messages to order like those on platforms. I could hear spirit, see spirit and feel their presence but not to order every week only when it was given to me. They then stated they could not visit or help owing to the long journey and dark nights, therefore two of us visited another healer/Medium, Bob H. who stated that Spirit were telling him that they had trained me and that it was to be in my home.

"But I don't do anything." I exclaimed. He then asked if I had stopped meditating and "Saw" things around people. I agreed. He then emphasised emphatically that Spirit said they had been training me to lead the Circle. He said he would come and sit in with us, for a month or two to make sure we were all right.

Meantime I decided it was time to inform my daughter that I was going to invite friends home once a week. I explained that she could have friends in any other day except Wednesday on which she could either visit her friends or quietly watch television in her bedroom.

"No Mum, we are not having spooks in my house!" She screamed at me.

"Whose house? The day you pay the rent is the day you can call it your house and they are my friends, not spooks. They will be coming next Wednesday and every week on a Wednesday. Surely you don't mind me having one night a week for my friends?

A friend of my daughter, Sue, who was staying with us sat in the kitchen, listening, and rather than argue with Kerri, I asked her friend if her Mother was allowed her own friends in her own home.

"Of course, but I cannot."

"Well maybe you can clarify and explain this as I seem to be having a problem." I stated and left the room.

Whilst sitting in Church during the service, Noreen came close and gave me a very wet kiss on my cheek exactly the same as the one she gave me the last day in her home. Then she caused my left eye to water, which is the way I now recognise that she is still with me and often helps me with healing.

We started the Circle on December 3rd 1982. Bob H. came to make sure we were all right and suggested we all concentrate on Gill, who was showing signs of trance. This was against the ways I was being inspired but then I was not a medium and thought he knew best. After a few weeks Gill said she wanted her husband and her sister to come in to the Circle. I was not happy about what was happening, as they had never sat before but this medium had years of experience and I was not even a medium. Years later I was to get confirmation that this was not what Spirit had in mind and that the reigns had been taken out of my hands. The harmony was now out of balance. We all sent our powers towards Gill and she went in to trance. I sat and poured out love to her, often watching my hands move of their own accord either pulling or pouring out the power. Little did I realise at that time she was working in the powers that built with and around me and was not attuned with the divine source that would build her own powers around herself.

My "voice" had stated that I needed the best teachers. 'Who were they?' I thought to myself. A brochure of various activity holidays arrived in the post. Nothing appealed. As I browsed through it wondering what I would enjoy as a leisure activity, nothing appealed at all. 'What was I interested in?' I questioned myself realising I had set my life on to a different path and was not interested in these other activities anymore but was searching for Spiritual truths and knowledge. I wondered if there were holidays where I could learn more about things of the spirit. I searched and questioned and found there was a place - The Arthur Findlay College that was residential and did courses. The President, Gordon Higginson, was the only Materialisation Medium who demonstrated publicly. I wrote for their brochure and asked Gill, if she would be interested too. We both decided to book a week containing a pot pourri of spiritual disciplines.

It was a Spiritual Awareness week called Canadian week, which we booked. I also wrote to Gordon Higginson, Charles Sherratt and the S.A.G.B. in London. I received a brochure from the S.A.G.B. and wrote to every Medium. Finding the best teachers soon proved to be hard work to find. I received no replies to several letters, including Gordon Higginson and Charles Sherratt, in spite of enclosing stamped addressed envelopes. This seemed bad manners to me, as a printed piece of paper would have sufficed, which I stated to Charles the first time I went to The Arthur

44

Findlay College and then received a letter after returning home! Some of the mediums at the SAGB specified they only worked in special situations in well-known places, and others declined home groups. One replied and was very interested in coming. She was Dorice Hannan, who I booked for the Saturday after Coral Polge.

Coral Polge was still booked for January and I notified her of the change of address for this booking. The day arrived and I had given circle members a choice of having two sessions each. I had asked circle members only and most had booked for two pictures and, of course I would also be sitting in both groups. At breakfast time I became aware of my Nun at my side, impressing me that her picture would be drawn today. I mentally thought to myself how nice it would be if this happened. I prepared the room and lunch then walked the dog, Tara. As I was walking I was very strongly impressed that the other picture would be that of my Grandfather. I must remember to remove his photograph from my living room.' I muttered to myself otherwise I would accuse her of copying the photo. In the rush to prepare lunch and have everything ready before fetching Coral from her home in Walton on Thames, I forgot about the photo. The lunch and afternoon went well and sure enough, the first picture Coral drew for me was a picture of my Nun. How on earth did Spirit arrange this and communicate this to both her and me? The mechanics of mediumship and the higher knowledge was astounding. We had a tea break before the evening session. This time Coral drew my Grandfather. But what a lovely surprise, this was my Father's Father and not the one in the photo of my Mother's Father. Here was proof I could share with my Father and maybe help him overcome his fear of the unknown. Everyone enjoyed the evening and asked if we could do it again. I booked Coral regularly.

The following week I had booked Dorice who drew Auragraphs, psychically, as well as working as a Medium. She came just before 10 am and each Auragraph took an hour with a lot of details and clairvoyance work. She was to visit many times after that day. She started work at 10am and didn't finish until midnight! I was the first sitter owing to not wishing to divulge any information about myself and test her mediumship.

This may help some readers who already receive symbolic pictures.

My Auragraph by Dorice Hannan. "Sometimes you look into the mirror and have a certain image of yourself but you never see the true you. You get a funny reflection: -

As she started to draw a Brook she said "A lot of water down here. It's a very quick bubbly brook. Water is the symbol for the sub-conscious. Your mind is very quick, very active but its very luscible and especially with your first years. You were very much in this brook. Spiritually you are very active anyway, but it hasn't been easy, especially in the beginning. I get little bubbles, they come up, but you cannot really catch them. These are your spiritual thoughts and were there as a child, fleeting impressions and quick impulses that pop out, but were put down to a vivid imagination. One sentence could come up and hurt very badly.

On the bank is a very very beautiful, deep blue bunch of blue forget-me-nots, growing in the middle. They are tiny flowers and they hide away, so deep inside you, regardless of what other people think. What about me hidden deep inside. Beautiful electric blue bright and gold centred. Many, many blossoms, many seeds and you don't regard yourself very highly. If you put the flower in proportion, they are very intricate and very deep. They are very strong and grow by the water. You hid and went into yourself. Now you are working with Spirit. Interesting new ways with you. A nice 3rd eye, a very strong root. Your whole life goes back into the root and pushed you up. Your psychic eye is right in your roots and you're hiding it your little diamond - your truth, it's very precious.

Couple of rocks your early years were quite hard, you hated being in the body. Someone had to bung rocks on you and you couldn't breathe. Difficult not sickly. You were strong but your body wasn't so you got out of your body and have peace and quiet upstairs - this worried your Parents - you slept too much.

Seaweed. Very fine tendrils. Your material life started it in the material. You very softly got into your body. Your mind was living around your body. An unusual child. I'm not leaving the water line until 5-6 years old, and then it's an uphill climb

Then you really climb this slippery bank. From age 5-11 years it was very difficult. Alone in a big crowd, one of the gang.

Solid ground 11-12 ish - lot of grass, short sharp relationships. The grass blade has very sharp edges, and can cut you. Always there was someone who could hurt you. You practice to feel inside yourself.

Dragonflies As you take off, you put yourself into a crystal body and your wings, bright and shimmering, kept you up. Your thoughts, very fast, were your life. You became almost like an automaton, what you had to do in your life. This worried you, you thought you were insensitive and didn't care about others but you were so sensitive, harsh feelings were too slow for you and you had to put this barrier on, otherwise it would have destroyed you. The body of the dragonfly is very hard but also very brittle. So you meet friends in the same boat from 15-17 years. You start meeting people on the same wavelength.

A beautiful pink starts coming up like a dawning. The sun is

46

coming up, starting to rise. It's not quite up to see. A lot of people get their enlightenment from upstairs but, with you, it comes from inside and you start breaking out of your shell and you understand the dawning. I feel its memories of past lives and things come up out of the sub-conscious. *(Very true)*. A lovely rosy glow, deep pink, meaning love and wisdom combined. You get into the stride and that's when the bubbles start to come up properly. All those that were here in the brook. Great big shimmering ones like the dragonflies. The crystal hard shell has disappeared and you are a clear soap bubble, unfolding yourself. With the first one, you went; Oh my God, I've disappeared!" Now you are free to float out of the body. Do your best. There are still quite a few little bubbles. They are your bank account that you are not using. Grow gradually. They stay static, and yet when you put bubbles into water, as oxygen they do their job. You are working on them.

A healing Drop - you started early and you didn't know what you were doing. A Heart - only one. *(I do not have a partner so this was true.)* You learned how to use the Kundalini red energy and convert that energy, distilling that and learning.

A Purple Drop. So you are using all the things that come out. It seems very selfish when we do that but it's what you are functioning for. That is your job done. A Healer and a Medium can change the energies, centring and really working.

Cup Spirit - is the Top Chakra energy. You put the energy up - the high energy above and you work with and channel it. It takes courage. The crown is actually less important than the cup. The cup says you have actually reached the grail and become a vessel for spirit. You had to earn that and you worked very very hard on it, a hard life, with no one else to help with the teaching. You held them, the truths, and kept them inside. Deep root - putting down. Water ability, upstairs, downstairs, you can do what you like, your foundations are down. You achieved your homework and got free time. Lessons accomplished in two thirds of your life - you raced through it. Stay in your reservoir - I'm doing it.

Little Fish - Your Daughter is very psychic too and is coming up underneath and is going to teach you a few tricks. Another fish and will take over where you leave off.

The Psychic Eye has three positions.

When it is at the Top - the higher self guides from above.

In the Middle - It's inside you and works out to others and you only use upstairs to store energy.

At the Bottom - Your whole being springs out of the psychic/spiritual. It's your truth and you cannot be anything else.

In the Middle - like yours, you are a natural medium half up and

47

half down - a very good balance and you cannot be knocked sideways. Wherever you go, just roll along with it. It hurts but no one can do anything to you.

If it's at the Bottom you are doing a high wire act. Always standing above people's heads. This reminded me of my recurring dream as a child. Maybe we change positions as we change roles, learn and progress through life's many challenges during our lives.

If it's at the Top - you are aiming, aiming, aiming but never quite get to where you want to get - always hankering.

You can now combine the deep red and deep blue - they are very fine and tough. You reach your own purple and can combine the white which is all the colours and handle the emotions. White is the next stage, a clear glass bubble. You can hit the bubble with red emotions and it will not break. It has nothing to hold but knowledge. Tremendous power to hurt but you feel the hurt harder. *(This was true because I always had to go inside, ask for guidance and ask myself if I felt comfortable with anything I said, wrote or did that might hurt someone else's feelings and if I felt guilty I couldn't do it because it would rebound back to me with double the power.)*

These things confirmed an awful lot of my life and helped me to understand the differences between using the psychic aspects and then the mediumistic aspects to clarify proof of survival too. Everyone who came that day commented, in the same way about her accuracy, and said Dorice had known things that no-one else did and proved survival to an extent that was quite amazing as well as doing some rescue work with one person.

My daughter had friends in the kitchen and made a point of slamming the door every time someone walked past, then made quite a noise talking and laughing. I asked her not to be so rude and to try and keep the noise down but nothing I said helped or made the slightest difference. Eventually, when Dorice had a tea break she asked if I minded if she went in the kitchen to speak to the girls.

"Go ahead, maybe you will have more success." I gratefully smiled. Then as I relaxed I began thinking that Dorice was a blessing in disguise, and how nice it was that someone else was going to try and help me quieten my daughter, laughter came bubbling out of the kitchen. I remained in the living room. Thank goodness something was working. Another sitter turned up and as Dorice saw her, and came out of the kitchen smiling, I returned to the girls.

"I like that lady. Can I talk to her again? Kerri questioned.

"We will see. She has been working all day and will want to get home." I responded.

At 9pm Dorice finished the couple that had been overstaying their time. I then said that I knew she had a family waiting for her and that she had been busy all day and must be tired, but if she wouldn't mind talking to my daughter again as she had asked to see her and talk or would she like to go home.

"Oh this work keeps me on a high with lots of energy. Come on, let's go in the living room all together and see what happens." She replied. My daughter's friends left except for Sue who was staying. Gill also stayed.

We sat down as Dorice described a man to my daughter.

"Talk to my Mum, I don't know who it is." My daughter responded.

Dorice then said she would hold my hands and transmit power for me to see. She held my hands and said I would see whom she was talking about. I then saw a clear black and white silhouette picture of my daughter's Father.

"Is he on this side or the other?" I enquired.

"The other - spirit side." She answered carrying on talking about him.

This would confirm my own experience of feeling him very strongly in my bedroom one night a couple of months before. He had come to me to 'get his leg over' and as I realised he must have passed on or be extremely ill, to come to me after all these years. I said 'O.K do with me what you will.' He then disappeared.

The power built in the room and Dorice suddenly began to glow gold. The room filled with gold. The carpet pattern began to rise. My daughter looked at Dorice in astonishment then nudged her friend Sue, pointing to the carpet; "Can you see that and look at that?"

"Yes look at that." We were all seeing the same activity and this wonderful gold in the room. There was a presence of pure love and a purity of spirit with this golden light. What was it? It touched the soul and our tears began to flow. What an experience. It was midnight before Dorice left.

At Easter I took the picture, Coral had drawn of my Grandfather, with me to my Parent's home. I placed it in front of my Father saying:

"Who do you think this is a picture of?"

He studied it saying; "It does look like Father."

My Mother commented; "Let me see it, I'll soon tell you if it is your Father or not." I passed it over after my Father suddenly noticed the date and said; "It can't be Father, it was only done this year and Father died years ago!"

My Mother studied the artwork, owing to her own ability as an artist:

"I didn't know him when he had hair - he was completely bald when I knew him."

"Could you draw a picture of him as good as that?" I enquired.

"No, I would need him to sit in front of me." She replied acknowledging a good likeness.

My Father's brother lived next door so I decided to show him the picture too. He recognised it instantly and said he would find me a photograph to prove it. Meantime my Mother found me a couple of photos, which definitely proved the likeness.

Circles and groups continued until, one day, the Medium Bob H. announced he was leaving to run other circles, and stated that we were getting on all right because we were very sincere. It was quite a shock to all of us especially as he had promised to develop Gill, the sitter we concentrated on. The following week she went into trance to say she, her husband and sister were to follow the brother who had left. I doubted this as being true trance and wondered about how she had done this in another voice. My own opinion was that she caused herself to go into a state of trance to say something that she was afraid to say in her own voice. What was going on? We let her and her family go and decided to carry on as we had done before we had been persuaded to concentrate on the one person, which was the way I was impressed anyway.

Then whilst concentrating on each person individually each week, I saw Alan turn completely negative, just like a photographic negative. What was this? I mentally questioned. Again I did not want to recognise my insights. I believed everyone had a heart of gold and wanted to be of service in whatever way they could so a 'Negative' was something I didn't want to see, as, to me, this meant they were working the wrong way round - misusing the energies and instead of giving their all to Spirit - they were actually out for their own benefit. The circle was definitely becoming more and more physical as well as developing more spirituality. The draughts, cobwebs and power of spirit held us in a time warp for over an hour each time. The candles began to jump in the room. The television often changed channels without aid or would switch on and off. The amount of love and power in the room was wonderful. My daughter began to accuse us of drinking the fish tank water! It was a large fish tank and my daughter estimated the amount of water that went missing during our circle times to be a gallon, but I had noticed that there was certainly a lowering of the water level.

My hunt went on. I needed to understand more about what was happening. Where were the 'best' teachers I wondered, little realising that only the best teachers would be interested in coming to our group in my home. They were led by Spirit, at the right time and years later I realised we were very privileged to have had the wonderful experiences and teachings we did at that time.

What is a circle? The Circle is about supporting fellow spiritual Light Workers throughout the planet, both on the astral planes, where we meet in advance as our true SELF, and are then linked in the flesh. Children, teenagers and adults meet like-minded people in most other dimensions as well as in the flesh. It is about manifesting prosperity and abundance materially, emotionally, mentally and spiritually. It is about going inside and discovering our own higher self and re-connecting that which is the inner personality self, to that which is the higher self. It is about supporting our own spiritual growth by understanding our unique process of giving and receiving. It is about making new friends and providing services as well as connecting with the guides and helpers who train and develop our mediumistic gifts of the spirit.

Why do we join Circles? To experience the joy of both giving and receiving the power of spirit. To be with people who support each other by expanding their love and light. Imagine spaces in a dimensional spiral. On the outside there are the natural GIVERS and HEALERS. Some people have cracked foundations and wish to re-align themselves from the power of a Circle. There are also Communicators and Light workers who facilitate, both on earth and from the spiritual realms, as well as RECEIVERS who benefit from the knowledge, information and energy of the flow.

As the groups continued we received some inspiring talks, from several speakers. One came through trance, from Muriel: -

"Bless you my friend, and it is a great pleasure for me to return through my channel, to return to say to you I am well pleased to see a circle - that is linked with the love and understanding. Now we know my friends that it is only a short time hereafter where each one of you has been sitting for developing. But it is not only the developing, it is the radiating out of the love of God from each one of you and it is to know that there are those in spirit that feel and understand the love that radiates and they too can receive a healing in the world of spirit. For my friends it is for us to say thank you to you for giving your time to us, to remember that we give back our time to you. But it is very distressing at times when the guides are with their channels for a period of time and they work very hard and then the channel suddenly decides to throw away the gifts of God. But it is, as I may have said before, it is not an easy pathway of developing, but it is the biggest testing time that one can go through."

At about this time I went with Gill and her husband for a private reading and what was said to me boosted my enthusiasm, even though Gill was no longer in our Circle.

"Your bracelet, *(a rheumatism bracelet that clipped around my wrist)* you know, I want to join it together and I feel that it's almost symbolic of what's happened in your life and I want to join it spirit are joining it together and you know it hasn't quite joined together, even now. They're working on it, to get the two parts lined up exactly. They are just a little bit out of alignment just a little. You are working on that and spirit are working on it. And when the time is right, and there is someone in spirit a lady putting her finger up, as if she wants to stress it. This is what she would have done. She was a leader and she's got a very long index finger. She's a leader - You cannot hurry it, neither can we but everything is right you know, because you have made it right, they've made it right. It's a three cornered golden triangle. I've still got this lady. She's a very forceful, positive personality and she's giving.... ooh I've got a breathless feeling. *(The description fitted Noreen very accurately and I had seen the room fill with gold similar to what happened with Dorice and whilst Noreen slept in her chair. Could this be to do with the golden triangle?)* Yes you have got her! As if she didn't want to leave any doubt. It was her way. Things have got to be exactly right. It's got to be your way too. You have had to re-shape your ideas so many ways, but there is a little niggle at the back of your mind. *(What had just been going on in the circle with the ones who had left)?* Will you leave it in abeyance? You see, always you have to do your best - you know that and leave the rest to us - so now will you leave the rest to us. *(Over the years the phrase 'It's all in hand, leave it to us' was repeated in my ear many times.)* 'The spiritual things are coming to a climax. This is why they're all gathering around because there is a very special work and you know it. Why have your doubts? This lady is getting rather cross. Why have your doubts as if well, it's so fantastic really, there must be something wrong somewhere. You've analysed it, torn it to pieces, now put it together again and let us get on with it and accept that it will be so. There's a young boy in spirit. It might not be linked with you anyway, but he is linked with you and he's looking up at you. *(Could this be Noreen's Tony again?)* And all the spirits around you. He has been training too. And a little child will lead them. This little boy here. You know he is just a little boy and yet all the wisdom of the years are here and he is waiting patiently, waiting, sitting cross legged, for all the grown ups to sort everything out and you, so that he can get on with his work through you. *(I couldn't believe this as everyone else in the circle was emphasising that someone else was the medium for it, whereas I thought it was a group thing.)* Love from above. The two will go hand in hand, the spiritual and the emotional, personal part of your life. They are, kind of, lining up and will go forward. *(It was another 10 years before I recognised the truth of this in a retrospective picture.)* They will be absolutely in alignment and will go forward. Levitation - but they are not enlarging on it. We will bring you gifts from the spirit apports, Levitation *(This actually happened some years later on my own.)* Now whether they're talking about you, I don't know. There is a young man in spirit who was very badly scarred. It's not a scar, he was marked to denote the trials he had undertaken. Now spirit are marking your face to denote the trials that you have undertaken. They are scarring your face, so that spirit can see for them selves what you have undergone in a very difficult incarnation. Always the hand that holds the reins but know that spirit have their hand over yours and so, over the reins. They are not being allowed to slip away, as they did once! *(When Bob H had us concentrate on Gill and she brought her husband and sister in.)* There's movement all around you as we go through the month of March. So much will have been swept away by spirit *(this confirmed that the ones who had left the circle and been swept away by spirit)* and the spiritual path will be wide open and ready for work to be WELL DONE. Yes there has been a trickle but we are getting ready to open the flood gates!!"

The trickle began to get into more and more as physical activity happened. We laughed as the lights in each room dimmed and brightened as if in answer to questions or to confirm spirit listened to us, as we discussed the circle and spoke after sitting.

# CHAPTER 5

## THE ARTHUR FINDLAY COLLEGE

In July Gill, the one, who had left my circle, came to the Arthur Findlay College, with me, for a week's holiday, to learn more about this spiritual work. I felt I was going home the minute I drove in the driveway. We were in for a treat. The lectures were very interesting as we learnt about energy centres and colours as well as the ribbons and facets of mediumship.

My watch began to go haywire! It was either an hour slow all day or an hour fast and I could not rely on it at all. We shared a room with a Scottish lady who linked us to several lovely people from Glasgow, with whom I bonded and remained friends for some years. Strange co-incidences began to happen as soon as we arrived. There was tea and coffee being served and I glanced around the hall looking for someone without grey hair. Seeing one in the little room at the side I walked over and spoke to the group she was with, introducing us both. This was the group of people from Glasgow and one of them turned out to be our roommate.

As it was Canadian week I decided to sit with some Canadians and listened for the accent as we looked for seats. I found two seats at a table. It was here I met Carole who arrived at the table later on. We remained friends over the following years following similar interesting pathways and sharing experiences. She said she trained Trance subjects in her home in Canada.

A Commitment to sharing, is what moves each of us from giving to receiving, from the 4th, to the 5th to the 6th, to the 7th dimension and Carole and I shared a mutual developmental process in our own Groups, at Stansted and at work. Our enthusiasm was supported by working with other Light Workers that can move us into receiving encouragement in many ways. As each person helps two other people, the Circles grow and move smoothly. When we teach and give more, we reap the benefits, increasing the momentum, making new friends, empowering our goals, sharing abundance and our services.

Charles Sherratt did a talk the first evening and commented by saying:

"So you have all come here to become Mediums?"

I turned around and looked for the door - I was in the wrong place as that was definitely not why I had come. The last thing I wanted to do, was to become a Medium giving messages off a platform! I was only interested in the Spiritual development and where the prophecies and dreams came from, but not in giving messages of the level I heard in the

54

churches and playing psychic energy games like many did working with ribbons, psychometry and the such. The door was quite a way away and it would disturb everyone if I got up and left so I remained and did enjoy the meditations, lectures and exercises.

On the Wednesday Gordon Higginson arrived out of the blue as he had no plans and was not even booked. He was in time to replace Robin Stevens, who had not turned up. This was an added pleasure, owing to his spiritual link to the other dimensions and ability to teach the truths I was interested in.

At the end of a lecture he came off the platform, looked at Gill and I then asked which one of us came from Camberley. "Both of us." I replied. He requested we both listen as he talked of listening to Direct Voice tapes in a flat. I thought he must be talking to Gill, owing to her own admission that she was to travel the world and become a famous medium as I taped the message and gave it to her. Also because Noreen thought that Direct Voice was to do with her trance. When his message proved accurate for me, the following year, whilst I was visiting Glasgow, I was flabbergasted at the prophetic connection. It was in Glasgow that I listened to Physical Mediumship tapes from the wonderful circle, *(which included all those I had met at Stansted during this week, who were involved in it),* for over 8 hours in the friend I had just met with the group of people from Glasgow's flat. We had tried to have them in the owner's house but couldn't because his wife didn't want them played there!

During a question and answer session Gordon told me I was developing like he did and that although I was at present walking the grounds with people, I would be walking alone one day and have an experience from which I would have a revelation at a later date. I didn't know what he meant about developing just like he did as I did not want to give messages off a platform.

The experience happened this way. My watch eventually behaved beautifully, keeping perfect time all day on the Wednesday and I hadn't altered it at all since arriving at Stansted. Therefore on the Thursday, when I awoke at 7.10am, by my watch, I decided to make a pot of tea for my roommates and coffee for myself, I did not doubt the accuracy of my watch. I boiled the kettle near the lift and made the tea.

On returning to the bedroom I was about to place a cup near the bed our Scottish friend slept in, when I noticed the time on her watch. I couldn't believe it. It was 6.20 am!! My watch was playing games again and I was wide-awake. I couldn't wake them up now. I decided to slip out and enjoy the early morning sunshine. I was walking alone, as Gordon had said I would be. The birds were singing and I appreciated the still beauty of

55

the early morning, with the dew fresh on the lawn, as I sensed the atmosphere and energy with each tree. Towards the end of my walk, I approached the sanctuary when I suddenly felt a deep sadness in the pit of my stomach. Was this me? Was this the tree? I couldn't make it out. I stood for several minutes puzzling over these strange feelings. Eventually, I returned to our room and made another drink before waking everyone. I laughed, explaining my crazy watch and what had happened in the garden. Was this the experience I was to get a revelation on at a later date?

Hilda Martin was running the week and I had a private reading with her;

"This seems to be a period of time where they are now expanding the spiritual work. A Rabbi works within a circle or group to do with the scrolls in a temple. *(I wonder if he is the Scribe people have seen over my face, who came once in trance to speak and writes with me - or rather my writing comes from this level of altered consciousness and I just feel he is on my writing level.)*

The immediate 5, your reforming nucleus is 5 and 5 is your number beginning a cycle of 5. 1983 finishes an era. You work between a spiritual and a natural law and the Rabbi sees you don't break either...." Interesting as I had investigated Spiritualism for 5 years and sat in Circle for 5 years.

Mary Duffy also gave me a private reading, which was to astound me, with the accuracy, 8 years later!

"Spirit are taking you to a mission or chapel. Teaching you within the very beauty and simplicity of life. How we can reach the Godhead, especially over the last 6 - 7 years. Nearly the end of a cycle of 7 years. Seven is important it is the number in a house. I am informed here that you are, either have some official part to play in a committee of organisation of a church, possibly, or society or if you do not have this position, you are going to be asked if you will take this on because I saw a building there with you. I felt I wanted it to be not I or Spirit necessarily. From you was projected a thought that I want to enhance this way. I want it to be known to many people. I want to build this place. I have a gentleman come into your vibration, who also knew about buildings and he says 'You don't worry because the plans are drawn up.' Obviously spiritually but symbolically also. Part of a spirit plan is such. You conform for a little longer with the ideas, if you like, or the people around you...I have the perfume of flowers, which I bring to you on the spiritual level where you are working. Will you watch for it - healing - compassion. The perfume of flowers with the healing. *(We were to have perfumes in the room at a later date.)* The lady who helps you. Spirit want to take you to London City, beautiful Pembridge Place,

56

beautiful church conditions. You will see wonderful ladies. The atmosphere is so beautiful, a place for the future. *(This turned out to be completely different to what I thought some 8 years later!)* You will try to pattern the atmosphere on that place. Healing. A Mission, a spiritual organisation. Healing of the mind............ This lady in the spirit world who did know indeed a great deal about development. You have a wonderful old Medium lady here. She belonged to the place you are working in at the moment. You have church condition please? *(My home is often referred to as a church and Noreen was the wonderful Medium lady who started us off).* You belong to a spiritual organisation. Lady Presidente for quite a lot of years, she was in charge *(This described Noreen very aptly).* She is still in charge of like El Presidente, She will make everyone toe the line, very strict, very much the conformist. So we cannot have people treat lightly this work. She will continue the job that she started but you must help. She will do it with you, through you. She tells me 'If I have your co-operation, will be able, they will permit me, you see'. And it will be like a liaison between you two is good. The Indian that belonged to her, he stands here *(I have his psychic portrait).* If ever she put a foot out of step, she tells me in the beginning he was the one to say Oh no you don't ............ *(Noreen had often said exactly the same thing to me!)* Your footsteps will be guided and your mind by these in spirit - spiritual. All these things will take you to a point where it will produce a retrospective picture. You managed beautifully. Apply to Spirit. You can only succeed."

Ivor James drew me a picture of my Nun commenting on getting the mouth right. This touched a nerve as I felt the mouth was a little out of proportion in the picture Coral had drawn, the first time she came to my house. Could my thoughts have caused a second picture to be given to me? He continued saying; "Spirit dress anyway. There is a guarding, steadying influence with her. You need protection against the pressures. Very delicate pale colour, lilac and rose pink, nothing very strong. A very delicate person altogether. Her dress is soft white, I fancy. She is associated with colours - very pale, very brilliant. Important - there is some kind of anniversary. August is pin pointed. Think about August - Jerry - something to do with Jenny or Jerry. It could be a family link, psychic link. Is free of all entanglements and is helping and is interested in something else and anticipating something good and effective. A build up of something here. Something will be achieved by someone who didn't think it would happen. Someone is saying; 'I don't think it is possible' but in a way it has been diverted slightly but suddenly something someone wanted to come off and it didn't. They have sort of wrote it off mentally. Not at all - this person is saying; 'It's very good and it will come off' - some one is attached in with a circle or group who is very physical. There is a lot of energy and activity there again something is building up and is in itself quite an achievement. Has Albert got anything to do with this August quite possible. The pattern has changed half a dozen times and won't change again. It was laid down before you ever knew about Spiritualism. Quite a change now" The accuracy yet to be proven about Jenny and Albert was quite an achievement in itself.

When we give Energy it interacts with the Universe in our movement toward a Worldwide Spiritual Consciousness, we vibrate at a new level. We receive in return. When we give or project Energy into someone else, a void is created in ourselves, which fills up through this connection. Once we give constantly we receive more than we can possibly give away.

Our natural pursuit of truth enables insight's to begin to come in on a global scale. The demand to end any economic activity that threatens the beautiful natural spiritual world causes intense introspection and higher values of truth, love and peace which create profits of Joy, by living dangerously and often isolated from those around who still play emotional games, owing to helplessness and ignorance. Setting an example that others may wish to follow is the goal we set for World Peace.

LOOK WITHIN, GO TO THE 'I AM' PRESENCE AND ASK IF YOU ARE TRULY OPEN TO RECEIVE. Do you have faith that you are abundantly prospered in divine order? If anything other than joy, enthusiasm and gratitude are present, do affirmations, prayers and ask for help. Keep in mind that whatever things look like on the outside, they are a perfect reflection of your own inner beliefs. This is the perfect opportunity for you to bring forth your inner joy and faith in abundance.

Shortage of Energy can be remedied by connecting with the higher source. The Universe has unlimited Energy and can provide all we need provided we open up to it. Opening up to the source and switching on the power flow is a progression back to that ultimate raised consciousness that brings about co-incidences which actualise a new level of awareness on a permanent basis. Adventures marked by co-incidences can be stopped if we manipulate for Energy by playing a drama game. These are familiar scenes for which we wrote the script as children. We repeat similar scenes time and time again quite unconsciously, without being aware of playing a game to manipulate a situation and gain energy or attention from someone exactly as we did as children.

Once flowing with the natural and spiritual laws of the Universe we find a movement from one occupation to another because people who receive clear intuitions and inspirations of who they truly are will find a way to cut their employment hours to pursue the truth. My own meditation and circle work was already cutting the hours I worked, although the amount of work I was doing, was equal quality, if not better than before, and life became easier - as being refreshed and on a higher vibration enabled me to produce a higher quality of work in a much shorter time period. Although I found I was risking all in taking time out for Meditation, the fact that I was rewarded 10 times over was proven time and time again as I was moved to the right place at the right time and life became less stressful as I moved in harmony with the Universe.

There is a tendency of some people, to steal energy by controlling another person or situation, it is a crime many of us find we have been engaged in at some time or another, when we feel depleted of energy and cut off. This happens because of a lack of knowledge about the high energy level that can be reached through meditation and raising consciousness to the source of abundance. We all learn the hard way. Some thrive on negative argumentative attention energy. Others absorb other people's energy. They can only work on other people's energy and often pick up their pains, depression and illnesses too. They can sap us like the elderly who have no energy left or the psychic vampires who deliberately draw on other people's energy instead of building their own powers around themselves.

When we take co-incidences seriously and become aware of what is going on with our situation and feelings - with regard for security, we open ourselves and become wide awake to what is really going on. We then view life with new eyes defining the Physical Universe of pure Energy that responds to how we think. We can be knocked off guard and lose our energy when we are afraid, but this feeling often helps us to attain what destiny is leading us to become.

The level of energy that started it all off, is instituted inside us. Once the higher source has been reached and switched on through attunement in meditation, we exist at a level of higher unlimited energy and vibration, which serves us as a new outer limit.

Whilst on my first visit to The Arthur Findlay College, I received two readings relating to my Energy field, which showed the hard work I had accomplished over several years of personal development and introspection. I was then able to work with other people. For it is priority to handle oneself before setting an example for friends and acquaintances. Many choose to overcome their own weaknesses by working in an environment field where they can help others with the very same issues that they themselves are handling within themselves.

I thought these examples were flattery at that time and too good to be true, but these have since encouraged me to believe in myself, when certain people have attempted to destroy me and squash my spirit. Both were Canadians who were psychically working with energy fields. Note that no communication with spirit was made.

Carole 22 7 83 It's beautiful, such a beautiful vibration here. It's so outgoing. The energy is so full there's no blockages here. I don't think I've ever seen this before like that. An awful lot of joy, mauve green, a lot of progress in the last couple of years. Field of Corn - harvest. You have sown so much. There's so much you have to do. Everything is just falling into place for you. It's unbelievable, I've never seen a beautiful vibration like this. People have a lot of love from you, all humanity, animals and children. You've done a lot of good work on yourself. Circles - really going to go a long way with this. I don't know how you feel about platforms but I really feel you will be working from platforms. I don't feel it's right away. I don't feel it's for a few years. A question mark over the top of this very high energy level with you............

Doug July '83 I'm not getting a person I'm just getting a feeling. There seems to be a tremendous radiance from your personality. You're a person who gives tremendous warmth of relationship to other people but also without saying anything, give a lot of support and encouragement through your volition to those around you and I gather you may feel a lot more than you express. You reserve a lot more than you actually say. Your feelings towards other people and the way you regard them, your volition is very pure and what you want to give, the best of yourself to those who you care for, those who you relate to in order to draw out from them the best person that they can be. But you do this in a quiet way but underneath is a much deeper and much firmer energy that you try to evoke from them as much radiance from them as you can. It's not something which you try to get something from them. You're trying to help them to become as full as they can. That's why I get from you as much radiance. It's like a golden light which booms out and it seems to come from the chakras in and out here *(heart and tum.)* First a golden glow with a head on top. A huge sun there and I feel there's some disappointment and sadness in your life from the past. What happens is that you've sort of capsulised and sort of, well, you don't hang on to it. It's not worth hanging on to and rather than interfere with this strength that you have, you put it out and it's just evaporated. You give love and, not in anybody's direction, resentment, you let it go where it can do the least damage. You don't think your thoughts are of a lot of value. You don't have a lot of thoughts to add to things and you don't pride yourself as an intellect but none the less it's one of your strengths because it means that other people can support you, can adhere themselves to you and be your friend and you give them support because of your own strength. Well on the whole I feel you're fairly healthy.

There was no spirit contact therefore what they were picking up was from my energy field; by feeling and sensing Psychically - no Spirit was present and this was not mediumship although very helpful as a psychic reading proving that mediums could also use their psychic abilities as well as be in contact with the spirit world. Both ways need developing.

During an exercise one afternoon, we had been asked to concentrate on a partner. As I looked at my partner in her sleeveless dress, a shadow appeared over the top of her left arm, like a dark grey sleeve. This told me that she had a problem in that part of her body. When I explained this to her she denied the problem. She said it was a case of mind over matter and she had no problem there - even though she could not even lift her arm! This taught me how blocks in the energy field could also be blocked by our mental activities, rather than allowing the physical body to express itself and share the emotional trauma that was causing the original pain.

When we left the College on Saturday full of the wonderful things that had happened I wondered what would happen that night when I had a visiting speaker booked. As it turned out the speaker did not come or phone to cancel. The first sitter to arrive chatted then suddenly started to describe a Nurse from the First World War and said I had bumped in to her in the grounds of Stansted. She said she had overwhelming sadness in the pit of her stomach and used to say her prayers in the early hours of the morning around the grounds of Stansted Hall. And that I had bumped in to her but she didn't want me to know it was her at that time. Quite amazing - proving Gordon had been right and I did get a revelation on an experience I had walking around the grounds of Stansted on my own and not with people!!

As I sat and reviewed some of the experiences at Stansted I suddenly saw a clear Technicolour picture in my third eye of one of the ladies I had met there and was told to contact her - Mary. I looked up the addresses I had taken from the members of the Glasgow party and wrote a letter to Mary. A reply came a week later from Cathie who said Mary had died and her husband had given her the letter to answer owing to them having been together that week. The strange thing was that it was Cathie I had had a picture of and now realised it had been Mary who was giving me the push to contact her. Cathie suggested I join them the following year on Caledonian week.

After my first experience at The Arthur Findlay College, Stansted, and the way the circle was progressing with several signs of physical phenomena, I decided I needed to learn more about developing phenomena and what this entailed. The Physical Phenomena week, in April 1984, at the College, was fully booked. Maybe I wasn't ready to learn more yet. I decided to book a week in August for Caledonian Week, with some of the people, from Glasgow, I had met the previous year.

Then I had a surprise, a couple of weeks before the Physical Phenomena week, I received a cancellation and was offered a place on the

Physical Phenomena week. I could not afford two weeks in one year and was already booked to go to Caledonian week in the summer for fun. As chance would have it, I also had an opportunity to achieve a cash bonus for the very first time, at work, which would actually cover the extra cost of attending twice in one year. This meant extra hard work but I put my shoulder to the grindstone and achieved the bonus. Afterwards I was to find the money was always provided in many other ways, whenever I was to be trained, learn more about spiritual work or be involved in anything to do with Spirit work. One Medium had said that all my holidays would be spiritual holidays and this turned out to be true - even if I thought I was doing the choosing.

When the time came for the Physical Phenomena week my Parents agreed to have Tara, the dog, and were meeting me at the college on the Sunday, after I had dropped off one of my Saturday night Demonstrators in Essex en route to the Hall. My parents had arrived and helped me take my luggage up to my room. We met the two ladies; I was to room with, in the lift. One commented on knowing I was their other roommate. We checked room numbers and she was right! She must be psychic - I was in good company! My parents enjoyed visiting the hall and stayed for lunch, which I had previously arranged. Then they left with Tara.

When I spoke to Gordon about the previous year's experience, after what he had told me about walking in the grounds and the revelation I would get afterwards, he remarked: "Didn't you know there are nurses buried in the grounds?"

"No."

"There is a bench dedicated by one."

This I had to see and check if anyone else knew about nurses being buried in the grounds. I found the bench but no graves or proof of burial.

The lectures held me spell bound. I felt Gordon was speaking to me personally when he said: "You will find yourself unable to wear synthetic materials." .... "This will happen...." "You know why you need so many baths and showers? It enhances the psychic energy and replenishes you ready to work." It was good to know someone else had experienced, what I was getting too and clarified my baths and conking out prior to going to the Circle at Noreen's. During question time where I always had many questions and always wanted things clarified, he said I was developing like he did. Was he a Light worker from these other planes too? I learnt quite a bit about running circles and what to look out for as well as what happened.

Before arriving, I had been doodling faces and had one picture where the nose was unusually large. No one had a nose like that. I tried rubbing it out and changing it but it didn't look right. Imagine my surprise when I actually caught sight of the face and nose I had drawn, when a lady turned sideways on and the outline of her face was exactly the same as the picture I had drawn!

After one of Gordon's lectures Irene Sowter, a lovely Medium and Healer, turned around and spoke to me saying: "You are a physical medium." I turned my tape recorder on to record what she said:

"Oh, no!" I argued, "No I just lead a physical circle."

"Well I'm telling you - you're a Physical Medium. If you could smell ectoplasm, it is there with you. I can almost smell the ectoplasm with you; that is if it could be smelt. Haven't you had flashes of light, when you go to bed at night quick flashes? This is a sign of physical mediumship but you have got to get the right group around you. Carry on as you are going. It could go forward into spring, then one by one all the sitters will be removed. A lot will be cleared out and all new sitters will come in. Carry on as you are now. You have earned it - what you are going to get. Carry on with your circle then one by one they'll fall away. Then you'll have a blank time. It could happen by the end of this year. It could go forward into the spring. One by one they will be removed, then you are without any sitters at all. Don't panic, take each day as it comes, then you will find the urge to sit in quiet contemplation for physical work. Start in quiet meditation."

I had no idea of this and still argued that it was nothing to do with me as I was only the circle leader and one of the sitters was to be the Medium for it, not me. *(The others certainly would not like to hear what she had said, as there were two already telling me that they were the mediums for it)*. Spirit hadn't chosen the Medium yet.

"Mark my words" she carried on. "I could never sit in anyone else's circle and had to wait over a year for my sitters. One by one they will be removed and then you will have a blank time. One by one all new sitters will come and you will begin in quiet meditation for the real work."

These words were a great comfort as before Christmas and during the following year one by one left the circle and tried to put their problems on to me instead of taking personal responsibility. Obviously they were not ready to move into the next dimension.

During the week I was in Dorothy Patten's group and the first thing she said to me was that I had a Psychic rod behind me therefore I must be sitting for Physical Phenomena.

A private reading from Dorothy Patten on 13 4 84 When she said: "A life that's been, shall I say, shattered. Nothing to do with passings, people, and twice you've had to put one brick on top of another to re-build it. Well congratulations from someone who didn't give congratulations easily. I mean they were very kind but um a bit like my Mum they would say 'Yes you have done well.' All they say is Congratulations and this lady also had, not an easy life - the easiest of lives - but for different reasons to yours and she too, in her time, had two lives in adulthood. She had two lives - you've had to re-build your life - you've had three lives more. So she is really saying Congratulations. There's some more sorting out to be done on a different level and you cannot please everyone now. Never ever will you please everyone in your business, personal life or in your psychic work or whatever, so don't try. You try, but don't grieve too much; when you cannot please everyone. You can be firm when you choose but you don't choose very often. Well it's good, it's very good to be able to hang on to your temper but that's not the right word. There does come a time when you have got to plunge for one side or the other. You have got to be firm. You have got to be very sure to use the right words."

On April 9th 1984 Betty Wakeling gave me a private reading, which gave me food for thought when things began to happen to confirm what she said.

"What's happened to a baby? I've got a baby here. She was born then I am cradling a baby. Somebody that was very close to you. Would do a lot for you because she is making a contact with you and she knows your little girl. Well she's not little now because she's quite grown up and very often at night when you have these beautiful feelings coming back, you have been with your girl and I feel this love is so strong with you but I feel, with the lady that isn't your mother but is still a very strong link with you. *(This was Noreen again)*. She was the one that looked after you and you looked after her. There was a very strong bond between you and you were very sad when she passed to spirit...

There's a strong link somewhere that is pulling you over water. Have you been making contact? *(Yes)* Are you a little concerned about your daughter because I feel that there are some thoughts going out and there's thoughts coming back from your daughter but she seems to be somewhere special? It looks to be more like a spiritual journey than anything else. I feel that it's not all been in your hands. I feel that whatever she's doing, it is for progress. I feel that it's experiences she is having. *(Proven when my daughter returned and told me of her experiences, which changed her life.)* I feel there is a lot of love between her and you. I feel that other sister, She is something to do with it and she is getting satisfaction too, from what is happening to your daughter. I felt somebody with rather gingery hair with you *(my daughter has red hair)*. I can just see the hair. *(My daughter was in Los Angeles, seriously ill with a blood clot on the lungs. She nearly died twice and altered her whole way of thinking in a flash when she was drawn out of the body, so this was a spiritual journey for her.)* Have you just moved home? Where do you go up steps then, in a home? You visit a family here living? Is there a house you go to with steps going up to it? *(She moved both hands up as though the steps went up either side, to meet at the top and I had no idea where this house was.)* Do you go to one where there's been somebody who wore a uniform? Do you live on the coast? There is a bay window overlooking the ocean. Who lives near the coast? Somebody in spirit knows something about it. A link with a uniform. Watch what you hear in that direction. *(Absolutely accurate the following year.)* Somebody singing. I want to hear singing, linking in with a choir. Do you know anyone who links with a children's home. *(Yes)* I want to go to a children's home. Have you been looking at this book because I feel somebody must have been with you linking with a children's home...*(I had worked in a children's home in Switzerland where I was given a book of children's songs and was only looking through it before going to Stansted. Schwester Inge, who had been in charge, had died)* .I'm smelling beautiful perfume. Someone is very fond of perfume. Something from the East. Do you smell a perfume? Watch - it's something from the physical. *(We had several perfumes of flowers and an incense the following year.)* Are you sitting for Physical? Have you had movement? It will come because there are the colours with you. There's quite a lot of red very active - you don't sit? Orange coming into yellow which shows you are very wise with what you are doing...but at the present time there is a lot done with healing. Does someone ride? I just see a horse's head. Something to do with a horse. Does Christmas mean something special. *(This was to prove quite amazing as I found a little silver horse apport after meditating, in training for whatever spirit were up to, on my own, 18 months later at Christmas time and thought someone must have dropped it but after checking with everyone who had been in my home, I found it could not be claimed and it was too big for a necklace or a bracelet. I took a photo of the horse, outside on the concrete in broad daylight, to publish in this book and was astounded to see the result a completely red photo with spirit lights proving the energy of a phenomena!)*

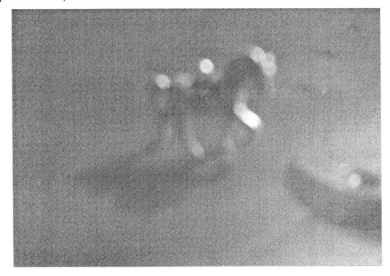

I feel it's something to do with the activity, but I do feel you're working on the right ways and you have a very strong Indian and then I see your daughter and she's the one that gives you the pictures because you get pictures sometimes. She is the one linking with all this. There is work you are going to do with spirit but it's not going to be easy *(Nothing worth doing or having is ever easy)* but definitely you are on the right way. Did you give your daughter something that has a chain in it? Watch where you are going to link in with a chain. *(I gave my daughter a long gold chain for her 21st birthday.)* A chain makes a link and a link is a chain and whatever is happening around her is making her link and it will become a chain and I know she will go on all right and your other daughter is very much a part of her."

*(Having taped all the lectures for my group members to also learn about the advancement of Phenomena, I was surprised at comments about not following what was being said, realising that the only way any of them were to learn, was for them to attend the actual weeks at the College).*

Gordon demonstrated physical phenomena on the Wednesday. We were all advised to rest that day. I lay on my bed and went into an altered state where I had a psychic dream about one person who had been to my house once. In my experience she had invited me in to her home for a cup of coffee and as she turned from the kettle, she flew at me with claws and nails, attacking me for no reason. I sidestepped and stopped her. My insight in to her true nature, this way, had opened my eyes to my own response to Gill, the one who had left my circle. I had responded with; "Oh no, not her" when she said she was now sitting with her. And slammed my hand over my mouth, when she had told me they were sitting together. I knew she had to learn her own lessons the hard way and although I knew what would happen - I could not do anything about it, for each had to learn their lessons their own way. This experience seemed to confirm what I had known.

Gordon's demonstration of Physical Phenomena was extremely interesting to me. The various stages of trance to direct voice and ectoplasm caused me to feel excited at the achievement and cleverness of Spirit working with this instrument. To hear independent voices as well as deep trance was a priviledge and very interesting. A voice asked for a 'Warner'. I waited for someone else to answer, as no one knew I was associated with a Warner and I was unwilling to accept it was for me. No one answered so I said; "I know a Warner."

"Do you know a Kerri?"

"Yes, she is my daughter."

"Do you realise how ill she is?"

"I think so."

At this time the direct voice of Kuku chipped in with; "I've just been to Los Angeles and it's beautiful out there!"

The other voice carried on with; "We, on this side have been very concerned about her. It has been difficult but she will be all right now. Do you know Tara?"

"Yes, is she behaving herself?" No reply.

"Would you go to where Lee is?" *(I thought to myself; 'What on earth do we want to do with him anymore.' As I remembered a Lee my daughter knew who was in and out of remand homes.)*

"You're thinking of the wrong Lee - would you go to where Phil and Fay are that is where we want the Lee." *(That was clever as my next door neighbours were Phil and Fay and their 3 year old son was called Lee).*

"Something to do with some fish" the voice carried on. *(Well that was true as they were looking after my tropical fish whilst I was away.)*

The fact that my thoughts were being read and answered immediately was the most evidential part of the message to me as well as Kuku saying Los Angeles was beautiful.

Even more evidential was a materialised head that came out of the cabinet showing every hair of his head. Voices all around began to say, "That's Jack." "Look at that - that's Jack." Several people muttered at the same time. Betty Wakeling was at the side of the cabinet outside of the viewing range. The head was moving around to the side of the cabinet, as Betty leaned forward to see her husband Jack looking at her. The most impressive thing was that every hair on his head was clearly showing amazing me with what Spirit could accomplish with the ectoplasm.

The following day I had a message on the breakfast table for me to phone my parents. I phoned to find out what was going on. Tara was destroying the place and was to be put down! I went to Charles and asked if I could have her in my car for Thursday night and I would then leave on Friday night. He agreed as long as I didn't let her in the building or walk her on the lawns. I drove off to fetch her from my Parents. She slept in my car. The following morning I walked her up and down the drive, after feeding her. I then realised the sun would be on the car and without thinking about my tape recorder that I had propped against the wheel of the car, I moved the car under some trees. As I got out of the car someone came running across towards me with my tape recorder shouting; "Look what you've just done."

I had run the car over the tape recorder and squashed all the buttons flat! "Oh, no!" I couldn't believe I had done this. I desperately tried to pull the buttons out and make it work again, with no success. I went into the Hall and asked a man to mend the buttons and make it work again. He tried for several minutes, then said; "I think you will have to buy yourself another one, this is broken." I couldn't believe it; "But Noreen gave me this recorder - it cannot be broken." I said to myself. I tried again and handed the recorder to another man who also tried his best and said exactly the same thing. By this time the lectures were about to begin and I had no time, to take it back to my room. I went into the Lounge and propped it at my side, as we listened to Irene Sowter's trance. It was a shame I couldn't record this work. At coffee break I went into the cloakroom and my 'voice' said; "Try another tape." I had another tape in my handbag and took it out and tried it. It worked!! If that tape would work then the other one should too. I put the original tape back and it worked too!! A phenomenal power had mended my broken recorder whilst we listened to Irene. Just to prove what Spirit can do when everyone is not trying to do anything. The tape recorder is still working to this day! Miracles are possible or was it a law I didn't know about?

In the August of 1984, I attended Caledonian week and enjoyed a brilliant week of fun and laughter. During the week I had a private sitting and received more guidance, which took several years for me to understand completely and prove correct: -

Ruby Webster 14 8 84 Linking with you, I would say if it was an older lady that you must have thousands of friends and relatives in the spirit world owing to the amount of people that are congregating around you. I don't feel they are blood relatives, I feel its more like people you've touched, not only touched but somebody you've helped to get in contact with somebody of mine - like you would have friends people that you were instrumental in getting them in contact. At this present moment it seems I am on the verge - I don't know whether this is really selected yet in your thoughts. There's some change - I'm going to open it out - it's a new avenue something new - I want to enlarge upon but I'm not sure yet. I haven't got it - its not clicked in yet. I'm still toying with the idea. Now you have been wondering whether it will be the right thing. Should I do it? Is it a bit ambitious? I feel, I want to say go ahead. You've got to that stage now where you must take the next step. I don't know whether money matters - after all it affects us all. We like to think it's not important but we cannot do very much without it in a material sense but the monetary position here, I feel there is going to be a new opportunity a new Avenue opened where you're not going to make so much personal effort to acquire the necessary to do the overheads. There's going to be some new Avenue opened when it can take this kind of pressure away from you. You don't have to look, do you? When the time comes it will happen. We can waste an awful lot of energy by thinking 'Well I have got to think if I don't do this then I had better do that because if I cannot get that then nothing is going to be successful'. I feel that your own sincerity your sincerity of purpose and if you prove this sort of depth of integrity, the door will open and that source of supply will automatically flow when it is for the right purpose because I feel that there have been so many times when you thought - You've actually felt that this is the right thing and then you've been let down, been abused and you've been very bruised by other people, their actions and their attitudes because you're like me - you are a big girl but inside you are like a little sensitive girl with a skin like a butterfly wing - so fragile that it's easily pricked and I feel, that there are times when you have produced and projected with such sincerity - these vibrations into your aura and you have allowed, because of your trust for people, to tear and cause little rips in this garment. Fortunately it hasn't put you off it hasn't made you so frustrated and destroyed that you think 'That's it'. You keep bouncing back in. Mostly everything around you has a spiritual orientation. It seems I want to be moved away from all the material conditions. Is there any thought of moving here? Are you moving house? I feel as though I want to be out of the summer I want to be in Autumn time when something new - Its going to be like a mushroom - its suddenly going to shoot up. You are going to think 'Now who would have thought. ' Out of the blue - something. Who would have thought just what I want. You know it's going to come - something like this. Now at the present moment you seem to be - you've got an idea in your mind you are teasing it about - you are contemplating doing something - I know you do meetings. You are going to enlarge or you are toying with the idea of enlarging this instead of just a little afternoon or evening. You are doing something a little more venturesome. Have you thought of a little school - workshop? I only want to be where you are. I don't think you have even suggested it to anyone. Could I do it where I am in a smaller way? Can I do it? There are so many ways. Even a few - 10 at the most. A one to one sharing and blossoming because I can see this in operation actually formed. I feel while it is spiritual it doesn't necessarily always have to be Spiritualist orientated. Spiritual is the keyword. This is the pivot on which it all works. It's the spirituality that each of us projects to get a better hold.

Somebody's mind is going too fast that I'm not getting efficient and proficient at something but I'm a Jack-of-all-trades. I'm not mastering one. I want to be a little more selective. I've dabbled and I've touched. I've investigated and I've tasted a lovely big bowl of fruit and I've had a bite out of them all. Some I like and some I don't like. Some I'll go back and finish but I just wanted to taste it all. Finish the piece of fruit you start because it would be a shame if you miss the sweetest part near the core and just nibble

69

around the skin; you're going to miss the beauty. I don't know if you sit or have an awareness group? I'm talking about a selected few for development or awareness or spiritual attunement and I feel here, the seating arrangement should be changed. Is there somebody not blending in. I feel there is someone not quite as good as I want them. You have an idea - I think I know where it is coming from. At the same time I don't want to hurt anybody's feelings - be diplomatic. There's something just not jelling somewhere. It's not bang on yet. Healing - I feel here that healing is an interest of yours but I also feel that you want to be away from the everyday little ritual that healing groups whatever. Because I feel that you are investigating other means, other therapies. Do you ever use a pendulum? What about Pyramid energy? Are you interested? I see this Pyramid and also a strong Eastern influence. *(I was attracted to a pyramid when I visited Canada at a later date and bought one which I sat under and had interesting experiences with.)* Something with regard to this beautiful soul. I feel a very strong power. Do you sometimes feel a little hesitant - a little reticent in doing something or putting something on? My skin is a different colour or it doesn't go with my hair. I feel that this Eastern influence, influences you over so strongly sometimes, that you could paint and garb and dress up. Is there anybody around you having difficulty or an uncomfortable feeling around the lower half of the body? Probably touching someone somewhere. I feel you are going to have to be very selective - a little more selective in the people you allow to be near you. You are going to have to be a little more positive. Admitted, when you are a friendly person - well if I can help them - I'll love them all but I feel you have done this and you haven't always been appreciated. Not that you are looking for bouquets but you have been bruised - you have been let down. Now I am touching a money situation and I feel I want to say to you are going to have to start and keep two purses and not be such a daft touch when people are a little bit hard up. Can you? Will you? Or I am hard up and you think well but I feel you will help this person more by saying I'm sorry I cannot. You are going to have to manage because I don't want you to become the crutch because they are not going to stand on their own feet. You're always going to be there - consequently they will think 'Och, she's always going to be there - she kind of helps me. I want you to be able to say 'No, I'm sorry I cannot this week - I've had a bill or I've had to do something and you're going to have to manage.' It'll be difficult and they won't be terribly happy about it but they are going to learn and by doing this - they are going to become stronger and you will help them more than even they realise

You seem as if at times, so anxious to open your front door. I don't necessarily mean the house - it is symbolic, and get a great big pair of stepladders to stand on the top and shout 'All you lonely lost hungry thirsty destitute come here I can show you all the way. I'll help you.' It seems as if you've got such an anxiety to be doing this. You get impatient with something; you know - you've got it all worked out here but getting it into an operative plan isn't as easy and you get frustrated. It isn't for us to see how hard or how fast. We don't care really if people are going to recognise what you are doing and you are not terribly interested, hopefully, that someone is going to bang on your door and you receive great mountains of wreaths and bouquets. All this because you've helped me - you know inside.

Do you know a little girl - a coloured girl that would link in with you? Whether she is a little helper, a little guide or she just pops in to lighten the atmosphere. There is a little coloured girl nipping about here. Two names Pansy and Daisy. I don't know whether either of them are significant. I feel here, you would need someone to help you keep the atmosphere fresh. You need someone I don't know whether you've thought about - as if you want to form - I don't know here whether you've got the plan formed - how you are going to go about this new little group sitting but I feel you want to take some weeks in preparation of the others before you actually start what you hope to do. Anything from 6 - 8 - 10 weeks and its a kind of education. If they lose interest then not to worry. It's been good they didn't get started but I feel want you to prepare and have this ready because soon the doors going to be opening and I must be prepared. I don't want to start fiddling about once I've got started, as though well do you think if we do so and so. I want it formed and I've got my lists made out and this is the pattern 1st, 2nd and so forth session and you are going to lead them gradually through these initial stages so that they're ready for what you want and hopefully are going to establish. I'm seeing a trumpet here and it's a new one. I don't know whether you've got one or you're thinking about sending for one. I'm seeing a new trumpet. Now I don't know whether - Now I feel as if you. You yourself. You are going to have quite a surprise. It's a new thing. Its going to be made manifest with you as the operative pivot - You. This is where you're going to have to be very careful, very selective, because you're going to have to have the right kind of people there that you can trust and that will keep that chain of protection of strength unbroken. You I feel it's with you. There's doors opening for you. I feel as though you are going to be led into another group. You are going to be directed into another group where these opportunities are going to offer themselves and you think 'Now these things could never have happened where I am.' You! You, something pertaining to yourself. Still conduct your own circle but this'll be one you're - I feel you're going to be invited or led in another group for you. You'll still be in charge of yours. You are very conscious of what's needed. You wouldn't drop them and leave them high and dry because you are very conscious and because of this you keep on doing. Others can drop out and, maybe, have a night off; you don't - you're always there but you are going to have the opportunity to go into another group for you yourself. Now I don't know whether this is you or its someone closely linked with you that does a lot of reading always wanting books and reading. Somebody is buying books and reading. Somebody is buying books I see. Don't buy anymore you've got all that's necessary and I feel I want to say for a little time put them away. You've read - you've dabbled, investigated, questioned - start and make it work because after all these books are other people's experiences. It's nice to listen, it's nice to hear and talk and read, but if we keep doing that all the time, we're keeping the curtain drawn across and not allowing the sunshine to come in. Put them away for a little while and start and put into operation - what you have learned - be big enough - have the daring to put it to the test.

Do you know where there is a broken wedding ring somewhere and while I'm handling this ring, there's a strain somewhere in the material that you've touched on - condition - there's a strain in a relationship not as harmonious and I want to say that you are going to be asked advice and because you're you 'I'll tell her what I think and I'm going to say...' Don't, make the right noises 'Oh yes it is a shame but not to worry it'll work out.' Interest yourself in things - don't commit yourself at all because I feel as if the strain - the weakness of it will link up again but then you will never be in the position for somebody to say; 'If it hadn't been for her this wouldn't have happened.' (She seemed to be talking about Gill who had left the Circle and did link in again in the September, when I asked her to come back.) You're so sensitive, you're so vulnerable, and you're misunderstood so many times. You open doors and half the time you don't even know what's coming through them willy nilly. You say; 'Oh you must come and see me - give me a piece of paper.' Anybody, anybody. You don't care who they are. Come and see me. You've got to curb this a little bit because you are being used and while you do benefit and you are quite conscious of being re-charged - I cannot afford for you to be depleted to such a degree - where someone is going to benefit from this energy and not know and appreciate what is happening. (Some, who left my groups actually commented on losing what they had gained at my home and had taken 9 months to get back to the same stage they had reached before thus proving this to be correct.) Its all right for the ones you are going to be able to school through these initial stages but some just want to know for the sake of just wanting to know. Curiosity is good - we all have to be curious before we start to investigate but sometimes people want the fairy off the top of the

Christmas tree before they've even got the tree in a cemented pot. 'I want that off there'. And these are the kind of people that you, sincerely, but not wisely, keep on doing this. Now I feel that there is someone close here, close to you who loves often but not always wisely. They love too well but not wisely. I don't know if someone is thinking of getting engaged or linked up with someone - thinking of going and setting up home with someone - to think before they jump. (This was my daughter but she went ahead anyway and learnt her lessons the hard way.)

Did you know anyone that drowned? Somewhere in your gatherings - somebody knows someone who drowned. (Some had picked this up in the circles too and it confirmed the little girl working with us in the Physical Circle that B M was to give later.) Now I feel here that I've been helped a little. Have you ever done any rescue work because I feel here you are going to be instrumental in helping someone that's sort of been plunged into the spirit world not prepared and you're going to be able to help these things. I think you attract and draw people round you that sort of take the wrong path and I feel somewhere in the physical you touching someone is going to open a door because I feel there's someone linking in now. They are showing me their arms. They are all pitted with injections. Somebody must have been taking drugs and for some reason or other - I don't know whether you just thought about this and I would love to help in some of these fields and I don't just mean when they have just passed over. I mean in the physical and it would seem as if you're going to begin a new Avenue, a new venture with your spiritual work and its helping people that don't know. Not the ones that come to you that's read a bit and had a few visits to various churches and Mediums. You're going to go through another door, a new Avenue, where you're going to help people that really need help because they don't understand anything at all and because of this - this is where I feel that you are going to be drawn into another group so that you can be strengthened, completely strengthened - for you! But even your own group - you can adapt this and get them to sit, once in a while for you. Not that you're going at that time or in this stage, into a trance condition but just so that they're going to impregnate, fill, surround, saturate you with their power and their vibration so that you'll be able to pick up these conditions so easily. It's like your antennae is out and you'll immediately pick up and you'll know where to go - what to do at the right time".

21 10 84 In a dream Gordon H arrived at my house to sit in circle. Although the door was the same the interior was different but as previous dreams with different rooms. A big old house with many rooms. He brought two women who were not of the correct vibration. I asked one of the women to open the Circle but she fooled around, therefore I stated there

would be no circle. I walked and talked to Gordon asking him how he knew, although I knew he had received the information in a private meditation from his inspirers. He said; 'Well, I knew you'd ask that.' I told him he had had a written invitation so I did not feel guilty turning him away and said: 'No-one can sit until they are invited and you refused the previous invitation. When I had invited him originally and written to Charles - I had an argument with Charles the first time I attended Stansted, about not replying with the stamped addressed envelope I had enclosed. A printed piece of paper would have sufficed. Gordon was definitely on the same link I was on and I knew he could teach me more about these things than any of the other Tutors. From then on I booked 1 - 2 - 3 weeks a year at Stansted for his Trance and Physical Phenomena weeks.

# CHAPTER 6

## PHYSICAL CIRCLE

When I had a private trance reading with Muriel before taking her out to lunch and then bringing her down for a group sitting, I was quite taken aback that the whole reading was for Gill who had left the Circle. I questioned Topsy on whether this meant I could ask her to join us again. "Yes. Just the one this time." (Meaning not her husband or sister.) It was whilst I was on my way to work one day, that I saw Gill and gave her my tape asking her to let me have her opinion after she had listened to it. Gill phoned me to say she had been getting the same thoughts herself and would like to talk to me. We met and I explained that we were going to sit for Phenomena but she was not to go in to her trance states, as Spirit hadn't decided who the Medium was going to be and we all had to give our love to spirit for them to do the work. She agreed.

My daughter had moved house in the September, when she received a full time position where she had previously been doing voluntary work with disturbed teenagers, and was happy to have a room in the house she had wanted, as I had forecast, and as she was happy, I was happy. This gave me freedom to open another more advanced circle and pursue the phenomena side of development, which was the movement of progress to reach higher minds. In September we started with 8 sitters, including those from the original Circle and some others who had sat elsewhere. The developing circle was now with the others who had come through the open nights on Saturdays and were interested in development. I still invited visitor speakers to the open nights on Saturdays for newcomers.

Bill Marie was recommended as a very good healer. He came on Saturday 29 9 84 and was surprisingly good with his clairvoyance to each of us, especially as he knew nothing about what we actually were doing in my home and claimed he was only a Healer and didn't do anything. He had asked me what I wanted and I suggested he spoke about how he came in to the movement. In the Saturday group that night he arrived and immediately told me: -

"You're a teacher in your own right. You know your own guides don't you? Push them aside and can I just talk to you about Egypt because I feel, very much, that this is the land that I would love very much when it comes to teaching the Wisdom of the Ancients and I feel very much there were many secrets that he would have known. He would have taught in the Temples, actually. He would have known a great deal about Spiritual Law and we talk of Jesus being a great teacher, which he was, but before Jesus there were these wonderful Teachers of Spiritual Law. Aspects of Levitation and that's why you laugh at levitation because levitation, you know is possible. He's moving aside and the China man is coming through and he says "Me too." I feel, very much, the Egyptian is a wonderful teacher and I would want for you to link with him because I feel that he also guides the groups you're working and he is trying to build. We talk of Churches and this is what it's all about because a Church is only another meeting place for Spiritual people and he says 'Church Meeting Place for Christian Spiritually.'

There's a new person coming - will help - will help - is needed. This is to do with your circle. They're looking for somebody to come into your circle. There is some to do yet but we are very close to the move from A to B one experience to another.

You've got an Aboriginee, you know? Well he's got a white face. *(Coral Polge drew his picture at a later date and I also saw him overshadow someone who misused energy before they left the group, proving his protection to me.)* There is a bloke who stands behind you and you know the white face, I thought he was an Aboriginee actually but his face is white and he also acts as protection. You need protection. There is difficulty at the moment with spirit people I'm sorry there's nasty ones. It's necessary for you to build a protective shield before we go in fully. There is always nasty approaches from all spheres. Not people on Earth - people in spirit. You've got to defend yourself and protect yourself. You're not doing Rescue work are you? Now that is the only reason I would have thought you would need the kind of protection that he's talking about. It's not long. It's being prepared now and should be within a month or so. It will be an extension of a circle you've already got, but there will be some from one and some others in. It'll be an extension from one to the other and you'll find they will be powerful people that you have already got who will want to come in to this other one, whatever we are talking about. That's what he feels but there is also one we are waiting for. Be still my child, we select, we coax, but we cannot force anybody to do anything against their will, so therefore we take you and hope you will come. If you don't then we must find another. This has been going on for a few years of time. We have one that we feel will fit. The trouble is, of course, if we say who, where, and what you will expect and no other will do, consequence until we know that that one will not only fit but accept that it's pure free will, then it would be foolish of us to tell you. Until such times as the acceptance is on both sides, it would be absolutely foolish because you would say it must be that and you would be extremely disappointed if that was to walk away. You ask for these things and we try but because we are in spirit, you take us for God.

We can only ask, encourage and direct but we cannot interfere with Man's free will. So therefore you say will this happen and we say if A and B and C works, it will happen but because we say it's a possibility you don't like it. You say it's got to be tell me. All things we can lead and direct but we cannot predict to the extent that it is going to positive because we cannot interfere with Man's free will and Man is fickle. It has taken seven years to achieve the state we have achieved up until now but it may take another seven years to achieve the state that we would want to achieve. If we say one thing that such as it will be and it doesn't materialise because.... you will have lost your faith in us, so therefore we say to you be patient my child for indeed it will be. You have your time, allow us to have ours. He says it will be. Man's fickle mind is the one that creates the problems rather than harmony. That's our biggest problem HARMONY. That's within the group. That's our big problem possibly. Harmony is an absolutely essential aspect of what we are trying to achieve and life on earth is so difficult no one can be in harmony at all times. Stress and fatigue and types of illness tend to make difficulties amongst each other and although in trying, personalities have a tendency to clash due to many things but we are doing very well but it needs to be better. Can I say everybody, before sitting should spend a period of time preparing before sitting because some still fetch in the outside world and that creates a great effort for us to calm it down and much of the power is lost, because we are trying to calm people, calm rather than work. But everybody must, before they come in, go into themselves in silence and leave away all efforts of the day chuck it out. Think only of the joy, of the communication, the excitement. Sometimes we are very boring and when we are you certainly show.... It certainly shows. We say to you please be patient - Attunement is absolutely essential - Preparation is also an absolute essential. We are doing well. We are moving apart to build another part and put one on top of the other and indeed all will be well. The reason You (P) cannot move. You've made a promise to your people that you will be prepared to do as they wish. At this stage it is absolutely imperative that we get this as it should be and we cannot, at this stage, afford to have you stop now.

This winter is very important. Can I talk to others sitting too. You've all talked about the world and how bad this situation is. This winter is very important for your team spirit to harmonise to get this off the ground. There must be an absolute 100% effort from everyone in it. Please watch for sickness because that is a problem, no can be a problem because when one-steps out it's very difficult to keep the balance of Power and we cannot progress as well. Are you lighting spirit lights in the corners of the room? They are lighting them in the corners of the room. What they are saying is that it's very important that you don't miss because it keeps an imbalance and when one drops back. It is hard to keep the balance so therefore look after your health. Do your meditations. Attune to your spirit people as much as you possibly can. Who is trying to fetch in Phenomena? You are that's all right - guidance from spirit. You want to see spirit, so there must be no change other than fetch someone in. But all of you that are sitting in it. You should make sure that you are prepared in Truth to sit as you should. Then there is a wavering and to be quite honest you would be wise to remove that one. *(I phoned her the next day and went to talk to her. She had been wondering how to tell me and was so happy that I had the same thoughts that she flung her arms around me and gave me a big hug for allowing her to leave.)* About the little girl. She's about 9 years old, pigtails, plaits that come down here. She is to do with the China Man. The China man is teaching. The Power is built up. It's absolutely imperative you get that solid. Get it solid. Keep your places. I don't have to tell you how to run it, it's essential. There was a time you were talking about changing. Keep everything as it should be. Water we want water in the middle. We want water in the corners, we want flowers, we want things growing and..... I'm getting all excited...and we want always to open in prayer. This is for the protection and the right type of spirit people. The little girl will be the controller of the people that come round. Please don't ask 'What am I doing in the Circle?' Just know it is important that you be there. Don't question your part, her part, and his part. Don't question it accept it. Just come as part of a group. Do give whatever you have but for God's sake prepare yourself. Don't just walk in and say I have had a heavy day. It's wrong. Do that outside. When you walk in the day has gone. Today is the glory, the excitement of today and don't be afraid to talk. Talk and sing. We are quite happy for you to sing and we want lively.... You can play tapes but it's better coming from you. What is needed is when they can hear your voice, they can follow it, they can link with it. Tip toe - that's basically - as you build that, you will expand into another field. This is a field that is for spirit; this is for man. We talked of Rescue. Organise it as such because one will enhance the other. What is important is that you have a situation here where we can have spirit control, but it is very important that the rescue aspect be considered too. Not in that in the other and a team from that will help you to do that. In other words it is one brick on top of another and it will work but be patient. Can I tell you the little girl is a cockney and can I tell you a little bit more about her? She died. How? She fell in the river and she was drowned. Does the name Abby or Aggie mean anything to you? Only as I'm talking I'm picking up the name that sounds like Aggie/Abby or something very similar and I think that's the kid's name. Has Jess got anything to do with it? One of them at least should be attached to that kid. When you're working some of you will pick up in your meditation, the river Thames and you'll either see Tower Bridge or something. This is how some of you work. You see pictures; you get visions of that. When you see the Thames it'll be her way of conveying to you that she is there. Each one of you, at the moment, needs personal convincing. You need to be convinced that you are playing a part within this and at the moment there will still be questions, so she will try to interpret to you, and come to you. Once she does you will see her by emphasis on the river Thames and you will feel like singing Cockney songs Lambeth Walk. That is the kid being trained to work within the circle. There is a Chinese Man that is extremely important where the kiddie is concerned. So I say to you all; Please, for God's sake, don't let it go, put some more effort in to it because I feel for sure it will be good. There is somebody already talking in the circle, someone is talking - instruction talk. There's two and I feel very much that this is important, that the music, the sing a long attitude is just as important in fact I think it - I'm excited to get this kiddie bit. The trouble is with the talking, it has a tendency to hold you back from your work and I don't mean to be rude but they're saying to me. "You asked us to come and we get carried away and we tend to leave little time for effort." That's really what they are saying. Look for the sing a long, so we can all work to produce the power that is needed to light the voice boxes, to produce the voice boxes that will also be the media. Bless you Finish. If you've got something just give it off - oh let's have another song in general conversation. Don't lay down a pattern. Sit down - prepare yourself - prayer safe - allow it to form. The guides don't need to come into you. Be still happy and contented. Help to build. Always talk about what you see - one at a time. You've got to have a leader to control it. Do you mind if I talk. Do you mind if I say something. I just saw this. I just heard that. Feel the backs of your neck coming up and she's on my shoulder. That will happen and each one of you will see a little - enough to convince you that you are part of what you are trying and that will come about this winter. Beautiful - lovely - it's a collective thing everyone works as a team and no one is greater than anybody and what you're trained to do is to.... It's some form of phenomena that you need to see spirit persons and that what we are trying to fetch forward and the kiddie is the one that will help and direct and we are trying to get the kiddie to be seen. That's possible. At this stage there is a lot to be done. What you are doing at the moment is working to build individuals and we don't want individuals. *(Unfortunately this remained the biggest problem, in most of the Circles, with most of the people only wanting to develop themselves and not work as instruments of the divine allowing Spirit to do the work).* We want collective effort, but each individual has got to give everything that they have, from which they will all be fully developed as Mediums anyway. They've got to express the way that they feel. According to the way he's talking, it will come, but it will take a long period of time to get the basics. The soldiers that were killed - that's the form the rescue will take part".

There was such a lot of excitement from Bill about getting everyone committed to sticking with this work. I wondered what the real problem was, as first one then another left. My writing had stated: "We are surprised at the thoughts that emanate from one of the sitters." Who? And what were they thinking? I read it out one night and another resigned saying; "It's me that you read about." I asked her what she had been thinking: "Oh, I wonder what this is all about and my part in it." I couldn't believe it after Bill had said specifically 'Don't question your part, her part, his part'. It was very sad that the harmony and balance couldn't be achieved. One left in the autumn and the other left before Christmas so Irene's forecast was proving correct.

The Circles carried on and I had opened another Development Circle for those who were just beginning, having been regulars of my Saturday nights and some had developed in other circles. I heard of a good reader and went to test him out before asking him to come on a Saturday.

Mick's reading on 23 2 1985.

"Basically money seems to be making money split in two directions. Money you are earning is going to the house but also going in other directions. *(My spiritual work, running groups, buying books and attending The Arthur Findlay College.)* Very much, a lot of strength from the point of view, you're doing an uphill struggle and not a downhill struggle. It's taking a lot of effort to motivate other people to keep the enthusiasm and almost, a wanting to stand back and watch things happen because you feel there is a lot more that needs to be done on your side, as a person. Also a lot of career opportunities arising, but you are not able to take the choice of because of the field you've chosen. Clarify. On past efforts and the work that has gone through, you have achieved a plateau. Now this is in a way, splitting two people. I've got one person liking what they do and one person not wanting to be there. You at work and half your mind is not wanting to be there. I feel the past efforts of one; in a way you've wished you had done more of the other to build them up to an even keel. Go back through time if one had gone with the other one, there would have been more stability of what you're trying to achieve at the moment. Very much, one is right - its level. The other one you are having to work at, to get to the same level basis and one you're having to put a lot of energy into, at the moment. You need to find, in yourself.

80

A lot more strength coming through from that angle. Around you there is a tremendous amount of emotions and you are seeming to stay in the middle. You don't seem to be going one way or the other. People around you see you with all these talents and they are wondering which you are going to settle for Spiritually. There are four different ways you can go spiritually, and you try each one of those four. People around you see you as a Magician to give other people those spiritual talents as well. This work will produce someone who will be quite renowned but this person needs to be forced into the limelight and it is almost as if one is giving love to two. In this way it seems to be giving adversity to the mind within. Although it is going ahead, it seems to be an area where someone doesn't understand. To someone around it has to be a closed subject. Someone who is doing extremely well to be renowned but there is an area where they cannot be as free as they would like to be with the discussions that they have. Not here outside area. Some one in a way frowns. I'm talking more of a gentleman than a lady. A lot of nursing to someone. They keep looking back on the past and not on the future. I feel there is a wheel of fortune that has been very cruel to this person. There doesn't feel, at the moment, anyway that this wheel is going to stop and that is how this other person feels about it. Someone in your family circle wants to buy a house but cannot. However much they sigh, the adversity seems to stop them from doing it but there seems to be ways being worked around where other people can help and that help will come a lot more than people think because there is an added bonus coming to that and the bonus is an idea that someone will give that will allow it to be done at that rate but in a different way. *(This happened to my daughter who, in spite of having the mortgage arranged and surveys done, lost three of the houses she was buying. The final house had been newly decorated, fully carpeted and had a new bathroom fitted by the builders, thus saving a lot of time and extra money.)* You've got a lot more to do. A lot of justice is going to come to you and justice will bring you money because there is an area where there's an expansion you need to do and you will find this will happen towards the end of, not this year or next year but the year after. (1987) There is quite a bit of money but I feel you don't own it. I feel it's coming to you. There is a lot around you, a lot of light. There seems to be more light going out than coming in. I feel you will be going to a wedding towards September next year, not this year. *(Quite accurate. I had been invited to a wedding the following September on the day Bill Marie was coming and was not willing to cancel him. This decision was taken out of my hands, when Bill cancelled with family matters, was rushed into hospital, had three heart attacks and died the next day.)* It is to do with someone you know very well. It will quite surprise you. Building is going on beside you but the energy that is there. You've got to be careful that there is always enough fuel because there is a fuel situation where if you run out of fuel, you can make yourself ill. *(I did this a few times before learning my lesson.)* Protect yourself there is someone around you who seems to be sapping your energy. I don't feel they are here, they are away. Don't go too far within. There is someone wants to take you into a very deep state of meditation, very much wants you to contemplate very deeply and by deeply, go within your very being. It is Spiritual but there are risks involved and I am being warned, you need to be careful about it. *(I realised the dangers and how it only happened on my own behind locked doors)* Anything you turn your hands to, is going to make money and I'm talking again, about 2 years hence. Anything you want to put your hands to will make money, but it's all for a reason. Not yours it's for other people, but you seem to be the principal King to do with the money. *(Could this be spiritual gifts I had 'caught' and not money?)* Don't go too deep within yourself. You have to find the level that you need and that's why the Jester's there, because sometimes you go too far below your level. When you go in, you feel you're not going to come out again. *(I had felt that too!)* I've got someone who would like to take you down a long cave. The cave has the Source but at the same time, if you go too far down, it is difficult to see things in the same reality that you went in. *(This actually happened in a transpersonal psychology excersise.)* The perception, that you would see, would be different to when you came back out again. Funny act with a deck chair. *(During one session of deep meditation, I was out of my body, aware that the sun bed, I was lying on, had been gently folded up underneath me and then straightened out again. At the time I felt it had something to do with levitation and control of physical matter.)* You are going to the seaside. Be very careful of disturbing the sediment - wine. Music, for you, is the right way to take you. *(Music played an important part in preparing the room before all circles.)* Clear the air locks before you sink the submarine. *(My lungs and breathing.)* A lady who would have been quite huddled up, very much, as she got older. She wouldn't have been able to use her hands. Her hands would not have been able to pick things up. Your hands will but at the moment they cannot, but what you pick up is precious and that is why they are saying don't move the sediment."

As the Circle progressed I was astounded by my own development from just seeing colours then a heat haze around people and being told that only very advanced Mediums saw the auras. I was seeing Spirit in the room objectively. No one concentrated on me and all my development came from giving my all to everyone else whilst I led the Circles. In fact the less I thought about "getting" anything the more things happened especially in my own private Meditations, therefore I realised that the more Meditational time we gave to God for these things to happen - the more we were rewarded in our daily lives and in being developed further.

It is very important to have the right sitters Gordon had said. These sitters don't try to develop their own specific gifts. The 'trying' blocks Spirit from working with their channels. They are then trained by the Spirit Guides and are being used as divine Instruments developing the power, which is used by the controls who, by extracting that power, the Spirit Power is maintained - it is a team spirit. Sitters reach the point of trance - when whilst giving their all to God and everyone else in the Circle, it just looks like they go straight to sleep. From a Circle of this nature everyone in the Circle is developed to the maximum of their own capabilities. The joy is that everyone is being trained and developed as Instruments for the Divine.

For Phenomena to be in the Circle - Cobwebs, will be felt, a moulding denotes physical energies. Ectoplasm is taking place and sitters feel breezes, which eventually bring apports. *(these things had been going on ever since my first circle.)* For Levitation there is a feeling of hot air around the hands. Table phenomena - very heavy hands. Sometimes the Power's there but not being used. The Circle maybe confused - they have got it all there but are not specific. Try table phenomena. Teaching Circle. Ask for controls - advice - direction. Normally one then the other. Always a reason for sleep in the Circle. The other body is used in Spirit - it may be a build up of power - not always trance - power goes back to the people and also out to mankind. Don't put light on after closing - cup of tea- something sweet replaces lost energy.

To have the powers so strong you find yourself moving - that's the relationship with your development - where the spirit is moving you. When you have given yourself wholeheartedly to the power and that is where the greatest effort is to start with. When you are able to see and listen to the greater minds of spirit. The spiritual beings that avail themselves to the great minds of spirit because you see Physical mediumship is not only the development of the great power - it is the movement of progress, beyond the basic stages, where gradually you are reaching higher minds and they are coming through.

Purely for God's reasons not commercial or personal. Energies there but not used means Spirit can tap in for good or bad. Test and try the Spirit mentally before talking. Mediums are working 7 days a week and not paid in monies. Ectoplasm in the beginning is liquid fluid and very soft. A Cabinet or a Curtained off corner is often used to protect the medium- to keep the power close together and the work goes on in it. Trumpet phenomena can take place whilst spirit people are working on the other side. Don't put a cabinet in a room until spirit instruct you to do so - work with sitters first - open the Circle working with you. When satisfied they ask for a cabinet then the real work begins. Lots of things are going on first to enable these things to take place. Red is the only colour ectoplasm can take never a direct light.

First Stage: Trumpet phenomena, table phenomena, things floating, and then trumpet

Second Stage: Transfiguration - moulding on face.

Third Stage: Direct Voice

Materialisation is the last

A lot of practice with table phenomena to practice raps - get intelligent responses - use an upright trumpet - a red light makes it is easy to see the ectoplasmic rod because it is very long and it has suckers on the end. It works at a tremendous speed. With the Discs going round, these are cardboard with luminous paint which is enough light - start with no light at all.

Physical Mediumship is a rare gift so put all effort into developing transfiguration. The Spirit people have got to build up a tremendous power of their own. The Face is covered with ectoplasm and moulded like putty. For those with a negative solar plexus, it has been known that they can draw on this ectoplasmic material from other sitters, especially when they speak or sing therefore this is the reason all the sitters hold hands in order for no one individual to be absorbing the power and then the power is used purely by the Controls. Talk and sing. For the action of the voice makes the body positive and conducive to giving out of it's substance for the Chemists on the other side and production of the ectoplasm and power.

The mechanism of Materialisation is bound up with the movement of electrons and their entry into or out of neutral atoms. Neutrons and other small physical and etheric particles are also responsive to the will.

The positive people who connect directly to the Divine Power for Healing and channelling the truth are able to produce phenomena without using any of the singing or drawing on substance from those in the physical body, that is so necessary to those with a negative solar plexus. Either way the Medium has the physical makeup from birth and cannot develop something that is not already there. The laws in the Universe are responsive to rewarding the Love and appreciation given, in dedication and service, by producing phenomena that may be classed as "Miracles" but there is no such thing as a miracle only spiritual and natural laws science has not yet found a formula or explanation for.

Nowadays the Positive/Negative Solar Plexus people are their own source of energy connecting to the divine source and resulting in many more achievements without a group format. They are often developed on their own during Meditation. Development becomes a personal choice and dedication in their own lives.

The principles are good for all Materialisation: whether they be for the Séance room phenomena or for the materialisation of some high ideal into practical and earthly reality. Nothing is created without a thought form nothing can incarnate without desire. Through meditation we are assisted in the materialisation of our highest thoughts and aims in service to the Universe. Those who take part should be very aware of what they are doing and their heavy responsibility to safe guard the Instrument/Medium and themselves.

A New Age Spiritual culture is evolving where the individual is raising consciousness to a higher frequency of vibration, enabling a wider range of knowledge and appreciation to be perceived. There are many born with both positive/active and negative/absorbent Solar Plexus actions. This explains the confusion in so many born in female bodies with masculine tendencies and those born in masculine bodies with feminine tendencies. Unfortunately many stay on the physical plane of material sexual aims, instead of raising their consciousness above the base chakra through to the heart centre, in meditation, to combine these qualities to a spiritual level, that is their natural birthright, resulting in beautiful unions with each other. The heightened sensitivity combined with both practical and intuitive abilities of bringing the spiritual planes down to operate on Earth, is the responsibility of these 'cuckoo' children, in this lifetime.

The more this aspect of appreciation develops and works firstly in overcoming selfish desires, then, within the immediate family and amongst friends on a non-judgemental, unconditional level of appreciation, the higher and finer the vibrations become.

When we appreciate each other through the heart centre, we all glow and radiate and have more presence. We can focus on each other, sending more energy to lift each other and ultimately move into another dimension. As we give of ourselves, when connected to the source, so we empty ourselves and are given more to give and radiate with the love, we then walk into, everywhere we go. Once we are radiating the Spirit helpers find it much easier to move in closer to their instruments and develop them accordingly.

Many factors are taken into consideration with various invisible Guiding forces and the many spiritual guides in a human body too. Several people forget that we are a basic core spirit within a physical overcoat and when that coat has been shed we do not change, therefore as like attracts like continuous testing and trying of the guiding forces is very important, before putting complete faith and trust outside of ourselves.

During our earthly life our Parents and teachers at school influence us. Again we test the relevance of their guidance and make our own conclusions - drawing from our inner observations. Along the way we meet a variety of people who influence our direction in life. These influences are both positive and negative and both teach us what we want more of or what we want less of. The free will choice we individually have is to reject one and follow the other. Either we choose a selfish destructive negative way or we aim for the selfless constructive positive path to freedom. Sometimes there is a constant battle going on inside; where the selfish side is prominent and at other times the selfless part wins. Commonly known as our conscience, our inner tutor and psyche are the best guides. The wisdom and source of all knowledge lies within connected to the selfless universal mind of all creation The God force. Also within each one of us, lies the temptation to follow the destructive selfish, devilish part. Both have a voice in our overall conscience, and we then have an inner personal fight for overall control.

Our Family members and guardian Angel often stands beside us on our left as well as our selfish materialistic attachments, whereas any who approach us from the spiritual teaching or communication levels from the invisible realms come in on the right hand side. They can be clearly felt or sensed (clairsentience) in exactly the same way as those with a human form and can be clearly heard (clairaudience) just as though someone in a physical body speaks, in the same way a friend might do. Sometimes the hearing is within the mind and at others outside of the body. They can be seen by those with clairvoyance - clear seeing beyond the normal senses but similar to the extended vision or hearing most animals have. This can either be subjective in the mind's eye or objective when actually out in the room or surroundings.

The aim of a Medium is to develop all the gifts of spirit in service to humanity i.e. loving, healing, sensing, seeing, and hearing and go beyond the normal five senses to the supernormal communication of the more advanced realms of knowledge and vision. They continue to sit for the rest of their lives. This development cannot be taken lightly and similar to any with a gift, whether music or art, it means a life dedicated to this purpose, often to the point of isolation, as far as families, marriage and children are concerned. For the higher finer advanced development it also means daily practice in the form of meditation until that is second nature and we walk in the state of meditation all day long to the right place at the right time for whatever service we are being guided for. The dedication is often too much for some who have a natural gift but are unwilling to devote their life to it and fail to fulfil their potential.

The tests and trials of endurance and stamina take students to breaking point, which often causes them to turn their back and give in to the pressures of life, other people, family and children. Many are called but few are chosen for dedicated work, therefore few achieve their full potential in this lifetime. There is no medium or healer that has had an easy life.

The complete development of these gifts of the Spirit often takes from 12 to 18 years or more. These souls are born with knowledge and a calling they cannot deny. It is interesting how the writings in the Bible speak of Jesus at the age of 12 and then nothing is heard of his development and training; until he begins his work at the age of 30 a gap of 18 years. The most interesting parts of his training and development have been completely left out of the story although there are many schools of wisdom around the world claming that Jesus visited. Did he learn from the ancient wisdom? The best teachers? 18 years went by with no information about his preparatory training for the work he was born to do for three years. Maybe few are as interested as I am in how Masters became Masters and what tests and trials they had along the way. This part of the story has been suppressed for there are many stories and legends around the world about Jesus visiting their shores and learning from the wise ones of that time. This part seems to be the part that is lacking and kept secret. The same as all the Schools of Wisdom and the secrets of Initiation, yet Jesus said that even greater things, than these that he did, we could also do in his father's name. How, if he and others never disclosed some of his training disciplines?

In my own development I stumbled blindly and searched endlessly for the information I wanted to know about. I read many books on Development Circles. The older ones had always held hands and the Power of Spirit made itself known. The comment by Harry Edwards books on Development "In the light of experience, I now see how much better this initial training could have been. By acts of concentration in any direction, the mirror of the mind was strongly possessively occupied with my own thoughts, thus obstructing any inflow of spirit communication. This word 'Concentration' is very commonly used during development. It is a wrong word giving a wrong idea. A much better directive could be found in allowing "abandonment" of thought to take place."

This tied in with my way of thinking for it was in the "Letting Go" of our own personal will that Spirit did things and definitely not when someone was trying. There are no guidelines for the activities that happen when Spirit begin to use the love power we build and the resulting joys Spirit devise to train their instruments - yet the work is similar for all who follow the Divine Path. The knowledge appears by word of mouth at the right time and in the right place from those who have gone before and walked a similar path. When the pupil is ready the Teacher appears. Nowadays the training information is dying out before it can be printed or passed on. This is sad therefore all I have stored and recorded, as information to help me in my own pathway, from some of the best teachers, that I met along the path, is being reproduced to help some of you, now reading this, to carry on trusting and believing your inner truth. I endeavour to help you with your confidence and confirmation, that you are on the right path and all will be revealed; as you meditate and follow the truth, in due time. No two stories are the same but there are many pointers along the way.

As Saturday nights progressed with some very interesting evenings - more people attended. Bill Marie came again and spoke to me saying: -

"Your Guides are very close but what I am more interested in is this person. Tall slim man. I'm only seeing his face; I don't know what he is. That's a bronze colour. You know a Red Indian fellow that controls the circle. I don't know whether he is a Red Indian or whether he is an Egyptian because, at first I'm seeing his face and as he shaped up, something on his head and I didn't know whether it was feathers or the turban of an Indian Arab Egyptian. I like the nose it is very prominent and I like his bronze colour. It seems to come out with light and I think you will find he is the controller of your group. Does his name begin with A? I missed it it's a very small name Assas, As. You'll see. Don't let anyone see. Don't let them listen because I'm sure, when he comes forward he will introduce himself and his name will be given very small one, about 4 - 5 letters - Azzaz. He should introduce himself. There is a tooing and frowing of attitudes and lovely people but not quite right at this stage of development. Is there a tall gentleman in your group? *(Yes)* A tall thin gentleman, very quiet, he should have more to say. He is very wise and will you listen when he has something to say because I feel, you'll find, that unlike most people, he works for the betterment of the group rather than himself, and his philosophy, he claims he is a healer and that he doesn't do much of anything else but actually, his communication is very good, according to what they have to say and they are saying listen to him. Don't tell him anything but if he has something to say, please give it a lot of consideration because much of what he has to say.... The symbol of your group is a crook. You must have seen it. That's the symbol of your guide, your teacher. That will be his personal symbol. So when someone sees or says there is a crook. *(Two people had seen this, just the week before, in two separate circles! One had clearly seen the crook and one commented on someone offering a goblet or glass!)* Be sure that the guide, who is responsible for the group, is in fact in the chair offering a glass. There are two people that see him. One of them very clearly. There's also one that's questioning too much and got a very analytical mind. It doesn't do the group a lot of good because it's negative thought that comes in with it all the time. We must at all times talk completely positive. Water situation we want more water. What they are saying is, not just to drink. We want water. It's extremely important. It's being used to..... Is there someone who keeps talking about colours? You should soon be seeing colours and the coloured aspect is important because that's the start. You should see the colours on the outer rather than the inner part of the group. So would you look as though you were looking over the head of people, not as an auric thing but as a circle thing? What you will do is see blue from here to there and you will see light shoot from here to there. When you see it - everything you see will you please mention it and make sure that everybody mentions what they are seeing. The vibrations have got to be kept up and a very light attitude, very happy go lucky but very strict. Time is very important, who keeps coming late? There's a situation of someone coming late the way he's talking watch for it. No way can we accept lateness. It's imperative and make sure everyone is closed down when they go. There is somebody who is losing strength. It's nerves, it's tense. A husband, wife situation here. One of them has a tendency not to close down efficiently and therefore is there one of them having tension. It's having an effect on the circle because somebody who is very close, who is good, then you have to look and see what's creating a problem with them because it's that which is creating a problem. Is she a healer? Then that's what the trouble is. She needs to close herself down. Will you tell her that it's imperative that she does? 'Cause if she doesn't, she will find that her healing capacity will tend to dwindle and illness will come in and you will find she will be suffering and eventually she won't be able to work. But it's not only her that is the problem, will be, it'll be the partner and he will fetch that around to the same. *(I had already told Gill this some time before Noreen had died.)* This is important. Listen and accept because you haven't the slightest idea of what is being done this side, to get this thing, as it should be. The circle is going better now than it has gone for a number of years, not weeks, years. We are very excited. The interchange of people has been a good thing, it stabilises and we fetch new and old and as we join together, we find that their experience consolidates the eagerness of the new and it helps. Do you put flowers? He is saying we would like flowers. It's the colour of the flowers that we mean to enhance the colour. We will take it from the flowers. That's why we need the flowers. Actual fact, put flowers in, we take colours from everywhere but it's nicer if we can get it from a natural source. Different colours. Who's got a tummy upset. *(One of the males commented on picking up this tummy upset with the same lady who was also having a problem with her partner.)* We've been looking in and healing, - doing what we can. Anniversary or something. Someone in your group is getting married. I feel it's something to do with your group, very pleased for it. I know what it is, it's the marriage of the spirit which is symbolic of what is being done here. There is a lady going into trance. This is completely different trance, where somebody will talk to you, that you knew on the other side........This should be very good. I love this. Look for this because this is the start of your absolute control. *(Unfortunately when this started jealousy or envy came in destroying the harmony and the circle disbanded.)* Then there will be no change, it will be a situation where it will have locked solid and we will say we are already seeing things but this will be the start and will gather momentum by a situation that when you start again...which is in the winter time...you'll see that the thing will gather momentum and by that time, it will be extremely exciting. That's as it is at this stage".

The circles progressed, we kept records, and I found the more I gave of myself the more I was given to give. Not many of the others were willing to give; yet they wanted to get. I puzzled over how they expected to develop as a channel of service if they were not willing to give and empty themselves first. How can you fill an already full cup? It needs to be emptied first in order to be re-filled. We have to give in order to receive. My "voice" impressed me that when I had a room full of people giving their all to Spirit, wonders could be performed by spirit and every single one of them would be developed from this remarkable divine power of the spirit world. I loved giving and helping in spite of being constantly put down for opening my home and organising everything for free. I loved the work, the unconditional love power that flowed through me and enjoyed the groups. I was never concentrated on but constantly gave the power for all the others and realised that my own development was speeding up by this constant giving and pouring out. Many said I was a fool but I, personally, learnt a lot and as long as income came in from my daily work, I continued this way, receiving some amazing co-incidences and joys which I related to the Universal help I was now attracting. The more we give the more we receive is a natural law and it astounded me with the rewards, happenings and training I was receiving.

The groups expanded each year and were showing interesting results of development. I felt that the healing development enabled people to become more aware of what was happening around them in their daily lives. Meditation calms the atmosphere in a home and releases frustrations and stress. My own meditation last thing at night also impressed me to write. I received lovely stories about ancient Native American's life in the wild, with a Silver Wing, and then attracted another element. As time progressed, every time I wrote the writing began with: "We are here...." I tested this out owing to the words flowing through my mind first. Then for days I could not write and when I did; I began to write faster than I could think! It became an interesting aspect in my own development. I questioned who "We" was but received no answers. The meditation part was always the most important and the power of spirit built from my completely letting go and letting it be.

## CHAPTER 7

## HEALING EXPERIENCES

My own experience of receiving Healing from Harry Edwards, in 1973, had left me on cloud nine for a couple of weeks afterwards and seemed to have triggered my own healing gift in to action.

Whilst playing Badminton my healing gift manifested further, without me trying to do anything. Maybe sitting in Circle and then putting my hot hands on Noreen's back had triggered something stronger into action. One day I noticed a player lean on me and fall asleep. I felt something happening as the energies flowed through me. I realised that I was being used for something but I didn't mind, owing to my wish to be of help but not to be noticed linking in with spiritual realms. As I let the energy flow through me I knew that it had nothing to do with me. I was only the instrument for whatever service was happening. I turned on the tap but the water that flows is not of me but comes through me from a Universal source. I seemed to have opened as a pipeline. If we truly live, as I believe we do, in a universe of infinite supply which flows from an infinite Source, then somehow I had opened myself to the abundance of that supply from sitting in Circles and constantly giving to everyone. All I ever asked for was to be opened and used as an instrument in the best way possible.

There was obviously more to this than meets the eye as she gave me a funny look when she woke and found out she had been leaning on me! She also felt the benefit. Obviously there was a need for this way of healing, as the following week one player was rubbing her aching shoulder and saying that she didn't know if she could play at all that night. I put my arm around her shoulders and rubbed the spot with my hand. This was the first time I actually rubbed an aching shoulder, the recipient turned to me and said "Ooh that was lovely. Can you put your powers on the other side and make it match please?"

"I haven't got any powers". I replied.

"Whatever you have just done has taken all the pain away so can you do the other side to match?" Laughingly I replied: "It is Spiritual Healing and yes I can do the other side."

"Well can you put your hot hands on my other shoulder please? It really feels good".

During my daily work I was often confronted with sickness and family problems, which meant I would have to work really hard to replace good workers. I was very wary of using my healing gift at work, until one day when I had a phone call to call by and visit one of my most important helpers. She had become agoraphobic and was extremely uncomfortable leaving her home or doing certain things and wanted to give up. I mentally sent my thoughts out to help her before I called to see her and discuss the matter.

On arrival, my hands immediately became very hot and itchy and I wanted to put my hands around her head. How could I explain that she needed healing of the mind? I rubbed my hands down my legs in an attempt to get rid of the intense heat and itching but it persisted. I then asked if she minded my smoking. I thought that if I had a cigarette in my hand I could direct the healing without her noticing. I lit a cigarette and directed healing towards her, in order to release the intense heat in my hands. As she spoke of her problem, she also mentioned 'doing her back in' at the allotment over the previous weekend. I then asked her if she would like me to massage her back.

"You're not one of those lovely healing people are you? Would you do my head for me please?"

I was quite taken aback and said; yes I am. Of course I will. I proceeded to give her healing. I then asked her to see what happened before resigning. The next day her son phoned me to say: "Thank you for what you did for my Mum. She says you have taken all the cotton wool out of her head and made her better."

During my work I received comments about my ability to motivate people with my presence. One house was a regular stop en route into my Area for a Loo call. She commented on being out of the door working as soon as I left the house.

"What do I say or do? I asked, thinking I could pass this information on to help other people.

"I don't know. I can't think of anything specific but it happens every time you call."

At Badminton I soon became known as the Lady with the hot hands that makes you better. Another Badminton player watched me work with people but doubted that there was anything in this healing business, even as I explained more about it.

"Bet you cannot do anything with my knees?" He dared me.

I laughed and said; "Don't dare this power. Are you asking me to give you healing on your knees?"

"Yes, go on then."

I gave him healing and as I linked I felt the same sweaty heat that Noreen used to give me, with her healing and I mentally thought to myself; "This is just like Konchok heat." When I had received healing from Noreen it had felt exactly the same so maybe Noreen and her helpers were also

93

working with me now.

Konchok had originally been with a Healer who gave up his work. Noreen gained his help with her healing, after this had happened. When a guide loses their channel, it often takes quite a time to link with another person on the same vibration. Noreen found that as she became weaker, he eventually made her too hot and she could not do any Healing any more.

After giving this healing in the back kitchen, at the Badminton Club, I was dripping wet with perspiration. His knees responded well - much to my surprise, and when I met him again, twelve years later, he asked if I still did that healing business because his knees have never caused another twinge since I had touched them.

After doing healing this way, I worried because I realised my healing was nothing like that, which some of the Churches directed. This caused me some concern. I must get it right. When I returned home I picked up a book on the Science, Art and Future of Spiritual Healing by Paul Miller and threw it on my bed saying; "I must get this right."

The book opened at page 196 describing a healer called Francis Schlatter, who shook hands with people and they were cured of all manner of diseases. When someone tried to organise a form of ritual for his healing, they found, the next day, a note on his pillow. "I have gone to my Father." He was never seen or heard of again. I remembered Jesus had said 'Even greater things than these can ye do in my Father's name.' Therefore linking to the Divine Source was the only requisite. Jesus didn't use a ritual either. This incident caused me to remember that the Christ spirit or divine source could take on any form. Was this an example of the possibility?

This story was also telling me that the simple, natural way was correct and that if he could shake hands, I could attune as an instrument, open as a channel, with the intent to help, rub someone's shoulders or touch their knees, as it was nothing to do with me, when something happened. I was only a pipeline connection from the divine to the individual. I became known as the lady with hot hands who made you better!

Then lack is a myth we have perpetrated on ourselves in the Churches with dogma and rituals, because somewhere, at some time some one had closed a hand and held on tight to something that brought pleasure. Love. And nothing new could flow into the closed hand. So it was believed that the flow had stopped. But, the river of plenty was simply flowing around the hand *(which held on tight to the thing that, somehow, used to bring more pleasure than it did now)*. A Mother loves and kisses her child better when it falls over - without any ritual - and the child responds. And as the rumours of lack spread through the churches, hands everywhere began to close and hold on tight to what they had. And when they did, they too experienced lack and wondered what terrible force could have brought such a blight upon then. The plenty they had known disappeared and they were left with nothing but what they held in their ever tightening grip. What was happening to the natural expression of loving and helping those in need? The Churches seemed to be busy training people's egos, by concentrating on them as being the doer, instead of giving themselves in service and allowing Spirit to do the work. As a result, they were losing the natural channels of service for spirit to use, as more and more opened their own homes and Sanctuaries.

During my visit to Muriel, the next day, she gave me a trance reading during which my Chinese guide came through and spoke of my work progressing. You have earned another guide." He commented. I questioned this comment; "Is it Konchok?"

"How you know his name? How you know his name?" He questioned and I told him that I felt the same feeling the previous evening, giving healing to the knees, as I had experienced when I had received healing from Noreen. He agreed and Konchok also spoke to me. The confirmation was amazing and I was overjoyed to have his help and Noreen's with my own healing. As a team we could work together in harmony to all and be of service healing and improving wholeness within the confines of the people I came in touch with.

Another top selling representative had a slipped disc and was in agony with the threat of traction at the end of the week and, of course, she was unable to move far. I talked about spiritual healing and she agreed to try it. I put my hands down her back. As I drove away afterwards and my 'voice' suddenly said: "She'll be in agony tomorrow but will be all right on Thursday." Oh dear, I will have to go back and tell her this, or she may think I have damaged her in some way.

During my busy schedule of appointments, I would need to fit in another visit to go back and tell her about the pain otherwise she would call the Doctor unnecessarily. I managed to catch her at home later on. I explained that she would be in agony and may want to see the Doctor, but if she could leave it until the following day before contacting the Doctor she would find she would be much better. She did as I asked and waited until the following day then phoned me saying; "You were quite right, I was in agony yesterday and would have phoned the doctor but waited, and all the pain has gone today. Thank you."

The personal recommendations for help and healing involved occasional visits to people's homes and hospitals during my free time. Quite often I was just a good listener and personal problems were eased, causing more success in their daily life. Many phoned me saying; "You know what you said last week?"

"No I cannot remember, please remind me." I usually replied. They then gave me an outline of what I had said:

"You were quite right and it did help, thank you."

One top lady was a Nurse and I had called to give her an award. She came to the door doubled over in pain. "What ever have you done?" I enquired

"Oh I'm a Nurse and have done my back in again. I'm always doing it as lifting and turning patients isn't always as easy as the book says. I'm off to the Chiropractor at 4.30 pm."

"Have you ever heard of Spiritual healing?" I enquired.

"I'm a Nurse!" She exclaimed.

"And I am a Healer. If you like I will give you 3 minutes down your back and if it helps - it helps but if not you are off to the Chiropractor anyway and no harm can come of it."

She went to the kitchen and got a stool saying, "All right I will try it." I went to the bathroom washed my hands, attuned and came back to literally give her 3 minutes down her back. At the end she just sat there and then said:

"Do I need to see the Chiropractor?"

To which I replied; "You're a Nurse, you should know."

Her children arrived home from school at that time and I left to carry on my busy schedule.

It was the following week when some of her friends phoned me saying that I had cured her - could I cure them. I explained that it was Spiritual Healing and I could not guarantee anything but if they would like to receive healing I would call and see them. We agreed dates and times that were convenient to both parties. From then on opportunities for healing happened every week. I seemed to be in the right place at the right time for these things to happen.

Obviously the Circles where I poured out love to help everyone had been my training ground to open as an instrument for the healing power to flow.

Muriel visited many times and through her trance we experienced another interesting group experience with a Pearly King giving us a few words of wisdom.

'Do any of you know who the Pearly King is? There's one standing here - there's a Spanish lady and there's a man with a kilt on too. Jock yeh Jock - Scots Jock. There's a Pearly King coming to you and a Spanish lady with those things yer know those things. I've got a crowd here haven't I love.

It ain't what you wear. I love my coat - I love all those pearls -

96

each pearl on that coat means something to a Pearly King and that's the truth. What I want to say to you is mate; if there is - if only you can do things, say things and mean things you know what I'm talking about - it aint the lip movement mate - its what's in your heart. How many people, they put themselves on a pedestal and they pat themselves - that aint spirit - its what you do behind the scenery to help somebody - to send out the love and pray for somebody that's hurt yer now. That's a difficult thing mate, on this earth - is to pray for somebody that's hurt yer. Yer don't realise what yer doing to that somebody, because yer creating the love of God around them and the feeling of their minds - helping them into the light. For God's sake don't bury yourself don't feel sorry for yourself - say thank God you've got a body, thank God you've got your two legs - you've got your eyes and you - can think - look around you and see those that can't. You understand my meaning - so bless your hearts and I'm going to say - that so many people can be posh can't they mate, they can put their best clothes on, they can put their best coats on, they can comb their hair and make themselves look beautiful eh but when you get underneath it eh what we can find sometimes - mate - eh this is where it is - it aint what you do it's where it starts from - and that's within your own hearts - it is to be humble - its not put yourself - as though you're something on a pedestal - now come off your pedestal - be a channel and a channel for good. As you sow so you reap your harvest and my God that's true! And in my life mate, I tell you now - when we had our stalls up the East End of London - yer know where I mean don't yer? We had little talks with each other. We never started what we were gonna do to help somebody - it was done - we all got together we didn't say 'I'm gonna do this - I'm gonna do that' but it was given in the heart eh and this is the truth - this is true love of one person to another but this is - again my friends, don't create all that of this earth, within yourselves and think you are somebody great - because you are not you are only a channel of God and by being a channel of God you've always got to link and think and look within and say is there something more on this earth that I can do to help somebody less fortunate than myself - and I'm going to leave those words with you mate because while I've been talking to you there's been a nurse standing here and I don't quite think it is - I'm not certain about her. A Spanish lady with them castanets as well. You're all right mates - well just remember don't go about this earth. Don't shut yourselves away within yourselves and think you are somebody great 'cause you are only a channel of God, eh - just remember my words. It is to love one another, help one another and share love and share God bless yer, from the Pearly King - God bless yer.

"My friends this gives me a great pleasure in returning - oh well I know there are those, who will never understand the 1914 war and I know there are others here that know and realise and know of my passing of the tragedy where I was shot. But again it is my friends it is I that was brought up on the foundation of Christianity of my father and of my mother that I never realised there was the after life until I passed to spirit. I was to help those lads over the borders, to help them through into safety. I could do this work in spirit. Never fear my friends that your work stops, no and I know there is trouble on your earth and there is so much more please God I want to ask even in this little circle - if each one of you had a two minutes silence and we know the armistice is very near and at the armistice there will be those linking with our loved ones and not realising the heavens opened and loved ones are standing by their side. At that two minutes silence; if one could only realise that power that goes out to help these lads; that have passed through the hands of God that are in darkness. It is not every soul that goes to spirit but I want to ask you once again each one of you here - could we have two minutes silence of your material walks of life every day - it is not much to ask. Send out that love, send out the peace and that power that you are radiating out will be gathered for the peace of your earth. So please answer my query, and to know that Nurse Cavel is of service to each and every one to where I can help or serve. But remember that you are the channels so may God bless you God bless you friends.

'You don't know an old lady, do you know what I am talking about. It was another house, another room like this, I feel I came in it. I feel she's decided in the higher life, you understand, it was a bungalow.' *Noreen had a bungalow and was still interested in what we did.* 'She's been walking round yer she's been having a look at yer and smiling, and she's brought me back to er house. Well remember me as I've said before it aint what you wear its what's underneath understand and I would say what you've got to remember is what comes out of that - you understand me - no-one likes to be stumped - think before you talk radiate a nice kind thought to someone, none of us are perfect because you bloody wouldn't be here when you know spirit and you're trying to live in spirit - get a little higher in your thought don't sting don't hurt - send out a thought of love eh! God bless the lot of yer eh look after yourselves and have happiness. There's far more powers up there than anyone knows of. I'm happy to come back if I can help yer I'm gonna help yer - until we meet again. Bless yer - God bless yer. Father God guide each one, as we walk Father let your light shine through. We just need the loved ones and these to know that this power will be done to help someone, so Father God grant unto us thy peace."

And so, as we have been together in this our little sanctuary. To where we know so many have gathered - may we ask a blessing upon each one represented, so each one will be a channel. May we say thank you for all your love for all your gifts and as each one goes our separate ways yes we know others will not be far from the love of God and they too will see the upliftment of spirit, and so may God be with each one - until we meet again, God bless you my dears God bless you and thank you.'

# CHAPTER 8

## GLASGOW

In July 1985 I was on my way to stay with a friend in Glasgow and decided to call in and see my Parents before continuing up to Glasgow on holiday. I also visited a cousin and her family. As I was on the East side of the country. I decided to visit the Medium Ruby Webster, in Hartlepool, whom I had been writing to. I phoned and her friend said she was out at present but would be back by the time I arrived. When I knocked on her door I was greeted with: "She has been back but was called out again with a bereavement." I left a little disheartened and then thought about the one I had sat next to the previous year. 'I wonder if I can find her house?' I thought to myself. I asked for directions and found the house. My knock was answered with; "You, fancy seeing you. Come in". We chatted over a coffee and suddenly she said; You cannot go on to Glasgow, stay the night, but I have put a knitting machine in my spare room and it fills the room. I know, I will phone my friend. Her husband has gone to Saudi Arabia and I know she has a spare room. She proceeded to phone her friend who agreed. We then drove over to her friends house, parked the car then I must have been looking somewhat stunned. There were steps going up to the front door just like Betty Wakeling had described in the reading the previous year in April.

There were the Bay windows looking over the ocean and it had been a Seaman's Mission at one time, accounting for a man in uniform telling her about it!!! Was I becoming a puppet on a string? This was all beyond my knowledge and certainly beyond anyone else's here on Earth. I had gone with the flow of inspiration and enjoyed every moment. The stay was beautiful and I hoped we would meet again.

The next day after a lovely breakfast and walk with the children, I continued my journey to Scotland wondering about the 'Watch what happens' part of the reading. I arrived and was introduced to many of the physical circle members. One had tape recordings of 100's of sessions. I asked if we could visit him. He chose to visit us in my friends flat. The message Gordon had given on my first visit to Stansted was for me! I was listening to direct voice tapes in a flat!!! I wanted to meet the medium.

We visited Loch Lomond *(which my friend had been told would happen in a church message prior to my arrival and plan)* and on our return called in to Langside Church. I parked the car as the phenomena medium and his wife walked past. He was actually the medium for the evening. A tug on my skirt caused me to look around and find there was no one there. I felt it was a child but no one was anywhere near me! Then at the end of the service I felt a hand under my elbow with an impression of Mary. Mary was his sister, so that could be possible. But later on I was told that the last person to receive a message as I felt the hand under my arm was the last person Mary had given Healing to before she died. I definitely wanted to meet this man. I went to the kitchen afterwards and requested to meet him. He took my hand and held it a good twenty minutes. I felt like I was 'catching' spiritual gifts like catching a cold, which were not necessarily for me but I was to be the carrier for them I certainly had something to watch for!!

As time went on and I became aware that the commitment and harmony was waning in the Circle. Bill M had tried to encourage everyone but to no avail. There was one that I had noticed earlier; who turned into a negative of himself. In one circle he had smelt sulphur, next to him and I wondered what he was attracting or bringing with him as this seemed to be a form of negativity. I realised that the group was about to disband but definitely didn't want to believe it, as I was sure we had something going for us as a group - meaning all were cogs in the wheel. This would mean Irene Sowter's sayings were true and one by one my entire physical circle would leave. I poured out more and more love and prepared with more care. In May we reached a climax with loud dings or ringing as on crystal in the corner behind me. In between the man on my right and myself. They sounded as though someone had...knocked on a lead crystal bowl. The tone rang beautifully. Afterwards, the man next to me tested the lamp in the corner but it only thudded. It was not anything like the sound we had heard and no logical explanation could be found for there was nothing else to ring. After that we received 'Dings' in every group. I realised we had succeeded in something and looked forward to confirmation of some kind.

In June I had an invited speaker who knew nothing about any of us. Brenda Lawrence came on 22/6/85 and this is what she said to me, involving the group too: -

"You appear to be the catalyst from which it all flows. It's almost as if the embryo of ideas are within you and then you pass that out like a parcel, all wrapped up in gift wrappings, to each individual and that is not to say you haven't had disappointments, where you felt what you had given to an individual should have helped them a great deal, but they have turned it round against you. *(I puzzled many times over the reason for this happening).* Because you are very sensitive that can really hurt, but you have outgrown that, because now you say to yourself, if that happens its because I as an individual, have not read it correctly and know that they were not ready for that particular part. So that's a growth, which is very good indeed. A lot of your .... You take your ideas and thoughts to Spirit in prayer. It's almost as if you're talking to them on a One to One relationship and saying "Well this is what I feel is right. What do you feel about it?" Getting a response as if you're trying it out on them first and then pushing out whatever you've got to push out and you push out a great deal and the Circle gets wider because this is a group here tonight. One of many groups and I feel too that there are times when you talk so much that your throat aches because you want to just keep on giving and giving to individuals. You not only give to individuals but you also give to individuals in a clairvoyant sense because I'm giving out little pieces of information to each member to which they respond. *(Several nodded at this.)* I would like very much, to place in your hands a flower and see you read up the stem because Flower Clairsentience is with you as clearly as anything. If you take a flower and you can read the Life Story as you read up the stem. The most lovely part, we come to, is actually the bloom of the flower because you can look within the bloom of the flower. That is the focal point because from there you can gauge the spirit the spirit worth. Individuals do need to know how they are developing spiritually. *(This seemed to also relate to the energy readings the Tarot produced too by combining the energies of the person with an object or living flower and being able to read the soul's purpose and present state).* They need to know this because sometimes, although they are in contact with spirit helpers and spirit within them, they need that confirmation from someone, because it gives you a strength. A greater strength and confidence to go forward especially when someone has just about laid you out and also it helps you as an individual because you are linking in, really with that individual spirit and you can gain from that. People in the Spiritualist movement talk about spirit guides and helpers. They tend to forget... "All those on the higher spheres." I hear them proclaim. They tend to forget that we are individual spirits too and that within us is knowledge as an individual spirit. Within us we can give to an individual, in fact to many individuals, something of ourselves. It's a beautiful thing. You can go into a room and feel spirit there, not discarnate spirit but incarnate spirit - individual spirits who are trying to go forward on their pathway and the exchange of energies that happen. You've felt them, I know because I'm talking to the group and I'm including everyone as I'm talking on this but particularly you. You can feel the exchange of energy and you learnt a long time ago your lesson of giving too much and I don't mean just for the day. Quite some time, no energy at all and when I recognised it hit me and you learnt that lesson from there because you give too much. You had no energies left, and then you cannot give when it's needed and there are givers and takers in this world. We all give and we all take but some people haven't learnt the art of giving and don't realise they're taking and when its all taken you feel sh...... and then you try to do the work, that you are doing in particular, and when all that's gone you've got no reserves. That was a lesson you learnt quite some time ago. I feel that as leader of the group, which I feel you are, that you are impressed during the circle. It's almost as if you can feel someone standing here, tapping in on here *(she tapped her right shoulder indicating where my voice spoke to me.)* As if something's on they're tapping in to my head and out I come with whatever I've got to give. Now you don't consider yourself developed. I mean in a Psychic Aspect and yet I feel there has been a pattern to your life, particularly in the last 15 years and it's gone in cycles of 5 and I'm up to the end of my 5th 3rd cycle. I am here and as I'm looking at your path, I am seeing the whole of those 15 years and realising the group has reached a zenith. I can see all that has happened in the last 15 years, particularly with yourself and what has happened within the last 6 - 7 months, within the group reaching this point and from there I am booming I'm going I'm jumping. When I say I'm moving, I'm accelerating. The group is accelerating forward. They are progressing forward and you are going to see in individual people, a great progression. It's almost as if over the last 6 - 7 months things have reached the head and now everyone is going to get it together because that's what it's about getting it together. Now I said you were the catalyst and that is right. And from you will trigger that big jump. The Catalyst is someone who sits there, great deal of power; it's the trigger that makes other people spring. I do feel there is a step forward and I do feel a big step forward for each individual, but then the group as a whole because then the whole group has benefited from it. It's not just one, it's the whole group is going to benefit. I felt I was talking, particularly of this group. I am not aware because different people from different ones are going to step forward. Whoever is here tonight is going to step forward but you are the catalyst to do it. You are the trigger that starts them all off and the whole group will benefit from it. It's got to because the whole group has got to step forward with it. If they don't step forward with it they drop out. You're the trigger because you are in every one of the groups. They are very pleased with the way that the work has been going, but there is going to be a definite improvement a definite step forward. The Cycles are important. Where there is an earnest desire it will be fulfilled. That's my last words.

This was confirmation indeed but as I became aware of a need for a summer break and thankful that I was already booked to go to the Arthur Findlay College for Caledonian week again. I was looking forward to that, as the fun and laughter had been a great tonic the previous year. When I returned home what Irene S. had told me actually began to happen as one by one people had left my Circle before Christmas and there now seemed to be an undercurrent I could not put my finger on. We still had some beautiful evenings with dings of bells and all saw many things. We all agreed to break the circle for 13 weeks until September. Then on the final evening I was unable to stop myself from going completely under the power. At the end when I spoke about it, a loud "You" emitted from the negative one, and my 'voice' loudly shouted Out" into my right ear. I mentally argued "Oh no not Alan." 'Out' was repeated. I was loath to say anything as we had been together for several years. "Out" came the reply. The one on my right said he knew I was going to go out completely and was prepared and watching as he had once before. I knew the Circle was about to disband and I wondered why as I always thought we were working as a team.

The following day I phoned Gill, as I was aware that her husband didn't want her in my Circle and only wanted a man to lead her. He wouldn't even let me speak to her and said they were going to find other Circles. I then phoned Alan and he agreed to come and talk at 2 pm the next day, but didn't turn up. I meditated and was told to give him permission to go.

Meantime On the Sunday, I phoned Bill M and explained what had happened to the circle, with everyone leaving, and that I was having difficulty talking to the sitters. He laughed and said: Who do you think the Medium for this work is?"

"I don't think Spirit have sorted that out yet. It could be one of those who have left."

Bill suddenly exclaimed, "Oh, it's beautiful..... It's You and you don't even know it!"

I argued, "But I just lead the Circles and each of the others thought it was them."

"Let them all flow like water under the bridge. You are in every one of the Circles and it is you that is being trained and all new sitters will be brought in for the real work. Let them flow, spirit will have it right."

I phoned Alan again and gave him permission to go saying that we may have reached a point where we each had to follow our own work and thanked him for being a part of my life up until now. We had come to the parting of our ways and he was not to feel he owed me anything or had upset me. I said that his work might be heading in another direction. He agreed to come and talk. Then he announced that he was joining a Reflexology group, I wondered what Pat had said to him as she was the one with a friend in Foot Zone therapy and I was sad as I let them all go their own ways feeling more than a little bit hurt that they couldn't stick with whatever Spirit had in mind. I knew Pat would resign that night too. She did and I was glad I was attending the Arthur Findlay College on Saturday for a fun week.

My daughter was going to look after Tara but for some reason her car broke down and she was unable to get to my home, whilst her car was being repaired. Luckily she had the dog with her and at least Tara had a holiday too by staying all week at my daughter's house. My home was obviously being prepared for whatever was to happen next.

On August 6th I had a Psychic dream experience. I was in a room with wicker furniture when a terrific gust of wind blew in. I leaned over and protected one person who I recognised. I seemed to be giving her healing. A lot of people were present. Afterwards I looked down and found my dress wet all around my tummy and dripping off the hem, resulting from the power of healing. The dream continued as I found myself preparing for circle work in a big house with people scurrying about when someone came running up to me saying; 'I think you had better come and see. There are some people here who shouldn't be here.' I went into the main room and saw some men setting up equipment. I walked over to them and asked: "What are you doing here?"

"We are Knights of the Black Cross and we have been sent."

"Who sent you?" I automatically named the husband of Gill, as a question and received the reply: "You got it lady."

"Well you are not welcome here. Would you, please pack up and leave."

They packed up their equipment and left. What on earth had he been doing to bring in such a negative influence obviously his thoughts were not positive constructive and supportive of our Circle.

For some years I tried to find out who the 'Knights of the Black Cross' were. They seemed to be an order opposite to the Knights of Templar. I suppose there is an opposite for every positive?

Another psychic dream happened, where I found myself amongst Players, Musicians and Poets at a Chateau or Castle. Although there were many different outfits and faces relating to the 1600's, I knew who certain individuals were. They were from my circles - especially the ones who had just left. One, a dwarf called Racimoto, was running in and out picking up tit bits from the conversations. I knew who she was and eventually caught her. As I did, the dwarf became the one I thought it was, who had just left my group. I talked to her about the black cross people that her husband had sent to break up the spiritual work. She disagreed. I then said he must have talked to someone else who sent them and she agreed. *(Was this the work of the Masons?)* I told her the work was around me not her and she fell back with relief sinking down on to a grass bank. I had always felt there was a previous life experience we had been in together but the dwarf also meant deception of some kind and I was aware of this too. I phoned her the next day, to talk about my experience but received a nasty reception and hung up I wondered if she ever received confirmation herself.

For Caledonian week at Stansted in 1985, I had arrived with a real need of spiritual upliftment after our first Physical Circle had fizzled out. During the week, Jean T. gave me a private reading which was most appropriate: -

"A lot of this is nerves. You get yourself all worked up. *(I always seemed to get upset and very nervous)*. I was getting an upsetting condition and then a calming down. You're too soft with those that are close to you. Those that aren't close to you, you bring a firmness and you believe there is no sentiment in business. You're putting a strict foot down somewhere and you're right. Downstairs I saw a beautiful gold light around you. Your spiritual development is taking a step up. You're beginning to understand now, things that you didn't understand and you're becoming much more involved. When you first came into it you were terribly unsure. Now you know it is for you. Now do you have two children? One in spirit and one on the earth? *(Correct!)* The one in spirit is progressing. Upsetting conditions with the other daughter. You're going to find that these conditions will ease out and the power of prayer is great but we cannot always get what we want for our family. They get what is good for them. Sometimes we don't think it's good for them but it's what their life, what is mapped out and they've got to go through things the same, as we had to go through things....... You're going to be given an unexpected gift. It's jewellery and something you're going to be delighted about. You're going to find that next year is bringing you into new fields and it's good. Don't be afraid of it. You are a very inquisitive person and you doubt as well like should I or should I not. Is this right or is it not. Keep that because with your spiritual development, it's taking you higher. If we are quite satisfied with what we've got, we'll never get any higher because spirit won't take us any further, but if you're not and you're doubting, is this right or is it wrong, they'll prove to you it's right and they will take you a step further. Keep that inquisitive mind. But you will do platform work in time. You will definitely do platform work and I'm not getting in what manner so I'm going to leave that and you'll also have, later on a link with abroad, but you will go abroad because I sense travelling abroad and I'm getting a step up for you. Your spiritual work, you're going to take an interest in something else along with what you are doing but it's not putting more time on you. It's like saying I'm hearing, now I can see something else is coming in, one of your psychic gifts is becoming much stronger. The other, there is a newness with it and I'm going to say everybody senses. That you will have all three. You will sense, you will see and you will hear but be patient with yourself - plenty of time. There's a Spirit child. You do have a few guides but there is a Nun very strong and I'm also sensing a Gypsy. When you suddenly feel like singing or dancing - from Spain. Leo who is Leo? Have a little forbearance with them, very annoying in some way and I sensed you getting all worked up. Try to understand them and you'll find that in understanding them it is helping them. But you could do what I am doing and in time I'd say you'll definitely do it........ Someone close to you is interested in the healing and I want to encourage this because it's good....... Something is going off with electricity. Sorry to give you that. It's just a plug, a wire being pulled loose that's all it is. Don't panic and think oh dear I'm going to have to get a new washing machine or something like that? I am only giving that as an example, but there is a little work to be done in your house and I get that being done.... There is also a dog in spirit. This dog is not a pedigree dog; there was another mixture in with it. That dog walks with you and protects you. *(This was a good description of my old dog Sandy who had been described by another medium, when I first came in to Spiritualism, with his tail going like a banner).* Now dogs do bring protection but you are going to see a dog in solid form but you are going to see a dog and it's like looking and saying I'm seeing things. If you think you are seeing things pat it and you shan't find it solid, it'll disappear, but it's solid for a few minutes and it's letting you know it's there. *(This actually happened some years later after Tara died.)* But you are well guarded and you're getting more protection around you. There's a new guide coming in who is going to take you into a much stronger aspect and you're going to find that the new circle is good for you. You will have things rising. It's like having this table rising up into the air. You will get things rising but go by your instincts as to whom you want in it. I feel there is someone who is going to pester you. Keep them on the outside. There is no reason at all, if you don't feel the instincts to bring them in. It must be your choice, nobody else's choice and 2 years ahead you're not going to know yourself...Continue in the pathway at the moment and the change that will come next year you'll be more ready for it. Don't try and make a change before next year, you're not ready for it. It'll not be good for you. Leave things until next year then make all your changes much better for you.... You're needing a rest and this is one way of resting you......Somebody's trying to help you by telling you to wait. Plenty of time. Wait until next year then go into the newness next year and it's something that's meant to happen. There have been upsetting conditions here, be wary will you of him because I feel he could hurt. Be a bit wary and you'll find, later on understanding him. In some way you don't quite understand him. You'll find that out as well and you will come to understand

107

him and I'll say next year is a better year.

*(How accurate this was to prove to be. It was three years later when I understood and was surprised by the negative powers that jealousy and envy can bring to people. The sulphur smell he had at the side of him in the circle was what he was attracting to himself and my voice saying 'Out' meant this part had to be cleared before any damage was done to the spiritual work. I then remembered how he always looked like a photographic negative when we concentrated on him in the earlier days. How blind and ignorant I was. It all made sense now, 3 years later. Therefore those who have any feelings of envy, jealousy or resentment will attract lower, like-minded forces, just as strongly negative, as those who give love and service, attract higher positive minds and loving power. It's all in the state of the mind. Laziness also plays a part for anyone who does not prepare, but brings in the outside world and falls asleep, exhausted, would also invite the wrong influences. Preparation and effort to clear inner debris and the outside world, prior to sitting, is a ritual we practice until it becomes second nature.)*

On the final day at Stansted, when I sat and prepared to give healing, brilliant shimmering and shining gold began to shower down over me reminding me of the previous times when the room had filled with gold at Noreen's home, when she slept on the sofa and the room filled with gold and with Dorice. What was happening now? Tears began to flow down my cheeks as the feeling of wonder and joy touched my soul.

"I cannot give healing in this state." I thought to myself when, as if in answer, my 'Voice' replied: "Your handbag is on the Rostrum. Take a tissue and blow your nose and wipe your face, wash your hands and begin".

Again a perfectly logical, sensible solution. I did as was suggested and felt I was in another world with my feet off the ground in the flow of the power. After the healing was over I put my chair away and could not get back to earth. I decided to walk around the grounds and ground myself but the wonderful feelings were still flowing through me. As I returned to the Sanctuary the Leader mouthed,

"Are you all right?" through the window. I nodded and decided to see if she had seen anything whilst this was going on. I explained what had happened and she looked at me saying:

"I don't see anything, but in between you and I felt a tremendous gust of wind before we started." I had had a tremendous gust of wind in the physical circle too and knew that feeling. Was it the same? I was certainly being realigned and healed myself for whatever came next. The results of the week's healing sessions were very very good as people came up to me and told me their pain had completely gone.

The front cover is an Aura Photograph of Cynthia Bradshaw taken by
Sue Wood on 28th July 2004 at The Arthur Findlay College.

Whenever I start with the reading of an aura photo I usually start with this
corner here, gradually working around the face, around the photograph
explaining what all the different colours mean. Now as you see me smiling,
your energy field is a little bit different and the blending and harmonising
shows really what almost looks like one totally homogenised, blended energy
field of a strong orange red power. The blending, as you would imagine, I
should think, is good. What it shows is that your cells, your aura is blended.
That there are no separate blobs and splodges of colour. It shows that all of
your energy is actually working in synchronicity. So it shows a harmonisation
of energy really. We could possibly ... had you not been quite as experienced,
developed or whatever, as you are and I'll look in to this a bit more in a
moment, we may well have had some reds and yellows and possibly a tiny bit
of blue or something like this down here - violety blue. That could all have
been quite separate but because of the way your energy is and this comes
about with experience and learning and, well, long experience and ability, so
it's all blended into what looks at first glance almost like one complete colour
without any variations. We have to look very, very closely to see this slight,
just slight variance in colour that you can recognise as being there in addition
to what is obvious red. So red is vitality, red on the physical shows someone
who has a good grip on life, a good physical hold on to life. That is not quite
the same as saying that you have as much energy as you would like because
people with this sort of energy on the physical aura very often give out a lot of
energy and therefore get depleted as well as it being replaced. This is the side
the energy comes in. On your left hand side energy is received and constantly
coming in and this energy you give out. Now you can see what is happening
here. What comes in you give out so it is being replaced. So you are a power
giver. The orange tells me - orange is sort of overlaid on top of that vitality.
This tells me that you are extremely sensitive. You will always have been
sensitive, even as a child you will have been particularly sensitive. Now in
your circumstances of your family, they may not have had much patience or
time for somebody who is particularly sensitive but that sensitivity was there,
so it could have been uncomfortable to be as sensitive as you were as a child
unless it was totally understood. You would certainly have had a psychic
awareness all through your childhood. You would have known more than
your five senses. That will have always been with you so somebody with this
sort of energy, we would say at the very least, is someone who is naturally
psychic, a born medium/psychic. The very fact that it has homogenised the
way it has, we will say it is more than that because it's been years and years
and years of yellow, which is learning, absorbed in to the red, which is the
psychic vitality. So we we've got the two together which creates the orange,
all right? It's actually yellow overlaid on to the red that gives us this sort of
... But it isn't yellow that is just up here; it's yellow that is part and parcel of

almost, like, every cell of your body now. So the learning has been taken on board in almost like osmosis - almost like our perspiration comes through our cells. You've absorbed OK? Which means that your sensitivity would alert you to so many situations that other people wouldn't be aware of consciously or sub-consciously and your learning helps you to realise that. You couldn't actually explain because it would actually have to be you to actually know. I understand what I'm saying but I'm not saying it very clearly. You know it's a little bit like when the spirit world come back and say to us 'You should see the beautiful colours here'. They cannot tell us what they are because we don't know it. We have never seen those colours and couldn't understand. All we can do is accept that there are beautiful colours in their world that world and when we do get to that world we will then know about the beautiful colours. It's like trying to teach a blind person what colours look like and it's as though with this knowledge, that you have absorbed over such a long, long, long time. So Spiritualism isn't something that is new to you, is it? You've actually absorbed this knowledge over such a long, long time along with this psychic ability so it really is producing something that you will have awareness of that you cannot explain to somebody else therefore you have to somehow or other find a way of coming to terms in your own mind that you tread a separate path and it may well be that your path and the paths of others, your friends or others that are on a journey, occasionally will be in sync but you're really only just crossing that path, you know, just crossing over. You do have to walk, in your life, a solitary path through your life. Ther's somebody that actually shows themselves as somebody of the desert who is with you. Now they are showing themselves there in the symbolic way - in that way. They are saying you walk through the desert. You occasionally come to an Oasis and that's lovely. You can stop and ease up. You can be refreshed. You can take on supplies but then you can't stay there. You'd be bored silly staying there. You have to move on and therefore treading through this hot deep sand is just your path. You have to keep going.

Where your health is concerned in knowing your emotions are what will sort of affect your physical. So when you are ill it's almost always not through a physical cause initially but through stress or perhaps a feeling that originates on an emotional level through hurt or a feeling of disappointment or let down. Something that continues for a while lowers your emotions and that's when you are open to infections or illnesses on a physical level. Again with this synchronicity we've got such a close connection between the Mind and the Emotions and the Physical that the one will affect... but the Mental and Physical is the stongest and if those are affected that's when the physical resistance drops and you're open to infection. So when you feel a lot of stress building you have to deal with it. Don't just bear it. If you have deadlines or pressure or something that is mentally burdening you, deal with it so you can breathe again.It's a bit like teaching my grandmother to suck eggs. It's intrinsic within you anyway. You know what is right for you. I suppose I'm trying to prove I know a little bit about what I'm talking about as well, so perhaps this is for my benefit more because you know this. But maybe what you get from this is a confirmation as your energy field shows what you know to be true so it is a reflection of you. You are somebody who actually... If I had said just sit there and build up the power and I'll take the photograph we would have had exactly that but bigger because when Spirit come and bring their energy, their power is exactly like that so it would be just theirs added to yours whereas this is yours. It wouldn't have made a ha'pennyworth of difference. It wouldn't have brought in any different colour because spirit power comes just like this. Q. Why do some people get different pictures when they build up the power of spirit? A. Because they haven't got this sort of energy of their own. They may have an energy. Mine is different when I'm relaxed and I'm not working with spirit. Look it couldn't be more different to yours. That's me on my own. It's with you You are naturally like that. When I build my power I go orange and red then come like white beams - just white rays, that's all but I have to get to that position first. In this situation spirit might come and talk to me spontaneously. Somebody might come in and give me a message but it's not me working. To work I have to build up my energy. It might only take a minute or so. I have to get to that stage. Now you are naturally at that stage. That's really what I am saying. That is your energy and if spirit come in it wouldn't change, it would just increase but it is exactly like that. One thing you said to me was that you don't have a physical energy. You thought I was talking about physical as in Transfiguration or ectoplasm on that level but in fact if you were sitting for physical you would need that energy field first. That is the energy you would need. That doesn't mean it would just be automatic. You would have to have been sitting. You would have to work but I can tell by the orange - the golden overglow on top of that red - the yellow blending to create that gold that orangey gold, many, many, many years absorbing a little bit like osmosis has been going in. Not by sitting and studying for two years or three years or just by taking on board, but like taking breath gently over many, many, many years. This will also give you this sort of energy, will give you stubbornness with an energy like that in this area. Very, very determined. It gives you this linking on a health level emotional and mental. This colour in this area gives you the sort of energy that helps you to sort of connect to people on a sensitive level to know what somebody else feels to be able to just automatically. You haven't got to stop and think about their circumstances and what's happened. It's just in naturally and normally because this is connected - people connection - where you would connect to people. So if you only had that there that would be the bit I'd be telling about. I mean all this is what you have so being able to connect to others working with people although I'm telling you you walk a solitary path. You are walking your own solitary path but with a lot of other people coming in and out of your life because this is like a magnet. This sort of energy is like a magnet. People are drawn to you and some just take a tiny bit and that.s all they can cope with and they go. You will attract people of all types and they're accepted whether its people who are very intelligent and wealthy or whether its people who are penniless. There's something there that you would connect with, so that they don't have to be within a particular boundary for them to be somebody you get to know or like. You will know weird people, lots of different people, very strange people, very exotic people, very spiritually aware people you will meet in your life. You will have those experiences because all comers would come in to that sort of an energy field. You've got this lovely golden colour here, which is really around the heart chakra. Can you see the little bit of violet just around the side of the communication. There is a little bit of violet there. Again this is somebody who can speak of spiritual things, does speak of spiritual things - so speaking on behalf of spirit. The line is actually going all around your inner energy. The amount of power and red is overlapping it but I know that that is blue and violet around there and down here. This is energies that you give out and down here behind the red is giving power; is giving energy to others therefore being somebody who would quite happily be somebody with leadership qualities; somebody in charge because you've got those energies, those dynamic energies but I know behind that there is the blue of communication which creates the violet because blue and red create violet on a spiritual level so I know that a lot of the energy you give out is helping other people through spiritual things; through talking, which is here but also what I say, which is not so flattering or complimentary as everything else suggests about your aura. You are carrying hurt from the past. What you've cleared is the anger and what's left is just the hurt. Leftover hurt sort of will probably always be with you but it doesn't get in the way of you moving forward or doing what you need to do because the anger has been dealt with. You blend with spirit. Do look again at how my aura ends. You can see where Sue ends. With yours it just merges. You see I've got a clear-cut line. Yours just merges. It's like a fog that's getting less and less and less which means that spirit again just blend. Those that work with you don't come in with trumpets and bells. You know that's them - this is me. It's just you; it comes in through you and just works through you and just works through your energy quite naturally. So you don't have this clear cut Cynthia speaking this bit and spirit speaking that. It just merges and therefore even if people came to you because they love to hear what those in the spirit world, guides, teachers of philosophy have to say, it's got to a point now where you can just say it because you become as one with them. So you're working; it's just merging, it's lovely. It is lovely and it's an absolute confirmation really of what you already know but it's nice to have it in confirmation. You may catch it in the light that where the orange and red ends it does go into the purple. You may catch that on this foggy bit, a sort of purpley effect. It is the spirit you see in there and you may see it better in sunlight when you're outside or in the daylight but it's there, believe me, it's there and it's blending in with your energy in a very natural way.

Many readings do not make sense until much later on and I was glad I tape recorded the information and checked it out. For me to place my Trust in the unseen realms, I needed proof beyond a shadow of a doubt, from different sources, beyond my normal knowledge. Even then I questioned and tested all other solutions.

About this time I realised that my life was splitting into three distinct separate existences, although it tied up somehow. My Family knew nothing of my spiritual work or the demands of my working life. My business associates knew nothing about my family or spiritual work. And my spiritual associates knew nothing about either my family or work. The spiritual work seemed to help me sort out all the other realms of my life, and helped me cope with ever increasing demands. Years later I received a retrospective picture of my inner development regarding a purpose I was being trained for in this lifetime. The purpose was to do with my first picture of a nest of snakes. I was being built up, tested and set tasks with smaller snakes before I could handle the major ones. In all my activities at work and at home, I was meeting manipulative controlling people who surprised me with the games they were playing.

Once I recognised that fact in my groups, I questioned the reasons. 'It's all in hand'. "A voice" reassured me. I could even see the likeness in some people to the ones who had gone before and puzzled over their spirituality. Jealousy, envy and anger brought out the worst in people, which had to be cleared before progress could be made - hence always coming to the foreground quite early on. Why me to deal with so many incidents? I puzzled but carried on knowing that nothing could be as bad as the first instance of losing people who I thought were sincere and dedicated to being of Service to the whole, from my first physical circle. My constant questioning helped me with handling difficult situations. The stronger I became the stronger the opposite forces seemed to be in those led to me for help or service of some kind and I was only the instrument for the work. Sometimes as we met I would just know that this was going to be a tough test and remembered that all are children of the divine so where else could they go for help? I had given my life to God to be used as an instrument and knew I would be led and guided even though I didn't really want the negativity any where near me or to become involved in their manipulations and control games for attention.

Dorice H was back on 24 8 1985 and told me: - "It's like two hands holding something even though at first it looked like a ring, it's not really a ring and it's like somebody coming to help. It's like one hand and this other person is the other hand. It's like a plug suddenly. *(This could be the plug that was pulled out as J T had spoken of before at Stansted.)* It's like somebody suggested something and you weren't quite sure of their integrity because of the work you are doing and now it's going to come into place but not in the way it was first suggested by some other people but by different people that are coming in. Three to four months ago some people were saying about new ways of working group joining. It's coming in another way. The idea was right at the time because you've been wondering if you've got it right or wrong. *(Quite true)*. There is concern about your health you are pushing yourself. Diets you make little attempts and then fall back. Important you've got to be in good condition. It's building up a different level of work. Tidying up and it's going ahead. The newness is there. It's O.K. you're concerned in case it's going all over the same ground again. (I was owing to new people coming in all the time). Worzel Gummidge look a like person, is showing himself, with a pointed beard, a sense of humour, neat hair, narrow face and wizardy look. He's wearing a suit, almost clerical, it's Puritan, like a little bit of white underneath, straight buttons, a scholar. Books in yourself you are also collecting knowledge. I am being shown the same thing in different angles and they're both right. He is helping evaluate the chaff from the wheat. The name Dominique, he's not a Monk he's a Quaker, a Puritan. They called each other Brother. He's telling me the story about Glastonbury, the stick, and staff sprouting. The symbol of the Staff is what they are giving you. *(The same symbol Bill had given years before and sitters had already seen in my home.)*

My concerns about losing the sitters for the physical circle were somewhat put to rest by the following reading from Muriel on 29 9 85

"A Zulu with you here. He's bringing in a terrific power for Direct Voice. There's going to be many changes of the vibrations but I want to say this time the Foundation is going to be strong and you're going to build up but the Zulu man is going to be in charge of the vibrations to say where others shut the door, others will come in and not shut another door. One that has shut the door but not really shut it - something there I'm pulling a door open and I want to come in. Hold on with all love and faith. He's here, do you know that name Konchok, he sends his love and is with everyone in the circle. I can see something. There's lights building and they're all going round, at the present moment. So lady they give you every hope, every thought. But what has happened don't let it frustrate you because now the concrete is going to be there, so hold on with love. God bless you".

My healing in my everyday life carried on and I was asked if I could help the sister of a Badminton player. I said the request had to actually come from her and in due course her father phoned me. I began to visit her 2-3 times a week. Gail was only 32 years old and cancer was rampant throughout her body. She had her baby girl 2 years before and the cancer started in her breast at that time. She had now lost her hair and had so much treatment from the Doctors that she was exhausted. After the first healing she said she felt wonderful and really looked forward to my visits. I had booked a week off in the October and felt I was going to be involved with healing every day that week. But the Thursday prior to my week off, her father phoned to say that I was no longer required as she had gone away. I then thought to myself that I had picked up my impressions wrong and must have been mistaken. Then on the Sunday afternoon her father phoned and said she was asking for me as I was the only one that helped her. He asked if I could come to see her in the Hospice and I told him I had a week off and of course I could come and see her. That week I saw her every day and the family bought me lunch as I refused to take payment whilst working full time and coping. On the following Saturday I finished the healing and was walking around the beautiful grounds thinking it was a shame there were such lovely gardens that those suffering inside would never see. My "Voice" came in and said "The urgency is over" to which I realised whatever I had come daily for had happened. I went back and explained that I was back at work on Monday and couldn't come so often but would come on Tuesday and maybe Thursday if that were all right with her. She then said she was feeling so much better and of course she would like me to come when I could. I went back on the Tuesday and she was very sleepy saying she felt really good. On the Thursday I lay in bed and suddenly went in to a 'hold'. I knew this was for healing and asked whom for. 'Gail' was the reply and I let it happen. As soon as I was released I got out of bed and the phone rang. This was Gail's father saying that he would like to get hold of me before I went out to cancel that day as Gail had just passed. What a co-incidence my being in a hold for the power to flow and help her at that stage. This seemed quite amazing to me. Healing is wonderful for releasing all the panic and fears and releasing the spirit from the body peacefully.

Near Christmas we received more trance from Muriel: - "Eh Eh I know you lassie don't I eh eh I've spoken to you many times eh when I say you're one of the girls of the old brigade eh yes well pretty well like that eh. Well there's a few of them here you know? I'm going to say that eh yeh well you've been a bit of a lassie in yer time too ent yer? I'm not gonna give away any secrets but you've been a bit of a girl of the old brigade eh? I know ne're mind, it doesn't matter what you say what you do you've got to live ent yer. You can live it as spiritually as you possibly can. Er you know, after the war they don't want to know yer they don't want to know spirit, they don't want to know anything to do with Christianity. You know, but you can operate the good when you want something, eh ain't that true? Yer know, but its true and you got a get your thoughts right. What that thought can do to somebody else. I'm not radiating that one out. Not that One is perfect. As you go through earth you get these thoughts and you know you can say - just get out! I don't want yer so they get out. At the same time it's wonderful to say well please God, as I'm looking round 'ere each one of yer can be of service, cause you're healers and yer mediums and I want ter say to yer well it's only the peace of God that each one of yer can receive and therefore develop the gifts of God to help others of this earth less fortunate than yerselves, so may I wish you a Happy Christmas. In our country we celebrate a lot yer know in Scotland, eh in Scotland yer know. It's New Year. I can still do the highland fling lassie eh I can still do the highland fling. Well God bless you. All have a happy time. All unite together in the love of God. So good night and God bless yer.

# CHAPTER 9

## NUMEROLOGY AND PAST LIVES

Carole and I shared our experiences since we first met at Stansted and I was able to get a picture done for her from Coral Polge for Christmas, which was of her Indian "Strong Bow" then Carole asked me for my full name and date of birth for her to get me a Numbers reading from a very good friend of hers who was a polish lady well known for her accuracy which was on a tape as follows:

NUMEROLOGY AND PAST LIVES Given Early 1986

"Numbers, numerology is a science A study with Zoroaster a Persian Sage and the Kabala in Judea. The Science of numbers that comes to us today is based on Cabbalistic principles. I would say if I was told that evolution is the law of life, numbers are the law of the Universe. Energy is the law of God. Everything in the Universe is sacred to progressive cycles. The cycles 1 - 9. Also numbers have significance apart from the values denoted by the value of the figures. Numbers are different from figures. Numbers represent qualities. Numbers operate on a spiritual plane while figures are for measuring things on the material plane.

In the beginning was the number 1, the vibration then began and the 2 appeared, the first pair. Numerology is the art and science of understanding the spiritual significance and orderly progression of manifestation, because every one of the letters in our names vibrates to a number and every number has its inner meaning. Now you have to understand that everything that is in the Universe is energy, colour, sound and vibration. Spirit is energy, colour, sound, vibration and light. That's what you are. Planets and stars illuminate the complete Universe. Everything else, animals etc. are Energy. God gave us a spark of his own energy and with that spark he gave us the sense of love and forgiveness. He gave us the Intelligence and the creativity. Intelligence, also, for thoughts on a Psychic sense. He gave us also the power of manifestation and free will choice. So the Universal cycle of life is synchronised. It is the Alpha and the Beta. The beginning and the end that never ends. The universal symphony starts with numbers 1,2,3,4,5,6,7,8,9, and again you are on number 1. The Universal Cycle of life starts and it takes 2,000 years for each Cycle to be completed and also takes 2,000 years for each cycle of life as Spirit in a body and re-incarnations, to also experiment on this planet Earth. At the beginning God created men and men came to earth. The first ones were the Jewish, who were separated from the other people for generations to purify the strain. They are the ancient race that you know on the earth. After that there were different people that came to earth from different galaxies and stars and planets to experiment on planet Earth. Many of them have more understanding of technology than earthmen and others who have less. Never the less all of us have some right and the same opportunity because we all came here to learn. Earth is a great schoolroom and lessons are learnt in many different ways. Now working with colours, sounds and vibrations I was given the following reading: -

"I find that I have two beautiful numbers with you. One is a past life as the highest form of service towards humanity and also, you have a past life that you gave - also, as a Master towards humanity, which is very beautiful that you did that because you are a very old soul. You have already completed the nine - I want to say the 2,000 years on experimentation Planet Earth. It has been hard, you know people, you have compassion, you are a very psychic person. You completed the cycle already but, for some reason you have to come to Earth again from your own choice. You came to this planet again for some reason, possibly, you promised someone to help in their next life. And you came with the purpose to help someone or do something for someone or take care of someone or be the support of someone because you did it from your own choice because you didn't need to come anymore to the earth. You also you came back to learn a few things that were important to you, like you say, you want to polish yourself a little more. You have a purpose - a very special purpose, finishing this life, this re-incarnation and after that, you have a very high purpose. That's why you came again, also just to polish little things on you - you have the master number. You express emphatic building huge, accomplish things in a big way and work with large groups or business concerns. You enjoy the import; export business, which could mean long distance travel, meetings with persons in authority. You like to take an inspirational idea and put it into practical use. Self-knowledge is very valuable to you and you have the promise of very much success in life. You know what to use in your everyday work to adjust the physical laws of life and living to the one state. It is authentic expression of wisdom. Then there is authentic self-training, banking, financial affairs because everything is with you. You already learn so much from life. You are steady and reliable and that is beautiful numbers. You learn everything in life because you have all the numbers - everything.

Past lives - I'm telling you the things you learned are all yours - no one can take these from you. You represent - you have the more principal you, it is the pioneer - the striking out alone seeking experiences to bridge it is distinct identity. You are always in the process of discovering the solubles. It is raw energy with you. Positive, general, creative - it is a state of perpetual motion. You alone can do anything. You are the real I am unity, the vibration, the measure and the self-consciousness. You are original, independant, aggressive, individualistic, creative, dominant the first in the start of an enigmatic operation. You are the activity, the leader, the pioneer, the boss who likes activity. You have earned the goals that for you also learn adaptability because you have also the unity masculine side, the feminine side of you which is tactful and understanding, gently cautious, a follower and also a leader. You can be a leader. You can be a follower. You also are expensive, social, dramatic, communicative - the vestige fire that creates you with enormous vital power, enormous strength. Also you are that which corresponds to the triangle, now corresponds to the square. You are practical, stable. You endure. You have discipline. You are practical natured through self-discipline. You know people - you understand people. Also you learn to be versatile, resourceful, adaptability - you adapt yourself easily, you change things.

Activity, travel, adventure, promotion, speculation. You are a person to discipline the physical side. Also, you learn the family, the social responsibilities, service, love, compassion, counselling, healing, creativity. You are quiet, introspective, intuitive, analytical, inspirational, reclausing and mystical. Also, you have the power, the responsibility for financial rewards, good judgement and also learn the brotherhood, the love, the compassion, the patience, universality, tolerance, selflessness, service, endings. You are quite a person. I have to tell you are quite a person. Your destiny in life is to give my dear, to give. You come to life to give. Now that's all these things you learn in past lives. You are also exercising these things because you learnt all that. You came to life just to polish a few little things and you have a few challenges. Now I'm going to tell you about past lives that you had that are important, somehow, for you in the present life. So that is the things you, somehow, have to finish in the present re-incarnation. The dates I'm giving you are very, very approximate. There can be a difference of 1,2,3 years, no more or less. I have a life here a man 1273. You came from Italy. You went to China with Marco Polo. You were a pioneer. You had the lightening power for spiritual energy and freedom. Again a man in Greece 1400BC. You took part in the writing of the first letters of the Greek Alphabet. You have the light yellow colour for creativity and material force. 925AD Lebanon. You spread the words of Christ you spread the truth; the love and compassion of Christ not the Catholicism of now, you spread the words of Christianity. You have the purple colour for higher-minded Master. 1500 Switzerland. You were an Alchemist and Astrologer working with Sulphur salt and mercury to obtain earth and gold. You have the orange colour for cosmic energy. 1640 in France. You were a friend of Rascine, also a poet and a play writer and a dosical age. You have the mauve colour for balance and harmony. Arstie. You are a healer and a prophet. You have prophetic power. Now I'm talking about all the things you learn. I have to tell you the things you have to do. You have three stages in life. It is a tuning from Katavras is a square, is a triangle in the centre and three squares. You have the sum measurements. That is a fabulous tune in that sphere. You remember from your high school. Now the first is from the age since you were born until you're twenty-seven - is youth. Youth is the things you have to learn - things you have to do because you haven't anything else but just youth. It is raw material. After, between the age of 28 and 54 - is the age of power when you can have the power to accomplish, to do things, and 55 to the end of your life is the age of wisdom, your destiny is the destiny. Your destiny age is communication. Communication is the tower of power and combines the quality of the 1 and 2. The number 3 is a fascinating and diversifying vibration which sprang into existence from Zeo aserp to usurp its individuality under 1 and felt attraction of number 2. It now awakens to give needs for social interaction. Three is the need to communicate and become involved in the pure joy of living. You have enormous etheric power also nubility is a triangle as life. It is a line between God, Christ and Humanity. I would say also, you have a great response to life. Three also bestows ridence and enthusiasm upon all three. Three is an extrovert and with personal magnetism, tells others and inspires them to expand and grow. It is the performer who prefers an innate appreciation of pleasure, art and beauty. It's creative imagination and allows all things to be possible therefore becomes involved in many emotions and experiences. Three is friendly and expensive, driving on sociability and validity. If any of the numbers could be called happy go lucky, it would be the frivolous set of three. Youth is your destiny age; the number is the number three. Your destiny age is thirty-three my dear. That is a fabulous number because it is a double number also and is very beautiful because, you know, that is your personal number and is your soul number. You are steady reliable, have a strong desire to protect others. You would like to live next to nature. In your youth you may like to choose a life in Agriculture. Your goal should produce food on a large scale to help provide sustenance for any of the world. That is the number of Christ. Also Christ lived 33 years. You have the Christ consciousness. Christ is within all of us but not all of us have the conscience of Christ, I shall tell you that I am talking, now, about the present. Now I am to tell you the colours you have in the present re-incarnation. You have the sun, the gold colour, the blue and the violet. The sun is intellect, understanding, mind power and knowledge. The blue; you have a dark blue for physical healing. You can heal people with your hands. You have the lapis lazuli for manifestation, and inspiration and

116

creativity. You have the lighter blue for mysticism and the silver blue for power of manifestation. You are a natural medium. You have mediumship. You have the violet colour that is connection with a Mastermind. You have the sun. I told you, with you, its not to do with astrology. The sun that is the intellect, the masculine side of you, the strength, the leadership, vitality of the outside life, the sense of authority; but you have also, the moon that is the symbol of the feminine, the soul, the inside life, the imagination and fertility. You have with you the four elements. I'm talking about Mercury, Venus and Jupiter; you have these three planets having enormous influence in your present re-incarnation. Mercury gives you the intellect, the form that you express, this cushion and creativity. You have Venus, that is emotional feeling for love, affection and a sense of art beauty and you have Jupiter with you that gives you - is the establishment, the order that combines the material - spiritual. It is also the satisfaction that you get from life. You have with you the four elements. The water gives you movement going into spiritual motion, growing and profilication.

You have the earth that is material for material love, nature and for balance. You have the fire for energy and power of leadership. You are quite a person, I have to tell you. You are quite a person - absolutely fantastic. Very rare I have a person that completed the cycle of 2,000 years and came back to earth again from her own choice. You did! Now I'm going, since I talked about your colours and elements and planets I'm going to talk about the things you decided to do in the present life for your own good - like life lessons that you want to take again. Life lessons all right? Between your birth and twenty-seven - youth age. You have the potential to exercise your life lesson learning, not learning exactly, but you know you have come to learn to be a good mixer, you understand? Its like you have a beautiful diamond that somehow, has to be more polished and you came to learn that lesson to learn that lesson to learn to become a good mixer and you should be a sporter in leadership role. More to help than be the leader, you understand and you can take five professions. They are open to you. You are learning to be adaptable. You select a career to be in finance, music, medicine or study scholarship, knowledge and research. You are very good on that but you've tried to do a little more but you have a challenge between the age of - until you are twenty seven - scattered energy - over indulge or took very much time for changes. If you look back you will realise that you have such could decide so much, do so much, because you could really put in power, all your knowledge. But you did so many things at some time that you scattered your energy and were a little bit over indulgent and was some change in your life You had to take a little bit - some time to do but I'm - look back and you see of it is or not. Twenty-eight to thirty three is your destiny age. You have to come to be very strong, very strong to be, my God, self disciplined, something to do something about yourself in that, to remain stable to be disciplined, well ordered, to conduct in everything, administration or something - sort of management would be the type, the thing you could do. You should become a diligent worker with very much success to do the things with very strong basis. Your challenge - you are very shy but you have Christ consciousness but you are very shy between 34 and 42 is another cycle. You want to exercise the keyword for you is freedom. You want to have freedom. You could have complete wonders. That I have to say. You could have completed fantastic things but, somehow, you have a little bit of laziness on you. You thought for yourself; 'Well I don't want to be bothered with much ach, why should I bother.' And now I see lady is 43 to 51 is now. Now is the time again that you've given out a choice to be self disciplined, to understanding's to have fantastic strong foundations in your life - the things you want to really do. It is the time that you want to be practical. You are very honest, detalient, economical, loyal, to understand pluralism of earth, to have the wisdom. You are starting to have the wisdom. You are very shy. Now you are very, very shy 50 - 54 my dear, you start with fifty to fifty four is the wisdom until the end of your life. Again the communication - you want to speak. You are a speaker. You want to give lectures. You want to talk. You want to tell people what you feel what you know but there is something with you that is a challenge or karma. You are going to be very super sensitive. You cannot take criticism and after you are 55, again you want to mix. You want to help. You want to be the Nuveator between people. You're going to be very shy, very much shy about - Oh my God, I cannot, it's not possible. Now I tell you that you should listen to the tape very often because when you know what is going to happen to us - what is the kind of challenge you're going to have, it's much easier for us to understand and gain the strength to overturn the challenge. I have to say - have to tell you that you are quite an extraordinary person. You are wonderful, a wonderful human being and I would say you have a strong desire to be the first - an ability for all the world dashing action. You have a great deal of ambition and oppositions with you to a great effort. Your enthusiasm is great. Your vigour and efforts are usually provided to good and useful ends. You are like a foreman and champion and your mind is quick and full of ideas. You are on your toes all the time and you can deal with any situation or emergency. Expediency is one of your great assets. You can make important decisions and good ones. I would also say, you are extremely independent and therefore a little proud sometimes. You resent criticism, be careful between the ages of 50 - 54 because it's the age of wisdom and you're going to be very sensitive about criticism. I have to tell

118

you that and about health. Usually you enjoy good health. You have a strong constitution that is somewhat delicate. You are prone to accidents, particularly to the head and face. Exercise special care when travelling in anything fast moving and also in sports. You are a very nice looking woman. You have long limbs and no excessive flesh except in old age be careful don't gain weight because you have endurance and a great strength and energy. What is a little weak with you is your nerves because your weakness is your nerves. You can have headaches and sometimes too much trouble. It is your nerves. You can have headaches, fever or something, that is something to do with your nerves. It is something to do about your nerves. You are very head strong sometimes and then impulsive okay. If you worry very much or have much excitement and anger tend, to upset your general health. You must learn how to relax and control your feelings. You need rest sleep and good food with plenty of vegetables. I won't have to tell you my dear. You have enormous driving force. You have enormous energy but you have to learn to relax and you can do that through meditation to control your emotions, control your nerves and you also have to slow down sometimes - a little bit and have plenty of rest. You are not entirely ruled by money. You just like the pleasures that money can give but you're not exactly the type of person for money. You like to earn because you give the money. You are not exactly very much for money. You like money for the things that money can give to you and you are a real home lover and family person. You like to have children around you. You look for responsibility in a home and you are very handy. What you can do - you are very handy. You can do lots of things in the house. You have very good taste and you are a generous friend but you like to have many friends, especially new ones and it's easy for you to strike up a fresh acquaintance. You are always ready to replace the old friends with the new ones because, in a way, you never give time. You place people on a pedestal sometimes. You have to be patient because you can become a little bit jealous and possessive okay. Because you start to bully people a little bit and you have to be a little careful if you want to have lasting friendships. You are enthusiastic and energetic in love as you are in anything else you do. A very passionate person. You are eager for attention and need it for all that extra confidence that will make you a true success of life, you are quite a person. Interesting - marriage for you is a very permanent affair. Oh my God Yes, but you have the good choice. You will be a fine Mother, a good housekeeper, a wonderful partner for an ambitious man you would be fantastic. You are witty, clever, a good cook, a social-minded person. You have a fine, brilliant mind. I see pride, be careful about your pride but I see more. Let me see - strength, energy combine it with generosity. You have plenty of personality, expediate

119

I see that too. You're not using your head very well. Brain not muscle - not muscle brain. A person of enterprise and plenty of go. You are a born leader, inspire others to action. Your enthusiasm and zest for living is catching and others follow you. You are a very interesting person you know that? A very interesting person just a little bit impatient sometimes - that's the only thing I see around with you and is a little bit impatient and that is what causes your nerves. Now my dear I'm going to do your music with your sounds. You have all the sounds - the seven sounds - the DO Re Me. I would say the A, B, C, D, E, F, G all the sounds with you and I'm going to make the music combine those sounds. That is not just your present life but songs that relate to past lives".

As the year progressed the second group became the Physical Phenomena Circle and I had more coming in to the basic Development group. It was always interesting that quite a few newcomers were applying to come in to my groups at the same time, when a Circle disbanded. They would always be applying at the same time. I wondered why no one ever applied in between. Then when Coral drew a picture of my Mexican Indian saying that he was the one who led people to me at the right time, it made sense for them to have been inspired and led by Spirit at the right time to me and had nothing to do with me as Spirit were leading and guiding their own instruments.

During or after several groups over the years, the candles used to jump off the unit at the end of the room. There was an intelligence behind this action, especially in acknowledging certain people by jumping to their feet. The harmony was better at the end of sitting, once we were all laughing and talking whilst eating refreshments and no one was trying to do something. One candle jumped to the feet of a visiting speaker, causing surprised looks from everyone present. Once a candle jumped on to my glass table in the middle of a meditation. Not one person jumped, in spite of the noise the clatter made. This surprised not only me but also everyone in the room with the control Spirit had over the rapport in the group, proving that meditation was the very best way to develop. Everyone had reached a stage of control by the world of spirit where they could remain in their inner peace.

The human body also vibrationally responds to impressions from the God within according to Pythagoras and other great philosophers. Another time after meditating on my own and going completely under the power I found my eyes opened to the view of the candle over a photograph of my baby and Grandfather, who were both in spirit! This was quite a feat, which I tried to copy with no success. The candle seemed to have been balanced against the force of gravity.

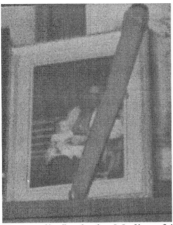

The candle that had stuck itself over the photograph of my Grandfather and baby

Eventually I asked a Medium friend, whom I visited occasionally, if she could tell me who jumped the candles. "It's Albert, he used to be a song and dance man and got run over by a run away carriage. He's saying 'You should see their faces.' He's laughing."

This seemed to tie in with Ivor James saying there was an Albert to do with physical phenomena in the group. I had been expecting an Albert to actually join the group in the flesh. I certainly hadn't expected Albert to be in Spirit!

There was one evening when we had finished sitting and were laughing and talking enjoying tea/coffee and eats when we all smelt different perfumes which was also quite amazing as none of us expected anything and it proved how spirit can work better when no-one is trying or even thinking about it. First one said; "I can smell roses, can you?"

Another "Yes but now its freesias. Can you smell that too?"

Everyone was sniffing and experiencing the joy and wonder of the perfumes in the room without any one trying to do anything. Excitement and wonder as each became a part of the joy of these happenings.

"Oh yes and this one is an incense."

"I think its sandalwood. Can you smell that one too?" We each nodded and agreed as we all experienced the same perfumes one after the other. The joy of these things happening when no-one was sitting for them or trying to do anything confirmed that the less we became personally involved in anything the more Spirit performed wonders for us to enjoy. Another confirmation of the reading Mary Duffy gave me in 1983.

The confirmation I received the following week was in a reading from Bob H. on 16 4 86 went; "There is a lady here who suffered a lot and I think she's coming back with thanks for all that you have done to help her for the period of her life and I'm being shown hands as though, from this I

121

feel that you've given this person healing and that they are now in the world of Spirit. They were ill on and off over a period of years - a lady - and I don't feel she's been in the spirit a long long time. I don't want to go back years. I feel around the last 3 - 5 months, maybe less and you would have visited her in a bed of sickness. You did actually visit her when she was in a real bed of sickness. *(This was accurate as I had visited her every day in an Hospice)*. There's another one in the spirit world that you visited for a period of time but you didn't visit her in a bed. It's the one who laid in the bed of sickness saying; 'You don't know how much you helped'. Perhaps you were disappointed that her physical body passed after all the efforts you put in and all your encouragement. Maybe there was just a slight feeling of being let down but you must have helped her over a period of time. You brought in to her awareness life after death. So you made her transition so much easier and also, they are saying, that what little bits you told her for some time she wasn't able to take it in. You've given her a springboard for her progress in the spirit world.

Now are you aware of a dark black who comes here? A Zulu or a big man like that. He comes with a lot of power and he's telling me to tell you; now look now don't worry about things starting, progressing and stopping and people coming and going because you are doing a lot of work to help people in the very beginning and I've got a strong feeling, also a China man there as well and he says, well you are going through this period of your life - when you are mainly with beginners - but there is going to be a time - I'm being drawn to that star - the six pointed star. I'm seeing a gentleman who is like that one up there in that robe. *(He pointed to a picture of a man like an Arab)*. He sometimes comes as a Druid or whether he comes almost without a form from the higher spiritual level, but he is saying that you will later on be not for the beginners but with those who have progressed that far and there will be more solidarity and lastingness in the length of time when you sit in your circles because sometimes you think to yourself, I'm being told, Oh, this is going well and it's been going well for a few months and all of a sudden it seems to disintegrate and then you are left with a little nucleus and then some more come in but it seems as though the nucleus is the same more or less throughout all the circles. We all work in different ways. You're going to have criticism but if it was all the same nobody would learn. If every circle was run the same and it was like a production, there would be no progress. I feel that you have come under criticism from various sources - they are telling me that your shoulders are broad enough to bear that and to go on the way that is right for you. A little chinese boy is here. He's very much like one of the boat children but he's got the sampan type of hat in Southern France - somewhere. *(I had only drawn this little fellow with a Sampan hat recently!)* You ever have the feeling that you have been guillotined at some time or seen a guillotine that is something to do with a period of one of your lives? Whether you were just an onlooker or were shown this scene. I was told you would be aware of it. *(I had had a visionary experience of myself with a group from my first circle, as an observer in a chateau. The people were all in costume but I recognised them from the present life. My numbers reading also stated a life in 1640 in France as a friend of Rascine, as a poet and a play writer.)* Don't worry about your daughter too much. She's got to go through her own knocks and bangs and sometimes it just concerns you a bit. Are the people coming for sittings and into your house gradually coming from further away, because I'm being shown spokes of a wheel? Look you are seeing more - I don't care what you say. It doesn't matter how it comes - it's an inner impression really and, truly, you've come a long way. Do you sometimes get a humming vibration around you, like energy, like under pylons? *(This happened many times, and sometimes it was similar to grasshoppers rubbing their legs together.)* Are you also instructing someone for healing? It's only the spirit world that teaches. We instruct. Somebody is very precise about this and they train. If they haven't got it and no love and compassion - all the training in the next 1000 years won't make them a healer. Sometimes you get them to practice on you and as they are practising on you, you're getting a feed back from the spirit world. I've got to encourage you on that. *(That was nice to hear as it confirmed what I felt and knew too!)* Also getting some people that border on the highly-strung too. You're doing healing on a high emotional level vibration. Some people work on the physical and they put back bones. It seems as though you do a lot to do with the head and mind, ingrained phobias which perhaps go back to childhood. Would you come in contact in the last 12 - 16 months, with people who have problems from child abuse? Spiritual mental healing - this is what I'm seeing, as though it's expanding around you and I feel you are having good results in a calming way. Perhaps more so in that field than in asthmatic conditions which are physical. Backs to do with this African and this Indian. Two powerful healers there. Sometimes, I'm told, you sit in a chair relaxing and you're here but you're not here and when you come back you think what has happened and I do feel they have taken you into a different dimension for either instruction or training. *(Very true!)* There is something new going on. I'm seeing a key now. It's a silver key and that's good, if its silver or gold. It is one of these big old-fashioned keys and there's an old fashioned door here, which you are unlocking. A very old, well built door. You are about to put the key in and open the door. There is something, actually, already starting for you. You've been given the key. It is already planned

123

and starting in the Spirit World. *(During an experience when I was in a deep meditation, with the cat on my knee, I saw a wall with a door in the middle, half way up the wall. The door was ajar. I reached out with my left hand, to push it wider, when an enormous Lion's paw landed on the back of my wrist and stopped me. As I came back to my normal consciousness, I became aware of the cats paws both holding on to my left wrist. He was sound asleep too and must have travelled with me!)*

I don't know if later on you are going to team up with someone, a gentleman. It may not be in a matrimonial sense. I'm not getting one way or the other. In some way I'm feeling you are coming away from the material way of life and I wouldn't be surprised if you don't eventually move from where you are and either be involved in some kind of a sanctuary - you live and work and, I feel you'll be working with somebody of the opposite sex. Now whether you are going to meet someone who is very much the same as you and you'll marry and this will come about, or whether it'll be just a spirit work relationship but I'm being shown that two in harness is better than one. I'm confirming it. They're confirming to me two huge Shire horses, which mean Power and Strength. Those horses are rock steady and not erratic or anything like that. They are really something and they are harnessed to this plough and I'm seeing Spirit hands on the other end and they are talking about two in harness is better than one. It's hard to say when this is coming about, but 4 - 5 years, but then things might start happening in '87. I don't know why I think the outcome is right but the time would be a little bit out. It seems as though it's an older type property, on it's own. Fair bit of ground and double frontage. It seems as though it's not in a town. It could be on the edge of a town or it could be in the country. Trees around about 8 - 10 rooms. People stay and is that the feeling you're getting inside - starting Centre? From little acorns great oak trees grow. They are saying also remember the Mustard Seed. Is that a big tree?

*(St. Luke Chapter 13 v 18. Then said he, Unto what is the kingdom of God like? And whereunto shall I resemble it?*

*V 19 It is like a grain of mustard seed which a man took and cast into his garden; and it grew, and waxed a great tree; and the fowls of the air lodged in the branches of it.)*

In Britain somewhere. I've got to say Britain not England why? Now they are saying not at the moment. Now my own impression was to say England but someone is saying "No Britain", so whether it'll be Scotland or Wales. I don't feel its Ireland. All will be revealed in good time because even in their little plan there has got to be little adjustments made. I've got to really say that I feel happy for you and I do wish you every success. The main thing is helping people to be aware of Spirit and the spirit of them and their inner selves and there's several ways of doing it, to gyrate towards their spiritual centre, which is suitable for them. We're all developing on different wavelengths and soul groups. You are not collecting books like your life depends on it? I don't want you to buy them, collect them. What I want you to do is just put it out that you're hoping to build up a library. If you are around the junk shops look out for some of the Arthur Findlay ones that are out of print. I feel you'll be drawn to them. You'll be given some. *(I was given quite a few from Aberdeen)*. Say 'Don't chuck your psychic books away.' I do see a library in this place. People are going to stay there. People will come to where you are, as a retreat. While they are there they will have psychic studies, lectures and things going on. You'll have your own circles several different ones, in the course of a week. That's why I feel this link up with somebody else. What is meant - the place will be provided. The future is a blue print.

In the May I was inspired to also open a Healing Group and we started with nine people. This was a truly wonderful evening with everyone in Meditation then each received healing, held hands and gave power as well as stand at the back and give healing. We finished by holding hands and sending out absent healing then closed before anyone spoke about what they had seen, felt or received. At last I had found a method of helping each to open up, build their own powers around them and constantly give out love to the realms of spirit. This became the most amazing group with everyone benefiting and developing at a fantastic rate. We used a candle in a crystal brandy glass where the colours shone into the room and raised the vibrations. Everyone felt themselves lift with the candle. By this time I was also writing quite a lot inspirationally. The writing always began with: 'We are here.....' I questioned who this 'We' was but it was to be several years later before I found out.

My own clairvoyance even amazed me, at times, especially when I saw the healing colours and received knowledge about each. I was also seeing guides with some people and hands going inside the body at specific times. I received information about their progress when they practised on me. The power of healing seemed to be the most spiritual phenomena developmental energy.

125

# CHAPTER 10

## CANADA

A lso in May, I went to Canada and stayed with Carole in Coteau du Lac on the edge of the Lake. Irene Griffey, a transfiguration medium was also staying and we spent many hours walking and talking. Irene was demonstrating to students in Carole's Sanctuary every evening. I was fascinated by the changes over her face from a mist that came from under her chin and the instant recognition of individual's family members. She showed me some interesting photographs of how the energies worked. My message was not from a family member and quite different to everyone else's. For my reading Parkinson said: -

"My friend, I greet you and thank you. You have been around my Medium and I wish

To say to you, that stirring within you is a greater energy that will begin to manifest.

Just give it 1 to 2 years and going to draw around you are 4 -5 people, who will dedicate themselves to sit for the benefit of the advancement of your own mediumship. For there lies within you deeper energies for physical mediumship. For do not expect in 5 minutes. To take time and your love and warmth spreads out to many people and will continue to do so and one young person will come in to the environment that you will be instrumental in helping them to develop. Go gently, encourage them. You have many souls and helpers; many from our side and you will find yourself, later on moving around more. That will bring more great joy. The purpose of life stirs with you. Your incarnation is to serve. One draws close here who wishes to manifest himself from the East.

'We walk together and serve. We have dedicated ourselves long ago. Once more.... So now we are together.... the beauty of the heavens spreads out to encompass you. It entwines you.... Another then showed himself and spoke as he manifested; 'Salaam let the sands of time walk each step...' This seemed quite different to the other readings people in these groups received from family members and confirmed the Arabian guide I was told about several years ago when I had been told I hadn't earnt him yet.

Could he be the one I had met in a Meditational vision experience where I found myself hurrying to keep an appointment? I was running along a corridor with one of the Circle members. She kept stopping and looking at her legs to see if her seams were straight and then stopping to look in her hand bag. In the end I said 'I am late, I have an appointment for 3 o'clock and am late already. I just have to go' and ran off without her. I reached the top of some steps leading to - what looked to me like - Paddington station but it was empty and I thought I was too late. As I looked out all around I saw a man in an old overcoat with a dark green baraclava helmet on and realised he had waited. I went down the steps and became blind as a bat. I couldn't see a thing. I stretched out my arms and walked in the general direction of where this man stood with his back to me. Then two hands were placed on my shoulders and a voice said: "Shalom Cyntia" with an eastern accent that could not pronounce the 'th' in my name. My eyes could see again and I looked in to the most wonderful love, compassion and literally melted. The vision ended and I then pondered over the meaning of the time. Was it years or months? I know I was about 10 minutes late so did this mean months or weeks? Who was this beautiful soul?

Carole and I attended the Spirit and Space Symposium held in Montreal. I learnt more in that weekend than several sessions could have taught me in England. This was certainly an important part of my development. When I first arrived and looked at the conference hall of some 500 people, an aura denoting Lemurian energies emanated over the entire congregation of people. I was taken aback saying to myself: "I would have thought it would have stemmed from Atlantis, not Lemuria, then these people are working more spiritually than many are aware." We had wonderful lectures from Marcel Vogel, Andreah Puharich and many others as well as some quite astounding trance by Marilyn Rossner who channeled Space beings. I was enthused before she even spoke by a ripple of energy across the curtains at the back of her as the control came through with a very tinny voice and with almost automatic mechanical sounds. We could have stayed on for more lectures and workshops but I felt two weeks of non-stop spiritual activities and learning would be too much. We took off for Stowe Vermont and went into a retreat, which was wonderfully relaxing and enabled us each to absorb and assimilate what had happened.

The only other place I wanted to experience was in the original Chapel where Brother Andre did healing in Mount Royal. There was a vortex of earth energy at this point, which helped the healing energies manifest, like they did in Lourdes. Pilgrims came from all around the world and left thousands of crutches behind. Marcel Vogel had spoken at the Symposium about the energy vortex in Brother Andre's Chapel and I wanted to experience this too. There was an enormous Church nearby and there were many steps leading to the door on which people prayed on every step as they went towards the Church or Cathedral, as it seemed. We were lazy and drove to the top of the hill then entered to walk around and experience this place. I was well aware of the thoughts of many with ailments purposely coming to be made well but the whole place was becoming a dumping ground for these thing and I felt physically bombarded by these thoughts and spent some time clearing myself before leaving. Carole then said she didn't like going in because she always felt ill afterwards and I suppose sensitive people would pick these things up. It is such a shame there is no daily ritual of clearing the debris and dispersing it properly.

The people I met in Canada were wonderful and I learnt a lot about a multitude of different ways of working, Carole and I linked on many similar subjects. This link shows in the photo of our connection to each other and the invisible realms.

Showing the spirit link between Carole and I Canada May 1986

When I returned from Canada I had a Wedding invitation for the same day that Bill M was due to come. I left it open and handed over to God to sort out what I was to do. The day before he was due, Bill phoned me and asked if he could put the booking off as he had family matters to sort out and I was able to go to the wedding. This was the last time I spoke to Bill as he passed away in early September. The next time Dorice came on the 14th Sept he was trying to come through to talk but Dorice said he was not trying correctly. She gave accurate details of how he passed.

One night whilst sleeping I suddenly became aware of a man in my bedroom, coming towards me. How on earth did a man get in to my bedroom? Who was this? I could see him clearly with my eyes shut and decided to open them and face whatever was there. To my surprise I was faced with a huge scene like an enormous Cinema screen right across the side of my bedroom, larger than life, which showed the same man, whom I had seen with my eyes closed, coming towards me, wearing an orange shirt, thick hairy braces and brown rough woolen trousers. With some relief I saw that he was not coming to me because right in front of me, was another man with a sword. He was really coming towards this other man with a sword in his hand, which was at my side, as though ready to fight. He wore trousers made of wool and hair, held up with some rough braces, over an orange shirt. He was also wearing a black Pilgrim's father hat similar to the ones Puritans wore. *(Even though the description didn't fit exactly. Could this have had anything to do with what Dorice had said?)* As soon as I had seen this picture, and realised that the man was not really after me so the screen changed to a ballroom of people dressed in crinoline Elizabethan dresses and powdered wigs. I enjoyed this scene and hoped I would get some more films of this nature but haven't as yet.

The Circles and Saturday Groups continued with new people attending. I was aware of a higher intelligence behind what was happening. The established sitters became the more advanced and the new ones brought in fresh insight's.

I invited new sitters into the Developing Circle, which grew to nine people. I opened another Physical Circle, with four of these, briefly, but although the power was there, it didn't seem to be ready to produce results, whilst each person needed personal tuition, adjustment and preparation. I decided to open a Healing Circle, which proved to be the most beneficial of all the groups.

Bob H had given me a private sitting on 28 7 1986: -

Have you got any links with Findhorn? I have got a feeling that its in Scotland is that right? I think so I have a feeling that sometime in the future you are either going there for a holiday..... Oh yes I am getting that very strongly indeed. And there seems to have come very much into the prominence amongst your guides. One's taken a step forward and he is a North American Indian - very powerful. He doesn't have a lot to say either. Your physical Circle is shut down for the summer but before it was shut down were you getting shapes? Moving about and a whisper like this - almost a breath. A little girl you might feel her pulling your dress. (This actually happened when I was at a service in Glasgow) and there is also a Doctor or somebody in the scientific side called Claude. If you can get your people to persevere because this is vital because I feel you can get it - most important is the dedication. I am seeing mainly people who link with it, a gentleman here in a turban and rather Araby Indian beard. You know he is grinning all over his face. Also somebody with one of those Fez's *(I had only seen him the previous week.)* They're all around. I feel that one is all right, everything is O.K. and as long as it's kept there you'll get what you are hoping for and perhaps what you've been promised but it is the dedication. The healing Circle that seems ... is there a gentleman in that that goes into trance? There's somebody in there that I feel could be a trance healer but not developed you know what I mean. Are you going somewhere similar to

Stansted to meet some interesting people? Do you feel your hands are not yours when you are healing? *(Yes)* People who come in your groups and sit in them, often you are given helpers who you think are new guides for you but they are often for them aren't they? *(Yes like the man in the Fez, I had only just seen the previous week, who I knew belonged to a specific sitter).* They kind of come to you first. You are also given the intuition, inner understanding who they are for ....... Your car is going in many directions in the future. I want to go westward down through Wiltshire, Somerset somewhere down that way Dorset perhaps Devon or Cornwall. Have you got old acquaintances down that way? Because as I said that they started singing that song 'Should old acquaintance be forgot'? I feel that you will go and it will do you good. I don't know if down there one of these Ley lines is supposed to be like Glastonbury or something like that but it seems as though you are going to get some benefit from a visit down there to renew old acquaintances....................

On August 3rd 1986 Dorice did an update on my Auragraph and this was a really interesting new way of working and very accurately described my work for the years ahead: -

"This muddy sort of Pond. All these green lentilly things on it and the tadpoles are people around you. They seem to be quite often, difficult people or funny people but they haven't developed yet, into what they are going to be. If you have the frogs they have linked the self-awareness with the physical self and then they have got the heart. You see there the front legs and things like that and it's like they are all seemingly loving, jumping around seeming to do it for everybody else but they're really doing it for themselves but they don't feel so happy about themselves. They haven't come to terms with themselves because if you think of the Piscean age, it is like people are swimming in the water. They are at the mercy of their Emotions. If the water is good they feel good but if the water is bad they feel bad and they are the people that are making the jump from the Piscean Age to the Aquarian age. As they develop and get their legs and make a big jump they take off but these are people that don't know that they are tadpoles. They are trying very hard to be fish but the fish keep eating them up. But people, like teachers and things like that, take charge of these people but instead of developing them they devour them and try to make them part of their own life. Like little rejects and some of them got so frightened of the big fish they stopped getting themselves big and strong. They hang about. So at the moment, and before you were working with them. You tried to clear the water. You tried to get emotionally straight with them but it is no good because tadpoles live in muddy water. They like their messes. It's no good trying to help them sort out their problems. You just have to

130

reassure them they are doing the right thing whatever they are doing. They are looking for spiritual things but they don't really want it. A bit of a nuisance basically but sooner or later they will start leaving the pond and turning into frogs. It's also to do with Circle Work where again you have these odd ones coming in for a while and they hang about and then get on with it. The trouble with those is they always think they know everything better. Under the heart level but really O.K. You mustn't smother them with love. The Lentil is symbolic for the love that they'll show in time, when they have grown up. Golden green and things like that. Toads and Frogs. This bit is like sand but it's got bits of slime on it. It's like a stagnant pond and it's a bit difficult to deal with, because it, like, gets up your nose a bit. You've just got to keep going. Sooner or later the water's going to start running down. Just give as many of them a chance as you can and see that they've got enough water and the right sort of conditions to grow, without giving too much love and emotions towards them. You mustn't overdo things there just accept them - that they are there don't fuss too much about them. That will take 3 - 9 months still.

Then the next bit is sort of like a marshy sort of ground, boggy and pond as well, very squelchy. You've really got to know where you put your feet. There are certain bits that are solid but you have got to really know where you are going. Lots of reeds denoting the emotional, spiritual, material and the world. These are like swords and some of them have got the bulrush like Moses a very interesting story and people are going through the same sort of development that you are going through. With the tadpoles, you are taking care of them, helping them through emotional trauma that you have been through, having turned into a frog, Parent frogs don't look after little ones, they just put them down and that's it! Bull rushes, golden brown are people that understand about their own darkness, their own fears, and their own problems. They get to understand others and you get the seeds of that, so red and black make brown then the gold of understanding why there has to be darkness and difficulties as well. You're giving them a chance to look further, rather than being stuck in the mud. Also a lot of yellow water lily things and the bulrushes. Three lilies and less of the muddy sort of things. Getting gold into it getting spiritual help and the golden colour. The other bit; the water lilies are people, like the crown of it. They are getting above themselves understanding spiritual truth and teaching it, expressing it spiritual awareness and learning. It's like a little cup with a top and giving it to others, starting to get results. The swords are mental strength. It's like people trying to get their own way. As long as they do it their own way it doesn't work. If they do it the right way, they understand what they're doing and do the right thing. As you learn to use your mental strength, your spiritual power to achieve your aims to see what you can do - you are worried about whether you are doing the right thing? It's quite a different way of doing things, more like relying on your own strength and making things happen/come your way, not for yourself but for people in general. Like being a farmer taking care of the land. Basically for yourself but for other people. They are all yellow ones. I thought there would be some blue. It's based on knowledge rather than anything else. The intellect more than teaching, quite matter of fact, a different kind of people coming in there. Emotions, say what they want and express themselves. They understand what is going on *(like your daughter.)* They know what they want and are doing it quite unemotionally. Getting on with it. This area is dryer, not quite a path but it is harder. So you have got to stay away from the emotional side of things and leave it to the people that are growing there. Pick these things from time to time to time, when you need them. Give them a purpose, like taking note but not too much notice. It's like you are letting them practice on and with you and people you know. One is woolly headed he finds it difficult getting across to people. 3 - 9 months it comes and goes. That phase almost 2 years again. First 5 months are a flowering time but it happens again and again and again. Not because you need it but they need to be looked after. That's not the only way knowing what they want to achieve. 18 months in that area, also water hens, ducks making nests. Reeds are personalities and birds are spiritual awareness hatching among these parts narrow minded to a certain extent. People who are very self centred. These nests in between are different, symbolising what is growing inside those people that are difficult, moving from tadpoles. That we are practising to those people that are more difficult but more approachable. You are showing them with the way you react to them, whether there is something you can accept or not. They are trying out their mental strength on you. Watch you don't get overboard with everything. You tend to then leave it alone again. You go through phases where you use things and before you know it, you have moved over to something else. You don't need it anymore. From time to time you are over enthusiastic telling people - link in with spirit. Do they need this or not? Giving the right prescription. You are your own guinea pig. Look at the person and see if they need it or not before you give the prescription. More answers. Some it's not good.

Very gentle hills go into the distance. Beautiful meadow with lots of flowers and it's like you are cutting this grass. Here you have got two different paths that are starting to define. One goes that way and one goes straight up to the top of the hill. The one is going that way, through a valley between two hills. It's almost, in a way, like part of you splits off. You can either go on that path to spiritual heights and they need somebody there or the other. More concentrating on yourself, doing what you feel is spiritually right and what you need to do spiritually. Another possibility, which you quite consciously choose is material conditions and then it's like you are in a physical personality getting on with the everyday job of being there for people getting all this living. That's more straight forward and it's like one part of you, in thought, walks until it comes back to yourself, like you are halving your energy. The third possibility is where somebody comes from spirit into your life. A cross roads where somebody comes to you and the two of you are walking together on the physical path as a team and it is a spirit person. It is not somebody physically alive. A very strong team of you and a spirit person. This path is a sandy golden colour and that is a sort of brown. How you are going to do it depends on circumstances that come when you are there. It's such a big way before you know it, but I've a feeling you'll make those decisions in your sleep, and you will just know what's the right thing to do then. What happens in your energy field? You've got to the froggy stage now Frog Prince that's your cup and you are starting to take energy in there and it blows you up more and more like a balloon and you are really something important and you are doing everything for love of others and for the sake of others but it keeps you jumping around and nobody knows where you are at any given time. Even though it's great fun and the right thing for you. Sooner or later, a frog can do it, but a Frog Prince is not the same thing. Now the Princess lost her golden ball and it fell down the well. There's your well, the muddy water. Her golden ball is her true self, the seed of her inner knowledge, awareness of true understanding. It's like a seed in the ground disappears, unless it starts coming up out of the ground. There is not much you can do with it. It dies off in there; it's no good in there. So, this little thing that can deal very well with the muddy stuff, actually pops into the well and gets the golden ball out. But he wants something in return. He wants to live in the castle with the Princess and eat off her plate, sleep in her bed and she's getting really cheesed off. Now that's your higher self, your spiritual self. Serene and calm the Princess and the Frog is your personality. The Princess is really cheesed off and would really like to get rid of the blasted thing. Most people think she kissed the Frog. She didn't she threw it against the wall. It banged and that's when the Prince came out. So when you get rid of that you get the Prince. So having connected your love and emotions and strength with your self awareness and knowledge yourself, to be part of the spiritual hierarchy and having come as high as you can in the world becoming a King or a Prince. You've got to take it one step further. You've got the completion, the purple. It's like, not enough. It's like a seed is a tree but it's not it has to grow. It's got to break through it's own barriers and the minute that happens, we've

133

got these three energies and those three it's like there comes a division and this thing is starting to get a head and a waist and things like that. It starts working from the heart. Taking spiritual energy in there. So it's not the Frog that's living in the castle. It's actually the Prince standing above the normal. So to get to that stage, there has to be a seeding of energy. If you are a root system you need the branches and the branches need the root system. You've got to work. It's like physically and spiritually in the earth sense, you're strong. In the everyday sense you're strong and you know what you can do but you don't know what you are capable of, given half a chance. You need someone to really pull you about. Some one from the really highest hierarchy and one of the Masters. You get one of them to take you through your paces but as an equal sort of partner and that is terrifying. You go down into the well and get the golden ball of the Princess.

Music Notes that one is the lowest of the high notes and that one is the highest of the low notes, which is exactly the same note. Every time it makes a jump or a step - the distance gets bigger or it doubles 2 into 4, 16 into 200 and something or other doubling in size. Having done the 1 - 3 physical completion 4,5,6 emotional completion, 7,8,9, spiritual completion, jump around and go through the negation's = spiritual death putting your life in God's hands. Emotional death loving others more than you love your own self 17,18,19, putting your whole life into God's hands and you get to the X. You only get to the X if you don't keep going because what you have done is; you go 1,2,3, 4,5,6, 7,8,9, 10,11,12, 13,14,15. You've got this thing done, getting bigger and rounder, making bigger circles around you, but it doesn't get you anywhere, except like a balloon threatening to pop. You're not blowing up you are taking no more in than you can cope with but your capacity is getting bigger like a tadpole. You've got a really big Toad then, but it's not just an ordinary one. It's got the crown. It knows where it gets its strength from. It knows where it is in the hierarchy right at the top but being right at the top of the low ones you're the same as the lowest of the high ones. So you are right in the middle. Being a Frog Prince is just as good as a Princess that is a stupid cow. Your higher self or the Master, whatever comes in there, is no better than you in the physical personality as such. They are only better because they haven't any problems with a physical personality but they've got a problem because they haven't a physical personality to refine it, to re shape it, to change it to set free the Prince that's hidden in the Frog. To do that, to get rid of the Frog you say I've had it with this thing. I cannot take it anymore - that's it, not how I want to be and you have to think; 'How do I want to be?' I want to be the Prince in charge. But you can be a good King or a bad King and to do that you need to marry the Princess. Mystical Wedding and all that. That's where you are getting to. You have finished with the Frog. Now from 1 to 2 would be 1 step but from 1 to 3 would be 2 steps, only by the time I get there, to go from there would be 2 steps. The level on a spiral - is always the same. It eventually gets faster and spins into a wheel like that, going bigger and bigger potentially to grow physically. Either you move upward and start detaching and these two move apart and you start dying or you re activate that by opening to spiritual energy and you feed that energy into the body. Then this makes this point stronger and this moves down very slowly again. You will return and journey until that is activated again. Then you start mirroring red, orange, yellow, green - all the chakras, all the energy of two people in one body. And when that jump comes, you pop like a balloon. It tears you apart. So if you let somebody help you through it. It means it becomes a spiritual experience that you can take. As big as the whole Universe it's like a drop of water being steamed up and you totally disintegrate, turn inside out and you start building up again with the heart as the base and the body, as a base and it's like here comes a core and makes your heart as big as that, and love builds up your body on that. These are Christmas colours mainly green and red. It's bringing that into a new potential and your whole body goes one step up. If I stand up my body is higher and the energy point is a different position to the rest of the world and that starts going again and then you start taking energy from earth powers. You start bringing earth power up into spirit power. Either you are giving some of your strength to spirit and give them the excess energy. Keep giving them the strength. They can do with it what they like, keeping yourself as small as possible, until eventually you meet yourself face to face every time, in other people and loving them as you love yourself. You suddenly understand that they are part of you or you go along your material path giving the strength that is in excess, to other people and into the world, planting seeds of understanding and knowledge. As they have their seeds growing, it is like you have given them 2 plants of roses. Now they get the seeds out of them. It is right saying I want 4 back. The next ones get 4 of them and you say I want 8 back. You suddenly double your energy, having prepared your body for it and you can either make yourself stronger. You've got the strength now and you can start planting it out and seeding it again but to do that you need somebody there next to you that knows how to do it. That person chooses you, rather than the other way round. You cannot pick. You put your whole mind and your whole heart, all your emotions into service of the Boss and that's it. Whichever Master of the race picks you as its student. The personalities of what happened to them are basically what happened to you. It sounds terrifying but it isn't really as bad as that. It's tough, very tough. Then comes the Integration and you keep going under guidance. You're allowed to complain what you like and what you don't like. That's basically what you are heading for, and until you've made that decision there; you cannot actually get to that part of another development.

# CHAPTER 11

## LEY LINES

An interesting journey to sacred sites and the connection to the planets all started when one of my Circle members, Bob, said he was going to visit Stonehenge with his brother that Sunday in August 1986. After several weeks he had still not been. I then suggested that if he was willing to go to Glastonbury I would go halves on the petrol and we could go the following Sunday. I had no idea why I wanted to visit Glastonbury at all.

We set off on a bright and sunny morning and reached Stonehenge. It was closed and there was no way we could even get near the stones. I had already been there as a child and sat on the stones and felt sorry for Bob who really wanted a closer contact. We headed for Wells and decided to meditate in Wells Cathedral. The peace and tranquility restored our energies and we arrived in Glastonbury raring to go to all the sights.

We began by searching for a map of Glastonbury and finding our bearings in the town. As we drove around, we decided to start where Joseph had when he first arrived in the area and planted his staff on a hill overlooking the town. The staff had sprouted in to what is commonly known as the Thorn Bush. We walked up to the Thorn Bush, took in the surroundings, attuning to the energies to see what we could pick up, and meditated, before moving on to climb the Tor. We chose the quickest steepest side and met several people coming down. Once at the top we spent time together and alone in the tower. We meditated at the top and spent time there admiring the view in silence. I didn't feel anything specific at the top and felt the prime energy was in the hill itself. We both decided it was time to move on and began to make our way down the steep side of the hill. On our way down I suddenly started to yawn and yawn - so much so that I said I would have to sit down because I couldn't breathe for yawning so much. Gordon Higginson had already told me the yawning was the way the power of spirit came, when I apologised to him for yawning so much in one of his lectures. As I sat down a "Voice" suddenly spoke in my ear saying, "You now have to go to Findhorn and Iona".

"Oh yes, in 5 years time, when I can save enough money", I replied. I knew that they were both in Scotland but had no idea where. What was this all about?

We continued exploring the Abbey and sensed the feelings of the place, and town before deciding to make a real day of it by visiting Avebury village encompassed by a huge prehistoric temple, on the way home. We were both in altered states of consciousness by now as we entered Avebury. This place had a gloomy air about it. Someone has misused the Powers, I thought to myself, as we wandered around the stones feeling the energies. If people could have been turned to stone by the negative use of the tremendous earth energies, then this is what had happened here. Now the positivity of a newer more knowledgeable age had arrived to turn this round for a benefit to the earth and mankind. We spent quite a bit of time with the stones and afterwards we walked over to the gift shop to see what kind of souvenirs were on sale. As we reached the shop a "Beep, beep" of a watch alarm sounded. "Oh your watch." I commented to Bob.

"It's not mine it's yours." Came the quick reply.

"Mine doesn't work, it has been disconnected." I looked at my watch and realised that the power and energy at the stones had indeed triggered my watch to sound its alarm.

Then I was sure this type of energy could be measured scientifically!! We finished our visit and returned home happy and aware of a spiritual link at the back of this journey. It had been a truly remarkable experience we both enjoyed.

That night I had a Psychic dream in which I was in an underground crypt with several other people involved with killing the personality self of people who had chosen one of us to perform this ritual according to an ancient astrology parchment, which they handed to me, authorizing me as the chosen one for this part, before I could do anything. As they handed me the ancient parchment astrological document, all tattered and marked from constant use, I discussed what they had chosen for me to do. I didn't enjoy the work, as no one liked their personality egotistical side being killed off, but did it as part of my role in helping humanity as a service because they had chosen for me to help them kill this part. My daughter was one who had chosen me and as she came to me with her parchment astrological chart, I talked about what she had chosen when she suddenly said, "Oh yes I know but we don't have to do it yet. Let's go and have fun first."

She wanted to delay the procedure and I was aware that eventually I would be instrumental in doing something I wasn't keen on doing.

When I forgot to buy bread the following week, I popped into the local V.G store, wondering how I could have missed out the bread from my shopping. As I waited to pay for the bread, I noticed a competition leaflet. I read it with interest. It was one of the few competitions I knew the answers to! I picked up the leaflet, filled it in and posted it. Imagine my surprise, when I won first prize. A free 1st Class railway ticket for 2 people, to anywhere in the U.K. Someone definitely wanted me to visit Findhorn and Iona before five years went by!!!

I hunted for details of knowledge and information about Iona and Findhorn, eventually receiving an address for Findhorn. I wrote away for a brochure and booked a four-day event for the New Year. I then had no one to go with me and requested another ticket to Oban in order to visit Iona from there. I was asked to take both tickets before the end of January. Who, in their rightful minds would want to visit Scotland in January? It was so dark. What was in store and what a coincidence it was in my winning two rail tickets to involve both destinations.

Meantime I remembered that Bob H had given me a private sitting on 28 7 1986:

Have you got any links with Findhorn? I have got a feeling that its in Scotland is that right? I think so. I have a feeling that sometime in the future you are either going there for a holiday...Oh yes I am getting that very strongly indeed! This reading gave me food for thought about where the directive, to go to Findhorn, was coming from. Was I a puppet on a string?

During September I caught a shocking cold as I weakened under stress at work, but continued to work right through it - resulting in getting much worse and succumbing to bronchial asthma, which took me out of the every day world to recuperate. The Doctor said I had pneumonia and that if the penicillin didn't work that night I would be in hospital in the morning. I dosed myself up and managed to stay out of hospital.

It was during this time, as I lay on my sofa watching television, that I found myself being pulled in to a "Hold" and felt that I was being "Used". I struggled against it thinking that all the Churches and mediums quoted that you should never go off on your own. As I fought this form of control, I was clearly shown two African guards, complete with a staff with a spear on top and a shield - one on either side of me on look out - like standing on a hill watching out for me. I felt so safe and with that I let go of fighting. With that kind of protection I was quite safe. I decided to test the wisdom of this form of control and set a clock up in front of me saying that 'God' could have half an hour to start with then said my prayer and let go. I was always brought back to open my eyes dead on the very minute. I would completely go out of the body and for me to come back dead on the minute proved a much higher and more intelligent control was present. This gave me confidence to extend these sessions until I gave God 2 hours a day, at the same time each day, for this to happen. I then set a definite time for this to happen and lengthened the time of sitting - always coming back dead on the minute. I called it my daily Meditation for training and development and allowed myself to completely let go, hand myself over and let God work with me.

This was to be the start of a much deeper sleep state trance where I was often taken out of the body to be shown things and always came back feeling enlightened, rejuvenated and completely balanced. There seemed a much higher purpose to this way of meditating. I would often find myself flying over the ocean watching the waves beneath me. Once I found myself on a plane behind an elderly couple that were going to Australia. Then I was with this couple in their son's home in Australia before sitting behind them whilst flying back again. How I had done the whole journey in one meditation I didn't know. There were many insights and interesting happenings as I became an observer and watched these scenes.

When enquiring about Findhorn and Iona, amongst friends, I was given an address for Findhorn and wrote off for details. I looked at the map and found Iona was on the opposite side of the country and this would make it difficult to visit both at the same time. As a one off Findhorn were doing a 4-day New Year Celebration called "Creating the New" which appealed to me as I could fit that in during our compulsory holiday at Christmas. Normally there was a compulsory Experience week before doing any of the Courses but this was a 4-day event without the need for an Experience week.

I always visited my parents at Christmas and could catch the train to Scotland after visiting them. I booked the 4-day event and arranged my ticket to Scotland. I decided that as it was a long journey I would break my journey with an overnight stay with friends in Aberdeen and visit some of the people I had met on Caledonian weeks at Stansted.

**Bob's story**

"I first came to Cynthia's in 1986 and sat with her regularly till 1993, mainly in the Healing group but also in the physical and clairvoyant group. My journey to Glastonbury opened a few doors for me and this area was just one, a powerful one. It was my first visit to Glastonbury and certainly not my last. The visit to Wells was of interest especially the grounds of the Bishop's house but I felt the purpose of the day was felt at Glastonbury. The grounds of St. Michel's Abbey was filled with history and a sense of interest within the walls of the ruin, especially the lower crypt where a well had been uncovered. I felt a strong energy connected to Mary. The walk up the Tor was incredible. The steps were weaving around and up. Much like a snake and at a particular point on the Tor it had a feeling of an underground chamber with immense power within. At the top of the Tor we rested within the Tower for a while taking in the feeling of the stonework and a glimpse into a past moment when floors and roof would have been intact with activity. We sat on top of the Tor for a small while in

140

silent meditation. I felt a rush of energy through me which, I felt, opened a new path for me. I became aware of certain energies and knowledge regarding the combination of earth and spirit energies and my later meditations led me further to thoughts about laws of light and D.N.A. I felt at peace on the Tor and looked out at the view and felt a dragon line running along a curve in the landscape through the Tor and across to another small Tor with the Thorn bush which was planted by Joseph of Aramathea. I purchased a crucifix from the Abbey shop which had a personal experience attached to it later on at home regarding dispelling a negative energy."

Lots of visitors came to Cynthia's which I met and enjoyed. Doris Hannan and Coral Polge, just two who made an impact on me. Both now gone to Spirit. Muriel Miller who probably had the biggest impact of all. So much love from all of them. - Thanks Cynthia.

Lots of love, Bob.

# CHAPTER 12

## TARA

Animal healing always came quite naturally after I had an experience with my sister's dog 'Lady' who was staying with my parents. One-week end I arrived to find Lady had been tearing her fur out and had a nasty raw patch of skin, which was really sore. I asked if she had been to see the Vet and my mother said she had but none of the creams, injection or anything seemed to make any difference.

Then whilst watching television Lady leaned on my leg and I mentally asked that if there was anything in this healing power, could it flow through my arm and help Lady. I put my hand out over the raw patch without touching her and left my arm there without thinking about it. About half an hour went by and I realized that normally my arm would have ached, being held out like that but I hadn't felt a thing. The following morning the raw patch had scabbed over and was healing nicely. Nothing to do with me as I had only offered myself to be used as an instrument. The fur grew back and she was fine.

During my work, as an Area Manager in the field, I visited a lady with a tiny dog. I watched it limp around the room and pointed out the limp asking what had happened.

"Oh, she jumped off the bed this morning and seems to have done something to her leg", came the quick reply. Owing to my insecurities about offering healing whilst I was working, I said nothing more. As I was about to leave she picked up the dog and saw me to the door. I turned around and reached over and stroked the little dog in her arms saying:

"Oh you poor little thing, you'll be alright."

She looked at me then the dog and suddenly said:

"Are you one of those healing people?"

"Yes" I replied.

"I thought so; because no-one and I mean no-one can touch that dog when it is in my arms. Not my husband or even my son can touch her when she is in my arms, so you must be a healer."

In many other situations dogs and cats just came and jumped on my knees, plonked their backsides in to my hands or lay on my feet to the astonishment of their owners who often said they didn't like strangers. They certainly had a sixth sense of where they could get a benefit and just took the healing powers that flowed through me and gave me their love in return.

One young girl had broken her leg whilst horse riding and after 9 months, of which several were spent in hospital, the leg was still in plaster and would not mend. She had been in and out of hospital and was getting fed up, when she phoned me and asked for healing. I arrived at her house and parked my car, just as a little black cat jumped down from a tree and ran up to me purring around my legs then followed me in. The girl remarked on the cat never coming in during the day but allowed it to join us. As I proceeded to give her healing through the plaster cast, I was amused to see the cat literally sucking and chewing the ends of my fingers and its owner remarked on never seeing anything like it. The cat followed me out, when I left, and went back up the tree. The leg healed and the plaster came off.

Tara, our Border collie pet of 14 years was a regular sitter in our circles and groups. She was always on time to the point that we often realised it was time to begin when she quickly settled in her spot. I found her to be a battery of energy, often sparkling with little lights, when she lay sleeping. With time she became older and had kidney infections. The Vet gave her antibiotics on two occasions and she duly recovered. In the September when she became ill again, I once again, took her to the Vet. This time the Vet asked me what I wanted her to do. "Give her some antibiotics and make her well", I responded. Come here and feel her heart." The Vet suggested also pointing out lumps on her underside. She then asked again, "What do you want me to do?" Refusing to believe she was indirectly asking me to have her put down, I replied: "Give her some antibiotics please."

"All right, how many do you want? Enough for 10 days," I replied. The vet gave me 10 days supply and then said "if you feel any different in three days time, bring her back." To which I agreed. Three days later Tara refused to eat, drink or go outside. She lay in her spot refusing to move. When the Circle members arrived, one by one, they asked where she was as there was no greeting from her.

"She is not well and has another kidney infection. I think she is on her last legs." I replied as each went up to stroke her and received no response. We held the Circle, ending by holding hands to send out absent healing. Suddenly, as though she had been kicked, Tara landed in the centre of the Circle, looking very dazed and bewildered, as she looked around at each person. I was watching with amazement. She then returned to her spot and lay down until we closed. Then she ran to the kitchen and was eating and drinking as normal. I realised she had been given an extension to her life and knew that the next time she became ill would be her last. At Christmas I had arranged for her to stay with my parents whilst I was visiting Findhorn in Scotland but she was not fond of being in their house.

Just before each Christmas I had an appointment to tape a trance reading for Muriel, the trance medium's, Christmas present where her guides and family members could speak to her. One control, Pearly King, came through and said he would like to tell me that he would be the one responsible for helping my doggie to materialise. How nice I thought to myself but she is not going yet. Then at the end the main Control stated that she had been asked to inform me that St. Francis would be with my doggie at Christmas. That was certainly reassuring owing to her dislike of being at my Parent's home. On speaking to my Mother, a few days later, confirming our visit, my Mother said my brother's dog was staying over Christmas. This was a blow, as the two bitches didn't like each other. I noted how tired Tara was.

When visiting my daughter, I explained that she hadn't much time left and pointed out her heart, lumps and lack of energy. My daughter exclaimed that Tara was all right and I couldn't have her put to sleep. As time passed and we were getting ready to leave. My daughter turned to me and said she left the decision to me but I was not to phone her at work with what I decided to do. I thought about the journey I was taking and knew that Tara would pine and be ill when I returned. It wasn't fair to leave her like that. She was going to die whatever I decided.

I thought it might be kinder to help her before I went away but I, also, did not want to come home to an empty house. I phoned the Vet asking if it was possible to put a dog to sleep on Christmas Eve. The Vet asked why I was requesting the information and I explained her history. The Vet discussed her history with colleagues who readily agreed. I made an appointment to fit in with my journey to my parents, in order that I would not return to an empty house. I came off the phone and couldn't believe my eyes. Tara must have known she was 'going home.' She ran upstairs, whereas she was too tired to run before. She became like a spring lamb. She looked around the garden as though saying good-bye to familiar surroundings. She certainly knew what was happening and we enjoyed her final two days. I duly took her to the Vets and stayed with her as her spirit left her body. My tears were uncontrollable as I signed the cheque. Amidst tears I drove away.

A friend had suggested I went to her for a cup of coffee before continuing my journey and I was able to let my tears flow freely before continuing my journey to the Midlands for Christmas with my parents. My mother greeted me asking where Tara was. I explained what I had just done.

On Christmas day in the early hours of the morning, I was woken up with pictures of Tara running through woods, across fields and jumping ditches, as she did when much younger. How could I be sad when she was so happy? I was so pleased for her and became happier now she was happy. I then remembered the trance control telling me that St. Francis would be with my doggie at Christmas. Could this have been already happening and why she was so happy?

My Sister also received some amazing absent healing through connecting with our group. For months I had not heard from my sister and husband. Then I received a note of a change of address from my niece, their daughter. I wrote to my sister at the new address in England explaining that I expected her to keep in touch. I then received letter on the Tuesday explaining that the reason she had not written was because of a lump in her mouth that had now been confirmed as malignant. She had only told her close family and I was the first she had told outside of her immediate family. She had been under torment, and to the very depths of despair with this result. Radiotherapy was due to start the very day I received the letter. I was angry that she hadn't told me as she knew I did healing and I also strongly believed my helpers and Doctors could do more if they could be invoked to help prior to killing good cells with radiotherapy and chemotherapy. Never mind I will send her absent healing now and proceeded to send out distant healing. On the Friday I phoned her to see how she felt after treatment that week. She started by saying: "A funny thing happened. You know I was supposed to start treatment on Tuesday?"

"Yes."

"Well the lift didn't turn up. I phoned the specialist and he said it was all right, I could miss Wednesday and start on Thursday so I have only been once."

"This is fantastic." I thought to myself as I knew the absent healing healers and angels had got in first. I then asked her to think of me on a Tuesday night at 9pm when we sent out absent healing as a group.

During the coming weeks I had a trance reading where the control spoke of my parents being all right and I commented on my sister not being too well. "Oh lady its here" she said pointing to her face and neck. "Keep your thoughts with her." The healing continued and I phoned again commenting:

"Do you ever think of me on a Tuesday night?"

"Oh I don't think of you but it doesn't happen any other day but on Tuesday at 9pm I just conk out and go to sleep." She replied. This was quite amazing, to me, what better connection to the divine source of healing than when she went to sleep. The months passed and she had a couple of teeth removed where the growth was. Swabs were taken at the same time, to see how far the growth had penetrated. Just before Christmas, she was called in to see the Specialist for the results to the swabs and tests. The specialist announced: "I think we have a Christmas present for you. There is no sign of any further malignancy."

145

At Christmas I decided to give her hands on healing and explained that what she had been receiving at 9 pm on Tuesdays, was what is commonly called absent or distant healing, which we had sent out as a group every Tuesday night. I suggested that maybe she would like to experience hands on healing - the laying on of hands. My sister, who had been holding her thumb in agony, since she arrived, said; "All right I will believe you if you can cure my thumb. I fell down and bent it right back. It is extremely painful."

I explained that healing did not claim to cure and although it had helped every known disease or problem, not every person had been helped, as there are many causes behind the problem. I looked to the heavens and said to myself that everyone expects miracles. I began to make my link to the source and proceeded to put my hands on her shoulders, as my sister remained open eyed, did not relax at all but turned round and repeated all through: "Don't forget my thumb." Eventually as I put my hands over her thumb and I reassured her: " I have done your thumb."

I finished and sat down wondering why people expected miracles immediately, before believing, when suddenly my sister remarked; "That's good the pain has gone from my thumb - it's better." I sat back flabbergasted and just marveled at the way the power of the divine spirit does work.

After Christmas I continued my journey to Findhorn for "Creating the New" over the New Year period. This was an important and very interesting movement into the future. I stayed with friends in Aberdeen before continuing my journey. On arrival I was interested in how trust was built up and the layout of the building. As I explored I was pleased to see a pile of blankets outside the sanctuary similar to my own sanctuary at home. They must feel the cold draughts here too. The exercises confirmed that the work in my home and at Findhorn used the same source of spiritual information.

One day whilst meditating in the Sanctuary I 'saw' a huge pottery coil in the corner of the sanctuary, which seemed to be similar to the ones on huge electricity power lines. This meant, to me, there was a tremendous power coming in to the sanctuary and building with everyone but it was protected and safe as it went through the safety coil. For our daily morning task, I chose to do Meditation each day with a group.

One day we were directed to do a walk up the meditation hill at the back of Cluny Hill house. We met in the Family room and linked together in silence, then set off in single file. I followed the others. As we were walking in meditation I looked up to the hill, we were walking towards and saw about 6 to 8 monks in an off white colour robe, climbing the hill. I was quite taken aback. 'There must be a monastery around here somewhere.' I thought to myself as I continued walking. On returning to the Family room, which we had started from, I looked around at everyone else and saw each person overshadowed by a monk. 'Had they picked up the ones on the hill or were they already connected from a previous lifetime as a monk?' I queried to myself. Afterwards I pondered on what I had seen and decided to ask a long-standing member of the Community about the history of the area, and where a monastery could be located. He asked me what colour the robe was. Off white" I told him as I described what I had seen.

"There has never been a monastery around here. Are you sure they are not Druids because what you have described could be?" He smiled back to me. "Of course they could be!" I exclaimed, as that would tie in with the tremendous earth power being fed into the sanctuary. I thanked him for helping me sort out the puzzle.

A day later I decided to walk over to one of the other houses, a short walk away. It was a beautiful day and I was quite wrapped up in the beautiful scenery, miles away, when I was strongly impressed to climb the hill at my left. I looked up and thought it was a bit too steep but puffing a little as I climbed the hill I reached the top. I stood 'gob smacked.' There in front of me was a tower, similar to the one at the top of Glastonbury Tor!! What was the connection? I wondered. It must have some significance to the pilgrimages the Druids made when they followed the magnetic ley line energy in the earth but why a tower in two places. What was the connection? I was certainly following an adventure in to unknown territory. I investigated further and found a map denoting this tower to be Nelson's Tower.

During one exercise with the main Tutors, I went flying out in space and on looking down towards the Earth, I saw a grid of triangles connected to, what seemed to be a space network. The facilitator called us to experience the earth and I flew back to see a timid deer come out of a forest. Was this the peace or me that was to come to the earth? The grid network reminded me of the North American stories about a Spider fashioning the Universe and linking the planets with its web.

On New Years Eve we went to the Universal Hall for an hour long World Peace Meditation. It took half an hour of raising vibrations, and consciousness to a wonderful height, in a band of light around the world and it took another half of an hour to gently come down again and anchor in the physical body. Even then I felt like I still had my feet off the ground. It was wonderful to be with such a lovely group of people.

As we waited for Dinner that evening, I went outside for a cigarette and looked at the clouded sky. Suddenly the clouds parted and a full moon shone through with a complete rainbow all around it in bright colours. It was pure magic and I couldn't believe it. I had never seen anything like it before. I then ran inside to tell the others to look out of the window and see this for themselves. Some went to the window and saw the rainbow just beginning to fade as the clouds moved over the moon and all was hidden again.

"Sunbow *(also known as a Sun-dog, or Whirling Rainbow)* is a rare natural phenomenon of light in a wide circle around the Sun. According to science, the circular rainbow is produced by the reflection of the sun's light on ice crystals in the atmosphere. Among the Hopi Indians it has long been understood that a time of great change would be signaled by an increase in the number of visible Sunbows. Traditional Elders say that the sign is warning the people to live in respect and harmony with all the creations that make life possible - plants, animals, water, minerals, winds and other human beings. The whirling rainbow will appear in the form of a Sun-Dog to those who are ready to see, which will be the Sky language sign that the Secret and Sacred Teachings are to be shared with all races. Enough of the Children of the Earth will be awakened to carry the responsibility of the teachings, and the healing process will begin in full swing."

There are many people who have rainbows signaling them as a sign already. If people act with respect, from their hearts, the time of transition, we are living through, can happen with less suffering, if we respect the Sacred Hoop of Life.

That night in celebration of the New Year, a Vigil was being kept from 8pm to 8 am, to bring the New Year in through Meditation. This was a very powerful beautiful experience, which was to remain with me for life. This was to be the only way I would ever bring the New Year in again.

Several people went swimming the following morning. I didn't - but wished I had when I walked too close to the water then slipped on the shingle and was washed over with a big wave, whilst fully clothed. I was soaked and it was freezing cold! Why didn't I change in to my swimming things and do it properly in the first place. What a Baptism into the New Year!

On looking through some old magazines I saw in an advert that Peter Caddy had organised and run a Pilgrimage to Glastonbury and Iona from Findhorn. What was this connection? My 'voice' had said I needed to visit Findhorn and Iona after I had meditated on the Tor at Glastonbury. There must be a sacred connection somewhere. Then I noticed that the Findhorn Trustees were care takers of the Isle of Erraid, which, was a small island overlooking Iona. Maybe I could visit Iona and stay on Erraid with like-minded people on a retreat holiday when I took the other train ticket. I looked forward to the next adventure and wondered what was in store as the next episode.

When I returned home I received a phone call from Bob who asked why he had been thinking of Tara and I all day on Christmas Eve. I explained what I had done and was pleased at the link we had in the groups. The next phone call surprised me when she asked if I could believe what had happened to her on Christmas Eve. She said she had been talking to a friend in the street when suddenly she had seen a dog just like mine and told her friend that this dog had been put down just before it had become seriously ill and died. I told her what I had done and she exclaimed 'But she wasn't ill was she?' and I said; 'She would have been just like you just said'.

In January I went in to hospital for a cone biopsy and was able to put off going to Erraid until June owing to the operation leaving cells behind and the Specialist said that would mean another operation. He arranged another appointment for a hysterectomy in April.

Meantime whilst lying in the bath one night I clearly saw Tara standing at the side of the bath. I remembered that before she had died the trance Medium's Pearly King had said he would help my doggie to materialize and here she was. The spirit operators were extremely clever in producing wonders when we least expect it and are not trying to get something. I also remembered that J.T. had also told me that a dog would materialize but if I put my hand out to stroke her she would not be there. I could see the whole of her head, back and tail but somehow knew she had no legs. What a clever dog!

Many, who linked with the world of spirit were accurate on a material level, others were mostly on the emotional level. A few worked telepathically linking with spiritual realms or even with the mental capacity of people in the audience but it was increasingly more difficult to find Mediums on a truly spiritual developmental level who had trained beyond these levels and worked from the heart connected to the higher realms. More and more of the best Mediums failed to pass on their wisdom and development aids, which resulted in this lack of spirituality. How could I help? I needed to learn more about where they were coming from in order to help to clear the debris and encourage the higher teachings.

I had booked a week at Stansted with five other members of my groups and hoped I would find out what was going on as I felt an undercurrent. Gordon agreed to assess us all as a group.

CIRCLE ASSESSMENT 26 3 87. By.GORDON HIGGINSON

To me "I take it you are the leader. Where do you normally sit? Right if you'd just like to relax please. The colours that you have produced for yourselves - that is all of you together. Your first colour is green. For some reason though you must have come from different walks of life and obviously your lives are very different; yet there must be a closeness with you. Are you close friends? I mean do you get on with each other? Yet I would have thought that you live quite different lives, because it's always similar, that in the normal way, I doubt if ever you would have crossed paths in your normal life. You only crossed paths really in your spiritual life because green denotes that. This is the case because it's followed by yellow. It seems to me as though you occasionally must have, I want to say, a heated discussion but I should think you do have quite a lot of chattering or talk. Do you find afterwards that you talk quite a lot? *(Always in every group etc.)* That does come in but there seems to be someone there that obviously has and is under the influence of spirit. Occasionally one of you must yawn quite a lot. Which one is it? Because the power that seems to come comes that way and it usually denotes that there is someone present that is trying to overshadow. *(My 'voice' and me).* So if there are 2 - 3 of you feeling it that means the power is strong enough for someone to go much deeper to Trance. Blue is a colour that comes next so that means there is harmony amongst you and I would certainly say that it is a spiritual thing rather than anything else because blue being the third colour rather denotes you are there. One of you has had some problems. Someone amongst you hasn't been able always to give their whole time or their life to it. Someone either had - I don't know whether it's a work problem or something happened. It seems to come in between these two. Which one is it? Are you on shifts of any kind?" Her explanation ... "That's what it is. That'll do. That's what I want because there seemed to be this there and you are fitting in but it did seem somehow as though one has taken more time to settle in to the power than the others, so you are obviously the one you see. So now we can put that right because we know why it's looking like that. That'll do fine. Red is your 4th colour which tells us that you have a very good power there and that you are using it well. I'm going through the colours like this so that we can get to this 5th colour, which is the orange colour, and one of you definitely must heal. *(Me at Badminton and with people in my daily work as well as running the Healing Group)* because one of you definitely has been using this power and it has been used. You see a ray has been used. Its what we call a basic. I would have thought it was from the healing that a lot of things have formed since, *(Quite correct. Inspiration to form a Healing group where most came through to the developing circle)* because the orange ray is the actual foundation of your circle and means that power. It's followed really by red, which is the energy colour that One would expect to see with anyone using it and using it correctly. But I would have thought that in some way either you've all met through healing or in some way

150

where you became part of it and then you've opened up from it, you see here, because that ray is definitely in use and has been used and it is really one of your strongest colours, so I would think that when you do sit either for meditation or anything, you have also been sending prayer or thoughts out to people in many parts because that's really how the power has been working and it has brought about this strong red which means that you have been at the point then, either having absent healing or you certainly have been sending thoughts out to people that have been ill. *(Several cases were confirmed.)* I hope it makes sense because it has to. That is the ray it has built. There is also someone here that will definitely speak under the trance because its there. There is also one of you that will - I don't feel will go into deep trance or anything like that. I certainly feel that there is definitely clairvoyance there and it must obviously be developed. One of you will sense very strongly the presence of the spirit world and you'll definitely feel them and will become very much aware of them so that in the developing class I would expect that one is doing very well. I would think they are definitely having open vision and you have, because of the blue seems to be channeling, as though it is being used and it isn't a power that is static. It seems to be used. If I can get an order of the particular circles you have... There are three circles. One of these is used not only in the development class but possibly also there is healing as well. Then one of you here must not only give healing, one of you is being developed clairvoyant wise and mediumistic wise, probably feel or sense the particular illness there is on the physical body. It must be developed because this is a clairvoyance, it is a mediumistic gift. What really I would then suggest to you is actually then the developing class itself for the development. Clairvoyance should be a basis for them to develop because it is obvious that the colour is being used and it does mean that they should be developed clairvoyant wise. I would recommend you to have various experiments with this. I would get articles of people that are ill and articles of people that are not ill and let them feel 'till they get to know from the article which one they get the illness with and which one they don't and its a very good way of training them to become very sensitive so that they can channel the powers that they are receiving, because you'll need that *(Which we tried and most practised on family and friends)* I have a feeling that this particular part is going to grow in some way. *(And it did)* It is a very alive circle because you all obviously have potential and I would certainly suggest to you that you ought to keep together because it would be a very good thing for you to develop these powers and be able to move from one particular circle to the other.

Now I'd like to get these others in mind because I still feel that one should be developed for trance but you seem to have somebody else as well

151

because I have a feeling the trance, probably, could come deep for one but overshadowing for at least two because there seems to be a group of spirit people there that are trying to get through. I'd be inclined to do it away. So therefore I take it that there are three circles? There is a Physical one, which is purely physical. There is a developing class, which is the development of their power, *(the Healing Circle)* and then there is, I take it, a sort of private class is there? *(Looking at me. I shook my head.)* Well I think I'd advise you. May I just say to you that you should have a private circle of where you can deal specifically with trance? Now if there are those that are showing signs of trance plus yourself then you should take it that each week one person as you are developing, that you take the first half hour of letting everybody move into the silence but the next half hour is spent on concentrating on one person. *(But we were already doing that in the Development Circle and had varying degrees of Trance, from Inspirational speaking to slightly deeper. But this also seemed to develop the 'Ego self' which I didn't like seeing or hearing and puzzled about how to clear that part. Some started saying how good they were and picking others to pieces whereas I thought everyone was good at whatever their gift was.)* That is that only one tries to go deeper. Then, the following week another.

That is a very good thing because it will enable the people that are being overshadowed. Because as you have got the lead up to the physical, I do think that the powers have to be developed and I would think the 3 main things here would be to have the what I call the developing circle then I think you need this private circle where trance and those things can develop plus the physical circle which should follow - so therefore if you've got 4 then I'd be inclined to either have a teaching class or probably a beginners class or if it is that you're using other people then you need a circle where you could introduce people not necessarily people that are going to go deep into it. *(Which Saturday was for and later on Sundays to practice.)* And you obviously do need a practice class where you can have a practice. So, I would have been inclined here to have probably not permanently, a class where you can train people to give a demonstration of say once a month to another class where they aren't with those particular people - so you are getting that help. The colour is very good. I would suggest to you that it is going to take a while to sort it out. Because I can see here - first of all there are those who'd make extremely good healers *(those already in the healing circle who were already building their powers around themselves.)* And they should definitely develop that power and that you are already using it. And I have a feeling that someone will go deeper into healing than somebody else. *(Some became registered healers and others used their healing in their daily lives as well as myself)* because as the power is a basic they are bound

152

to find a channel for it. Red of course is the colour where the energy comes in and you will need it for your physical circle. Blue is that they are developing clairvoyance. If that is the case when it comes to the physical circle then only those that are, what I call going to develop trance should concentrate on trance. If you have 2 or 3 I would be inclined to let those 2 or 3 in the physical circle sort of move away. *(Which I did.)* So you will have to see that there is someone else there that is very alert, that becomes sort of the, either the watcher, that is watching everything that is going on and would be there to encourage anyone should they be going any deeper. You've got to have someone there that will keep alert and won't sort of concentrate and go off. You cannot have everybody doing that but you do need, this is a physical circle and you need someone there that is watching for anything that may come about. Be alerted to knocks and things of that sort. I rather feel that because of this red power there that you'll get results. *(And we have)* It's going to take a little time because you seem to have sort of yellow there. That means someone is trying to get through and I feel that you must let your circle concentrate very much on overshadowing. That means to train them that when they're in the beginning stages - train them to become more conscious of spirit and even in demonstrations to be more conscious of the spirit, than they are where they are, so that they're getting this very close contact with those that are working with them. Put that link first before anything else. I do feel that the young man here.... Description of his colours and placing's in the physical circle followed

To the next. Its rather strange here you're the one then that's going into hospital - that's why green is here at the top. I'd most certainly have said the month of April not at the end probably the first week. *(Accurate for her and me to go in on the same day both for a hysterectomy but he only gave me a glance when I said we were both going in on the same day. ....... More on seating and her Mother/family)*

If they sit in the open circle, keep the open circle to a sort of round circle, and give them space between each one. You see they are not on top of each other. And let them build their own powers. *(Hence my emphasis on meditation, building powers around each and preparation)* Because they will get all the power they want there. Then, when they come into the physi-cal circle, it really is to get your people well balanced. So that you've got the power that goes around.

To another. Actually you are a very sensitive person.....

And the next. You have changed your life. You are an entirely different person today than you were a while ago. Because you are part of the blue ray you see. And it's very manifest with you. ... *(This confirmed what we had all noticed.)*

153

And the lady next to you, because you are sound and balanced you have got some red and some yellow. I have a feeling you are not always yourself.

To ME - Yes, I would certainly say, you will definitely get physical phenomena. But where you will have to be very careful of doing, and that is that in circles you are helping others and therefore your development may suffer. So that you do need a circle where you can build your own powers. And you should have a very small circle of where the concentration can be on yourself. And these other circles - some, especially the developing circle, are having to share what you have. But if you can cut certain things out and probably get a little private thing of your own, it will be a great help to you in the physical one when you sit in that. I still think you need some tuition as far as getting you in the deeper state of trance. *(Which spirit trained me for in meditation alone.)* So you must think that up - of how you can do it. Your life is very full, at the moment, with circles and training classes. But, I would work them - that one is leading to the other. *(Which was the way I was already being inspired).* But don't miss out you see. You have got powers, but they still need to be given the opportunity. Are you putting a table in the middle? Are you in a room with lots of furniture? I take it you can't go into another room or empty another room? Why I'm saying that is, that every piece of your furniture is absorbing the power. Therefore it is going to take longer etc. etc. etc. on physical." *(I emptied the room upstairs that autumn and it became the most powerful room in the house but for me to develop in, alone or be watched and amazing things happened.)*

An outbreak of selfishness came after this assessment. I was unaware of the cause until I realised that each one wanted to be a star performer and one was definitely not happy that Gordon didn't pick up their stardom. Three of the others were disgruntled about how their own work was going to develop. This selfishness was not my idea of spirituality and I knew spirit would have it right. It is in giving that we receive and none of these were prepared to give anything - they wanted the fairy off the Christmas tree before they had even planted it in a pot.

Gordon's trance evening was superb with Paddy connecting five Jenny's in the College and his subsequent Phenomena demonstration linked each of the ones he didn't speak to the night before linking the two who were in our group very cleverly together, very, very cleverly, causing some exclamations at the accuracy and shrieks of laughter too, which caused Charles to fling his arms round me, afterwards, acknowledging the brilliance of it all. The atmosphere was electric. To have had physical phenomena communications from both of the Physical Phenomena weeks, I had attended, was a real treat. At the end of the week I was given a poem that seemed very apt.

## MEDIUMS RARE by Nick Nichols March 1987

Well as you all know, for the great Sunday show
Mary didn't half lead me a dance.
She insisted I play the hymns for the day,
But I nearly ended in trance.

With a wink and a smile, I melt in a pile
There was no way that I could repel her.
If you are like me, I'm sure you'll agree,
She knows how to get round a fella.

T'was with these words of charm that she twisted my arm
"Come on - Anything's better than nothing."
How was I to know, I should have said NO?
But too late - half the music was missing.

And not only that, there were half the notes flat
And I didn't know one of the tunes,
It could not have been worse if I'd lost half the verse
And played what was left on the spoons.

Now it would appear, although I didn't hear,
I've no reason to doubt it's not right,
Betty's voice loud and clear, called for all round to hear:
"Can I have all you young men tonight?"

So in answer to prayers, we moved all the chairs
Many times. Oh we were so busy.
One circle here and one circle there
And one circle - Oh I got dizzy.

Now in his position it is only fitting
For Charles to be so upright.
With a ring of his bell and a look that spells - well
"Did you see flying kettles last night?"

He takes care of the place with a smile on his face
All is cherished with such loving care.
He looks after the grounds, and you can sit down,
But mind you don't damage a chair!

The lectures by Gordon are something to hear.
He quite often talks about dying.
And we all finish up with tears on our cheeks,
But don't know if we're laughing or crying.

As mediums go, there's one thing I know,
You'll be pushed to find anyone better.
But one day I'm sure, you'll find on the floor,
Bits of wool that was once a blue sweater.

Well with this little thought in a week that's too short,
Tomorrow we all have to part.
But one thing that's true, of each one of you.
You'll leave with more love in your heart.

Now when you get home and feel you need lifting,
You can easily answer your call.
Sit down, meditate, let yourself float away,
Then come back and drift all round The Hall.

In April I went into hospital for a Hysterectomy on the same day and at the same time as Jenny, but after being prepared for the operation, the Surgeon came to my bedside and said he had another look at my slides. He had changed his mind and found he could manage without doing a hysterectomy. I said he had to go ahead now I was off work for 3 months and had been prepared. He laughed and said he thought I would have been pleased to only have a small operation as a hysterectomy could cause other problems. Maybe Gordon had somehow known this when he said about going in to hospital and my healers had gone to work on me. He gave the day as being important for Jenny but just gave me a funny look!

After Jenny's operation I was surprised to find that three of my sitters were planning to open a Circle behind my back. I let them move away. I only hope they have the right influences behind them, I thought to myself as I picked up they only wanted to show off what they could do and were not in tune with the infinite powers of the divine.

Because all the cells had not been taken away with my first operation

I now awaited a second operation. I phoned the rail ticket Company and explained the situation enquiring about taking the other train ticket. They said that I needed to take it before the end of June. I was then able to alter the date of my trip to Erraid and Iona to June, which was much better.

The amount of yawning I did over the magnetic natural earth energy ley lines had increased and become much stronger, since Glastonbury, causing me to think I had opened to being a Human Dowser of some kind. I also noted that negative energy was burped through me. I planned a journey to Scotland and stayed with the same friend, in Glasgow, I had visited before. I invited her to join me on Erraid and we journeyed together. The trip from Glasgow to Oban, by train, was out of this world in the most beautiful countryside. I constantly felt the power of Spirit and yawned continuously. Then after spending a night in a B & B we took the Ferry to Mull and journeyed across the island in glorious sunshine, with flowers everywhere, causing me to forget the outside world. The scenery was very beautiful. I seemed to be in a dream world.

A brief Ferry to Iona and we had arrived! We walked up to the Abbey and felt the marvelous peace and tranquility of this beautiful island. We stopped at the original small building, just before reaching the Abbey, and sat and meditated. There was such an overpowering feeling of oneness, I allowed myself to float like a breath on the moment. Time was getting along as we decided to quickly look around the Abbey before taking the ferry back to Mull and catching the boat to Erraid. At low tide you can walk to the island but the tide was coming in fast. I phoned and asked if we could be collected. My friend only stayed one night then returned to Glasgow with some others who were returning after their holiday. I stayed on and agreed to go back to her on the Saturday after the Solstice Celebration as she had booked me on a Psychic supper.

The Sanctuary overlooking the Isle of Iona was wonderful and full of Love, which I thoroughly enjoyed for Meditations with the beautiful power of spirit. I also decided to explore the Island and spent time walking over the mountainous countryside amidst beautiful flowers and the sheep that grazed the hills.

One day I returned to Iona and walked over the island to view the other side. On the way I noticed stones in a sort of Circle and sat on the rocks looking out to sea admiring the wonderful view. Suddenly all the hills and rocks took on a red outline - they were glowing and radiating red. I thought that they must be a part of the lost continent as none of the hills on the mainland had ever done this. They had a different format. A while later I began to walk back and mentally aimed to find out why the stones were not marked on the map. When I walked in the shop and asked what the

Circle of stones was, I learned that it was in fact known as the Hermit's Cave. I laughed and said I expected the Hermit's Cave to have been a Cave and thought I had somehow missed finding that. Fancy calling a stone Circle the Hermit's cave but maybe it had been a dwelling place at one time where a hermit had lived. Without realising it I was in a constant altered state and loving every minute of my stay. The summer nights never ended and we celebrated Summer Solstice with a party on the quayside, which was lovely with so many visitors from Mull as well as the locals. Too soon, it was time to return to Glasgow, as my friend had booked me a ticket to a Psychic supper that evening. I wished I hadn't agreed to that part and could stay longer on the Isle of Erraid.

Arriving back in Glasgow caused me to jolt and jar a little in the everyday world, after the peace and tranquility of Erraid. As I walked along the street to catch a bus, an Indian man walked past me saying; "I can see the light," as he turned and looked at me. I must have been radiating and he was clairvoyant as my feet were hardly touching the ground. At the supper, that evening, I could not stop talking and had a lively audience. When we left a little old lady came up to me and asked if I was a Medium. I answered saying; "Why do you ask?" She replied; "I have been watching you all evening and you haven't been in your body. You were standing to one side. It wasn't you doing all that talking because you were standing beside yourself so you must be a medium". I always thought that one had to be in pain to stand beside oneself. There is a saying about 'standing beside oneself in grief'. Well here was another way of standing beside oneself in an altered trance state of consciousness for communicators to join in. I seemed to be doing this automatically and often found myself talking non-stop until all of a sudden there wasn't another word to be said and I stopped talking.

As my private 2 hour Meditations progressed I found myself out of the body up near the ceiling watching my inert body beneath me and feeling a connection from my inert throat to the real me up at the ceiling and over to the garden door. As I took all this in I suddenly heard Tara barking over at the door and felt the vibration run along this line of connection through me at the ceiling down to my inert body causing me to exclaim at how clever this all was in making a human voice box bark like Tara across the room. Then Direct Voice was possible like all the mediums had forecast.

# CHAPTER 13

## ANCIENT SITES

In the August of 1987 I attended Caledonian week at Stansted and enjoyed the fun and communication of like-minded people. By this time my Circles were changing once again. I always had a core of 2-3 people who carried on with me in to the new Circles.

The current Circle group that Autumn puzzled me. In a meditation I became aware of a previous lifetime where we were all together. All the women wore long Grecian style dresses, although we were not in Greece but at a celebration with Standing Stones before recorded history. How strange it was that each group related to some other life time and, then, either in a dream or in meditation I received a clear technicolour picture of the time period. As I described my picture one person exclaimed that the picture I described was on the front cover of a book her husband had brought home from the White Eagle Lodge the previous week. I asked her if I might borrow it, as I had never seen one like my picture before. The more I thought about these connections, the more I realised there were strange links and connections, to help turn a misuse of energy around for correct alignment. I was beginning to recognize that the many Centre's of standing stones in this mystic Britain were where a great and perfect light has been accumulating for centuries. Years ago at these Centres sincere and Holy Brethren met to practice the mysteries of the connection to the planets and a universal theme. Whilst performing Ceremonies a blazing golden light poured down over and through them which impregnated the stones and the very earth itself.

We all agreed to take a trip to Wayland Smithy on October 11th but the two women couldn't make it. When we arrived I was drawn to one of the four standing stones at the entrance and closed my eyes to link with the stone. It seemed alive. Where as the others didn't have the same feeling. A voice spoke asking me what I was picking up. I opened my eyes to see a young man in front of me. He proceeded to tell me of his experiences earlier that year when he had stayed there all night with friends who all experienced a warmth in the middle of the cold night and the whole place lit up. They had stripped off and danced in the moonlight. He certainly had a wonderful experience. This tied in with many other people having reported lights at sacred spots. Even the Pyramids in Egypt did not have the smoke of man-made lights but somehow enough light had been produced to enable these men to see in the dark in order to draw pictures. This divine golden light seemed to be part of my journey.

159

The journey from Wayland Smithy to Dragon's Hill connected us to the Earth and the awakening Ley line energy, which reminded me of how the misuse of these ancient sights had caused the energy lines to be stopped. Maybe St. George killing the Dragon could have been symbolic of this event when the top of the Dragon Hill was removed and the blood of the Dragon, that was spilled will not allow anything to grow on that spot. We sat and meditated at Wayland Smithy and on the top of Dragon Hill somehow involved in reactivating the power for good to run freely again and hopefully transmute the misuse into creative use. There is a definite quality attracted by and which responds to the influence and the power of these magical places, within each one of us.

Here was another test for me in the current group, with a very strong personality misusing the energies. I knew he was as strong as I was and many conversations proved to me that he saw and received similar information. In fact the first day he arrived at my home I looked to the heavens and mentally asked; "What are you doing to me now" as I felt the negativity of misuse of power and energy from previous existences and realized I had another negative to deal with. Many of you reading this may wonder why I didn't stop these people from coming to my Circles. I had opened my home as a Spiritual Sanctuary and said that anyone who was led to me could enter and be helped. Where else could they go? My being of service as an instrument meant that I would always be guided and helped the right way although there was great difficulty and a need to be completely selfless in giving of myself for this work.

There was a great potential in the group but the power did not flow freely until I passed a pillowcase around requesting healing thoughts. The pillowcase belonged to a friend who needed healing. The room filled with love as each connected to the source and gave of their best. Why didn't this ever happen in their development? How could they go any further if they could not open up and give of themselves in service to the whole Universe?

One, a natural clairvoyant said: "I have just seen a volcano in the group which is about to erupt". Then there was something I didn't know about. This was in the group and I somehow knew that the explosion would be caused by this misuse of the power. I picked up my camera and said: "I must take your photo before you all leave."

"We are not leaving. You may lose other people from your groups but we are not going." Came the quick response.

"Alright, so you are not leaving, I always take photos of my groups and I haven't taken yours yet." I responded laughing as I proceeded to take a photo. We had enjoyed a great evening and were still laughing and talking at mid night. Before the photos were developed they had all left.

160

In the Autumn of 1987 a Hurricane blew across England uprooting trees and causing havoc. I slept throughout the blast only to wake up, at about 4am, to the sound of the Cat crying. I realised that it was windy and cold and decided to let the cat in. The kitchen door was shut and as I never shut that door I wondered who had been in my house. I opened the door and the cat ran past my legs "How had he got into the house and who else was here." I puzzled to myself. On walking into the kitchen I felt an icy blast of wind and saw a gaping hole where the kitchen window should have been! Too late, the window had blown out in the gale. I then heard a creaking and groaning, which alarmed me as I had two enormous Oak trees near the house. I put my coat on and went to investigate. The one in my garden seemed quite safe but the one at the side of the house had already fallen right into the roof of the house above my bed! I must have been dead to the world asleep. I had not heard a thing. I checked how much more damage it could do and decided that it was propped up by the house and could not fall anymore. I went back to bed and slept until morning. The neighbours had heard my window shatter and were very good rallying around offering to help board up the window and walk to the nearest phone for help with the tree. There was nothing more to do as I decided to carry on my work and drove off amongst fallen trees and blocked roads trying to fulfill my obligation to my appointments. I eventually gave up and returned home.

I took photos of the damage to my home and when the photos were developed I saw a white line, which I took to be the washing line. On further inspection I saw that it was too high to be the washing line and that it was actually a band of protection between me in my bed and the tree that had fallen - no wonder I slept right through the incident.

When the 12 men worked at removing the tree, it took them three days. The men who removed the debris and repaired the house couldn't believe that I had slept right through as there were bricks and rubble right over my head in bed supported by a thin plasterboard ceiling. Another small miracle they said, was that the ceiling had stayed put. Could it possibly be true that the negative forces were still attempting to destroy me and the band of protection I had drawn around me was protecting me from these outside forces. I realized that when we open to become Beacons of Light the darker forces attack and attempt to put the light out.

The Circle group disbanded after a few incidents with the negative man trying to take over my direction of working and did his best to manipulate me in order for him to become the "Star" performer, in control of what went on, where he could talk and do his own thing. He said there were a lot of people who wanted him to work. I remained calm, asking him where these people were and suggested he could do his talking on a Sunday when we had an open group or do it in his own home. He was adamant he had to do it on our silent night.

The final week came on November 4th. I was aware of trouble brewing, realising that something had actually happened. I wondered how I was going to handle the disharmony. Would it be alright to send each upstairs to meditate and clear their individual problem? In the end I decided that confronting the issue openly as a group, would be the best way. The first four arrived and emotions were riding high with three of these. What had happened? The last member turned up and as she walked into the room she said: "What is going on?"

I asked her "Why do you say that? What do you feel is going on?"

"It's three against three. Those three against us three." She added pointing to us three. I asked everyone if they still wanted to sit. They were unanimous in their decision to carry on. After a brief meditation each spoke of how they could not meditate and their inner realisation. The surprising part to me was the way blame was put outside of themselves on to me. I decided to risk all and accept this blame, knowing full well that it had nothing to do with me. I mentally asked my guides to draw close requesting help to sort it out. I then asked the group if they were willing to work with me and help me put this right, to which all agreed to help me. The Volcano blew up afterwards when one of the men began to whimper saying that the other man had been to him saying that the woman had decided she didn't want his fat body anymore and it was all my fault! I was quite taken aback as she was already living with one man, and had done for some 11 years. She had stated several times that there was nothing but a mutual interest between her and the astrologer friend, when I had confronted her before with my

162

suspicions. So there had been something going on between them and she had lied to me. Now she had chosen the other man. How on earth could she be involved in spiritual work of this nature with such base sexual desires. I wondered how this could be construed as 'all my fault.' Maybe the Spider she had seen in meditation was herself and the web she wove around each to sap their energy and manipulate each her way, was a misuse of energy from a previous time, which needed to be confronted and turned around into more constructive pursuits.

The events that followed were bizarre, the young man went to a friend for healing but abused the healer by shouting at him before arriving on my door step shouting and screaming at me. I had been in a deep meditation and calmly said: "Get lost" to him, as I closed the door, dispersing the angry energy by not reacting in any way. The nasty, angry thoughts flowing at that time became quite a handful and I was thankful to my friends as I went for healing myself.

Shortly afterwards I had a psychic experience in deep meditation of a big burly wife beater type of man standing at the side of a public bar, looking at me and saying: "I have tried everything to get at you and nothing works." He shrugged his shoulders and dropped his arms to his sides looking defeated. Before leaving he said: "I'm going now". This was to do with the negative one. What had brought all this on?

The young man had picked up some of the wrong influences by talking about psychic matters in a bar and this was one of them. I was actually thrilled to have been able to help one of them move on. This was a form of Rescue Work. I remembered how the young man had been proud of what he had done at work where he demonstrated an angry exhibition, destroying the place, and told us how he had frightened everyone by turning over tables of goods and equipment. There were many things I still needed to learn about suppressed emotions stemming from childhood that emerged as dangerous activities instead of being put towards constructive creative use.

In January 1989 I had to get my holiday dates in before the end of the month and didn't know what I wanted to do or where I wanted to go. I had no plans apart from going to Stansted in the autumn. I fetched my diary and worked out some dates at Easter and at the end of July in to August and sent them in. Then in February I received a phone call from a friend in Cornwall asking what I was doing at Easter and I replied that apart from the weekend at my parents I was free. "Come and stay with me" she replied adding "I have left my husband and now have my own place." This would be interesting as there were ley lines in Cornwall but how could I broach the subject of how I would like to visit these areas to a Science teacher who wanted physical proof? Then my Mother phoned asking if I would take her

163

with me the next time I went to Scotland. I replied that I had no plans this year but I did have a couple of weeks free at the end of July if she wanted to think about going then. She agreed that would suit her and my holidays were taken care of but what was in store?

At Easter I drove up to see my Parents in the Midlands and then did the long journey straight down to Cornwall. I took a book of the ancient sites I felt were part of my journey and wondered how I would broach the subject to Mary. I had no need to worry as the first thing I saw, as I walked in to her home was lying on the coffee table. Spirit work in many ways, their wonders to perform! There was a book on the ancient sites of Cornwall. As we sat down I pointed to the book and said: "I am interested in those." Mary laughed and said that although she had lived in Cornwall many years she had never visited them and was interested on an archaeological level. We agreed to visit some of these sites and take packed lunches for a full day out.

The first day we set off to see the Lanyon Quoit, which is also known as the Giant's table and is slightly off key owing to a collapse during a storm in 1815. One of the four uprights broke and only three were reused. I took a photo of this Quoit and felt one of the stones was correct even though it was a little out of line.

The next place we aimed for was the Merry Maiden's Circle. As we drove down the road I suddenly became aware of a stone in the field on the right but couldn't see anything over the high Cornish hedges. "We are nearly there. I know there is a stone in that field." I stated becoming aware of my friend's puzzled, disbelieving face. A view of the Merry Maiden's on the left caused us to pull up and park the car. As my friend checked the other side of the road she exclaimed "You were right there is a standing stone in that field over there." The fact that I had told her before we could see anything seemed remarkable in her eyes whereas I had felt the flow of energy go through me and just knew it was connected to a stone.

The Merry Maiden's Circle, is made up of fourteen stones which as legend has it, was originally nineteen maidens who were turned to stone for dancing on a Sunday, to the music of two pipers, who were also turned to stone. These Pipers can be seen in a field a little to the north of the Merry Maidens and were where I had felt the energy of the magnetic force, as we were driving down the road. I was very aware of something beautiful here amongst the stones that had a powerful spiritual content that had also been misused and reversed at some time. The time had come to allow the purity back through the earth reconnecting the positive blazing light and magnetic energy to these sites.

Tregiffian is a Burial chamber, a bit further down the road, beyond

164

the Merry Maidens. Unfortunately the road was built over the actual chamber and has cut off part of the original chamber thus stopping the magnetic earth energy and I couldn't feel a thing.

One site that really appealed to me was the Men-an-Tol, which is known for the traditional belief that the stones have great healing powers. The holed stone also has great prophetic qualities. If a child is passed through the hole three times and then dragged three times to the east, along the grass, it is said to cure a form of tuberculosis and rickets. Adults were advised to crawl through the hole nine times against the sun, but I found the hole a little too small to crawl through, so I put my legs through the hole. Definitely a power of healing, which could move pins, placed on the stone. As soon as we had finished experiencing and exploring this site and I had taken a photo, I knew that whatever I had come to Cornwall for, was completed and said this to my friend. "Whatever I came for is done, but don't ask me what has happened or what it was as I don't know. I just know I came for a reason and the purpose has been fulfilled."

We decided to walk on further and see all the sights. Further along the cart track, we came across the Men Scryfa stone, which has writing on it and is an early Christian inscribed stone from about the 5th or 6th Century. I didn't feel anything with this stone and we carried on walking to a wild part of the moor with several stones, which seemed to have lost their connection or maybe I was just out of tune with whatever was there. They were called the Nine Maidens. We returned to the car and traveled further to visit Carn Gluze Barrow, which is a symbolic entry into the underworld. Miners have seen lights there and dancing fairies. I didn't feel or see anything but a mass of stones.

The next day we took a picnic with us when we visited Carn Euny, a village settlement, which has quite an interesting Fogou, built of stone with a circular stone chamber at one end. The village was quite amazing and it was easy to imagine how life could have been in times gone by with goats and sheep grazing near by.. I didn't feel the power connection as much as a link with a quiet peaceful natural way of life.

The whole journey seemed to have a purpose beyond my conscious awareness of that time. I drove home and called by Spinster's Rock in Devon. This Quoit had a gentle happy feeling around it. When my photos returned I realised that I had captured some of the connection in the mist on some of the photos but what did this mean?

Lanyon Quoit
Cornwall
March 1989

Merry Maidens
Stone Circle
Cornwall
March 1989

Men-an-Tol
Cornwall
March 1989

A friend of my daughter asked if she could borrow a book on Atlantis. I agreed to look out one from my selection of books on Atlantis. I picked up one I had not read and glanced through. To my shock, surprise and disbelief, I read about another person taking photos with the same results I had just received on my photos. "In this connection Mr Williams remarks on a curious phenomenon that sometimes affects his photographs of prehistoric standing stones. Several of these are marred by what at first seems to be a photographic fault, an undeveloped patch covering part of the picture, as if a light mist surrounded the stone. The objective existence of this phenomenon was confirmed on an occasion when a friend, taking a picture with his own camera at the same time as Mr Williams, obtained exactly the same impression on the developed plate, a band of obscurity covering the lower part of the stone. Mr Williams believes that this effect may be seasonal and, if so, it may be possible, taking in to account such other evidence as the traditional date of the local fair or feast day, to predict the time when certain alignments receive their maximum charge of current."

It seemed that Festivals, legends and certain times of the year were the actual times that the connection was at it's most potent. It was true that the Churches had adopted Pagan Festival dates for their own activities but lost the truth of the Universal magnetic grid connected to the planets, fertilizing the Earth at these times with vital power from the planets. The grid of triangles around the Earth connected with the magnetic lines inside the Earth; which are anchored at specific places by stones and ancient sites. The Ancient mystical civilizations used these alignments, in sacred ceremonies, to acknowledge the life force energy and link the divine universal source both to the earth and to mankind. Unfortunately there are also those people who use the same energy source attracting forces of destruction, in order to have power over others and cause discord, who can also tap into the tremendous power that flows through these connections. This has resulted in a gross misuse of the power at certain places on the Earth and a resulting blocking of the flow until those of the Light and pure intentions were born with a greater knowledge. Today the flow is being reunited with the planets and once again flows through the Ley lines to the ancient centres, connecting the planets to Earth.

We are all individually, becoming aware of the destructive forces we somehow attracted in the past and are intent on rectifying the damage to ourselves and the Planet, through turning the discordant energy around into constructive power for good. The destructive elements have been withdrawn as the planetary grid alignment is being realigned for the 21st Century according to a Spiritual Intent. These mysterious lines seem to

167

trace the grid patterns which UFO's use as their source to navigate; and draw electromagnetic power of some description from them.

We are beginning to learn that apparently 3-dimensional structures such as crop circles are in fact three-dimensional reflections of multi dimensional tetrahedral forms.

The pyramids, which were built in a precise geometric form, contain the sacred geometry of a Divine Proportion, which seems to be an expression of Beauty in Nature. This proportion is important for the planets which are aligned to all the ancient sacred sites such as the Great Pyramid, which has been shown to contain coded information such as the size of the Earth, Sun, Moon, many planets and information connecting the Christ consciousness. Through using the pyramidal forms the vibrations of atomic and subatomic energy within our individual bodies, aligns us to where the actual atomic level radiates and vibrates. The atom itself may indeed hold the mustard seed.

Obviously my sitting under a pyramid daily for two hours had stimulated energy connecting me to the principle that was underlying the truth of this connection. I was now enjoying the connection to the Universe, the photos proving the connection and the basic truth of where these things were leading me within my daily life.

As I became more attuned to the divine source for inspiration and going with the flow of life so I was often led to various places at the right time. I didn't always believe it, and one time I went to a house, to which I was obviously given the wrong house number. The message in my head told me the correct number but I refused to listen and drove home to phone again. This time I was told the correct number which happened to be the one I had received in my mind teaching me to follow up my impressions and messages despite there being no logical thought behind them.

A couple of incidents happened which caused me to realize I needed to discern the difference between the connections I had with the thoughts of a living person and those that no longer had a physical body. Both ways seemed to be linking like telepathy on a radio wave.

One day I was driving down a road in Farnborough when I suddenly realized a friend was calling me. I turned the car around and set off to her house. I knocked on the door and she opened it saying: "You! I can't believe it!" She handed me her phone saying: "Listen to this." I listened to my own answer phone message and realized I had somehow connected to her actual call on a telephone line. This instance made me realize that the natives in desolate places could also send messages and receive them without the need for mechanical telephones or any other means other than attunement to this divine network of gridlines and thoughts.

When I actually turned my car around and followed my inspiration to the other side of town. I called on another friend, feeling she was having a stressful time, I arrived at her house and her son answered the door, as she was on the phone. He turned around and told his mother it was I. She called me in and handed me her phone saying "I can't believe it; listen to this". Again, I was listening to my own answer phone and she, too, asked me how I knew she was going through a stressful time and wanted to talk to me. After that I mentally said that in future I was not answering every phone call with a visit as they could all leave me a message on my answer phone and I could send thoughts out to help them. I was not willing to answer all my phone messages with an actual visit. It never happened again. This proved that we take personal responsibility and are in control of how much we want to do and how we can cut down on the work we do not wish to do.

At about this time my daughter and her friends asked me to run a group for them. This was to prove a turning point in the way I worked. They did not want any of the Spiritualist things, especially the concentrating on people, which I was also unhappy with after so many selfish results. I asked my inspirers for help and meditated. Eventually I came up with a format, which seemed to be getting back to the basics and the most beneficial aspects, which everyone always enjoyed. Gordon had also suggested we all went back to holding hands, therefore that seemed a very good idea to keep the power flowing from the Universal source going around the whole group, rather than some taking or absorbing the power from each other. Raising consciousness was also very important to me as the finer levels of attunement helped everyone meet the higher, finer vibrations of the spiritual world. There is a distinct difference between relaxing and going down in to Oneself and the subconscious This divine connection through stillness meditation would make the direct link to the source; build the power around each person enabling each to be moved by the power of spirit. Then I would talk them through an exercise to clear any debris, they currently had, through the heart centre, where men were strongly linked before they became civilized and could help each bring in a connection from their own higher non-judgmental self. I combined this together and was overjoyed at the resulting development progress within each person The first time we sat there was great concern about the hyper active dog disturbing everyone. If they shut it in the kitchen it would create havoc and disturb everyone and if they had it in the room they thought it would irritate and prevent anything happening. I suggested that the dog may well be all right in the room and began. The minute I started the dog jumped up behind me and promptly fell asleep for the whole session. After the Meditation I became aware that each had specific problems in their own lives and suggested we did an exercise for them to find their own solutions. I shuffled my Tarot cards and spread them asking each to take a card symbolizing their current question. Then spend five minutes looking at the card to see what came up. I then spread the cards again and said that the next card would symbolize the solution to the problem. Again time was spent looking at the card and allowing the answer to formulate itself. The final card would give a time limit on the situation. I then asked each what they received and was flabbergasted at the accuracies they received and answers to their own issues. This seemed to be of much more benefit than relying on someone else to do it for them. The power of spirit was so strong throughout the sitting that once their hyper active dog jumped up behind me my own controls took over and he slept throughout. Afterwards there was absolute amazement as he never ever sat still a moment and I was asked if I would come every day, if I could keep the dog as quiet as that!

I realised that this form of development brought the very best out of each person without the egotistical aspects of what each individual wanted for themselves, whilst, at the same time clearing, healing and preparing each for their own life's purpose. Each of these sitters went further in their creative, spiritual work from their own development and desires.

My daughter was training in Counseling and suggested I had counseling too.

"Oh yes, I will choose what I want. What types are there?"

She then gave me a book to read about the different types of counseling. It was very interesting to read about techniques, which I had already employed in my business life and daily work without knowing that our management development and training used various forms of counseling tools. In the training I had done at work were several techniques, as well as those I had already learnt in the spiritual fields of development too. At the end of the book was a description of working with spiritual groups called Transpersonal Psychology, which interested me because they incorporated Spiritual Group work, which seemed to tie in with what I was already doing. I wrote down the address.

During a phone call a couple of weeks later my daughter asked if I had done anything about the address I had taken. I hadn't, therefore I immediately sat down and wrote a letter asking for details.

When the detailed list of workshops arrived, I was immediately drawn to the first three workshops and wrote a cheque as a deposit, to book these dates. I filled in the forms and wrote the address on the envelope. This was the third time I had written the address. A voice, at my side, then said; "You've been given that address." I looked at it again and remembered 'Pembridge Place' as something I had been given in a reading some years ago. Immediately I began to search through the typescripts of old readings. I found it. The first time I went to Stansted Hall, Mary Duffy had stated that Spirit were trying to take me to London City Pembridge Place. This was a shock to my system, owing to my dismissing the reading as a load of rubbish when it didn't make sense, all those years ago.

What would happen now? I was really looking forward to learning from these workshops. The very first time I arrived I felt a jolt from the facilitator. I somehow knew he was feeling that I was a threat to his position. What rubbish I am here as a student. I explained that a medium had stated that spirit were trying to lead me to London City all those years ago. He explained that they were not even there at that time! This was even more amazing to me owing to no one on earth having prior knowledge of this venue. There seemed to be a plan and intelligence behind these events, which was outside of any of our consciousness or knowledge how clever!

An interesting sequence of events began to take place as I continued to learn more about our individual facets and behavior patterns. The fact that I was being trained and prepared for further spiritual work and an enlightening future path caused by tying in the differing ways of Psychology, the Psyche and spirituality didn't enter my head until I completed several workshops. That is another story of unusual developments involving the Universal symbols and archetypes in a similar way to the original Universal plan, which highlights the way Native inhabitants of each continent have always developed their communication with nature and the universal plan.

That Christmas I decided to go to my parents for Christmas and take the train on to Aberdeen stay with friends and go on to Findhorn again to partake in the New Year's Peace Celebration. I packed bedding to stop overnight in the car. When I arrived I met a facilitator from the previous year and asked if I could take part in the Peace Meditation and she affirmed that I could. Then I met one who had been there the previous year and, during our conversation, she offered me her bed right above the Sanctuary as she and her boyfriend were camping out that night. I was amazed at the synchronicity and enjoyed being part of the universal programme bringing in the New Year with like-minded people on a very spiritual theme. Nothing much happens in Scotland on New Year's Day and I returned to Aberdeen before getting home and starting work

When I received a calendar of events from Alternatives, a weekend retreat at Glastonbury appealed and excited me. I had already experienced a little of the power and energy of this area and would love to have more. In May 1989 I went on the retreat to Glastonbury with William Bloom from Alternatives This was to prove quite an experience from the moment I arrived.

In the evening we meditated together in the sanctuary of the Abbey House. Twenty-eight of us together and all strangers to me. During the Meditation my head blew wide open with light. Could this have something to do with the ley lines, energy, and the atmosphere in Glastonbury? I had never experienced anything like it in all the other groups I had been in.

We linked in to the energies and walked to Weareall Hill, in a meditative state as well as climbing the Tor. The most potent time was an early dawn meditation in the original crypt in the Abbey grounds. A bell was rung which woke us in time to get up early enough to walk down to the crypt. I lay in my warm bed thinking how mad I was, to actually go out in the cold and sit on the cold slabs, so early in the morning. Did I really want to go? Suddenly, in the blink of an eye, I was jumped on to my feet outside of my bed and I shouted; "All right I'm going, I'm going!" Moved by the power of the Spirit. What or who did this to get me out of bed? When this happens nothing and no one can stop it. I had never been moved by the power of Spirit to this extent before. What was the purpose behind this visit?

I joined the others and, in silence, we headed down through the garden to the Abbey. I went into a 'hold' for the entire meditation time and felt I was connecting with planets to this sacred spot or could it be me linking with a connection that was already there? It was pure magic. A blazing light poured down through me into the earth itself. I became a tube or conduit for this light to pour through.

The history of Glastonbury and its surrounding countryside was fascinating. Once again as I looked out of the side of my eyes, at all the other people on this weekend, I saw all the men as Monks or could it be the Druids again. There was a definite connection to what we had all chosen to accomplish in this lifetime and it was no coincidence we had all met under the same roof. The photos I had taken came back with more rainbows. Was this also a form of phenomena? The crypt showed what I call an upside down rainbow. See photo. The colours show blue at the top whereas red is normally at the top. The original crypt had the same link to the universal magnetic grid. Was this also inspired from a vision?

Rainbow at Glastonbury
May 1989

There have been many people involved in helping to release the earthbound souls who kept the earth plane bogged down with materialistic thoughts and actions. Their work has been an important, remarkable Rescue healing of great importance to the world today. In the olden days a Medium would go in to trance and let some of these souls talk but in this new age of more knowledge, there is no need for the talking as Light Beings and Angels are linking with many healers and using them as instruments as a link to releasing them without the need or danger of becoming affected by their conditions.

In the July I journeyed with my Mother to Scotland. I had noticed how my Father put his head in his hands and realised his time was running out. He was dying. My sister was staying with him and he would get a little peace, whilst we were gone.

As we traveled north, I became aware of my yawning over certain magnetic connections to the earth. I tried to explain what was happening, to my mother, but received a look of disbelief. Our journey took us through

173

beautiful countryside and we found places to stay from Oban onwards. The renewal of a visit to Mull, Iona and Staffa in brilliant hot weather brought a freedom and happiness to me. I heard music in the air and realised that I was often hearing things that no one else did!

We visited ancient sites and eventually reached the lovely Isle of Skye. My mother, as an artist, painted pictures of the scenery and buildings whilst I meditated in the open air. The yawning continued until one day I decided to track one spot down. I turned the car around and went back to the spot where I had started to yawn. I couldn't see anything that would link the magnetic energy across the earth so drove up a cart track to see if any standing stones were in the vicinity. The track led to a farm and there was nothing to be seen. I turned round and went back to the original spot. This time I stopped the car on the exact spot, I yawned on. I got out of the car and studied the scenery. There in the distance, by the shore of a Loch, was one lone standing stone in exact alignment to me. I felt the connection I was linking to extended to the Outer Hebrides, especially Lewis. I wondered if a map could prove this link. We never went to Lewis but a link was made somehow. During the following year I received several cards from friends who were visiting Lewis, showing the Callenish stones. Each card said the same thing: I thought of you when I visited these stones.' Maybe I had connected to them?

One visitor on a Saturday evening had a book about the original Hannan Swaffer Circle, which really interested me, especially when it stated that Direct Voice was caught like a cold from ....who caught it from..... Etc. Is this what I "caught" from the Medium in Glasgow when he held my hand for so long and I felt like I was catching things? It reminded me of the 'Begat' part in the Bible. So and so begat, so and so etc. The other statement that was made about the original circle splitting into two, in order for the phenomena to develop in one circle and for the teachings of Silver Birch to come out of the other reminded me of what I thought was to happen in our circles. Maybe one of the ones who left did take this further and develop to that stage. As development progresses and each is committed to the divine so we are led and guided to part at the right time and the work unfolds in new directions.

As the year drew to a close I decided to have a Dinner and Meditation to bring the New Year in. I invited everyone who had ever been in any of my circles - being impressed that only two of all of those would come. When only two arrived I was quite surprised at the accuracy of my impression. Another friend joined us and the photos show that invisible Spirit friends were present.

New Year's Eve
1989

The Circles carried on and we had many experiences which always culminated with something special before we had a break and I went to Stansted with a couple of sitters, to learn more and have the work confirmed. This time Betty Wakeling gave me a private reading as follows:-

March 22 1990 A private reading with Betty Wakeling.

It's a lady that is sitting there with you. She is definitely foreign. She is like an Egyptian lady and she walked in with you. I feel she's got a very good hold of herself; the way that she walked in with you and she is a lovely greeny gold. You know that lovely green and its very plain, the way she is dressed in it. She either uses you or she gets very close in contact with you. She has come in with you today but I feel in some way you have been disappointed. I'm not saying with her, yet I feel I keep going on you know - you're not turning back because you have opened the door. I feel also, as she links with you - do you do a kind of diagnosis but I don't feel diagnosis for healing. I'm linking in with someone - you could give messages but they are not given in the way that usual messages are given.

175

She helps you and as she links with you, you get something - but I feel you can get it up to 3 days before and don't know who it is for and all of a sudden because I was linking with you strong in a trance state as well. Have you somebody with you when you are in trance? Because I feel, I want somebody with you when you are in trance because I want somebody protecting you. I feel they are protecting you from spirit but you want somebody to protect you here so have you got a circle yourself? Your own circle, isn't it? Are they sitting for you? Well this is right and I feel that as she's linking with you, there is a lovely feeling there. I feel she loved to play string music. I don't know if you've ever heard it. It isn't a violin, it's more like a cello, that kind of... I get a very deep feeling with her and I feel she could take you but you are a little worried because you don't know if there's people there. You can't get right to the point you want to get to. The next 12 months are going to make a lot of difference to you.

I'm seeing pebbles on a beach. Have you lived near a beach? Water? Because somebody is bringing it back to you. *(One year at Stansted whilst meditating in my room, I went so far out and saw a pebble beach in the rain with a pier in the background and a puddle with the rain. My friends knocked on the door for over half an hour before I came back. I was still in an altered state arriving late to dinner, feeling I was 3 feet off the ground. Then drank six glasses of water straight off.)*

Somebody that must have given you that picture and I feel you have to be careful where you put your feet but somewhere linking - if it's not 3 children it's 3 people. Have you got 3 people in your family? Besides yourself? *(yes)* That's what I want. Has there been a little worry around somebody because they seem to be trying to get away they seem to want to - I don't know why you have got to be cut away from your family but you will only get irritation - so you are better away. Then someone is showing me this lovely beach and it's got pebbles on it but pebbles are hard to go on in some way aren't they? So I feel it's somebody giving you something, where it's not been easy for you. It's been hard but I feel you are coming through this now. You've had to do it yourself because there's been nobody else to do it with you and I feel that the Egyptian lady, do you know it's a funny name. It sounds like Aa. It's an A. It starts with an A It's like Ama. I feel it's like Alma. In a way the name that I'm getting with this lady She is definitely Egyptian and she definitely looks after you. In a way, perhaps it's you consciously. It's a lady looking after you and she comes back to say; "I am the lady that's looking after you." I feel it is part of what you have built up with yourself, so in some way you have been very drawn to - have you ever been to Egypt? I feel she is very dominant with you. I'm not saying domineering. She uses you quite a lot but I feel you can trust her you

176

sometimes feel you don't know where to put your trust don't you? In your spiritual work but I feel it's going to be slower perhaps than what you thought it was going to be, because I do feel they take you. They take you into a kind of a deep I won't say awareness of yourself as well but that is where you get pictures. I think if you wrote them down because I feel that I am getting pictures of different and you don't always know the people but that doesn't matter. I'm sure you work, yourself, out of the body. Out of the body is a lovely experience because you get experiences out of the body. You see you are working that way I feel it's a way the spirit people have chosen for you and I also feel you can do without discord or irritation so they take you out of the body and give you the experience. I feel it is the right way for you. You know it is a lovely way because you help a lot of people.

A lot of people do work out of the body and they don't realise they are doing it. Sometimes whilst our soul is out of the body talked about in spirit. Well that's the right way to go so you are doing it the right way but it's the experiences. Do you know, as you are linking there and I feel - Are you conscious of your hands? I feel your hands are important. Well they are to a lot of people. Well they are to you because you cannot do anything without your hands. It's a good way because spirit people use your hands. A little coloured girl, she is laughing. I'm sure that she has been in Africa. She is lovely - her face is a lovely colour black. It is her that whispers to you. She has been with you a long time. You must have been sitting for development quite a while; haven't you? I feel I've been sitting - you got it. You're sitting quiet you see. You have learnt yourself, how to do it haven't you?"

It was always good to get confirmation of the things that happened and I always enjoyed the break.

Whilst walking around the lake at Stansted I took a photo and when it was developed I was astounded to find all sorts of things in it, whichever way it was turned.

177

In the summer my Swiss friends came to England and we met in London to see the sights. When we met I was taken aback at the light they emanated and my friend also jolted on seeing me, which caused her to invite me to Geneva for a holiday where I found out she had also been working spiritually - although we had never discussed it owing to the language barrier. I took photos and was quite astounded to find that outside St. Paul's Cathedral the atmosphere on Easter Day was able to produce a rainbow of colours over the picture.

The following year I visited Cornwall once again. This time we visited Bodmin Moor on Easter day. We visited Dozmary Pool. The lake supposedly where the Lady of the Lake took King Arthur's sword, shows another upside down rainbow alongside it.

Dozmary Pool Cornwall
Easter Day 1990

The Cheesewring
and Hermits Cave
15th April 1990

178

We then walked amongst the Hurlers stone circles on our way to visit the Cheesewring, which stands high on a rock, overlooking the moor. The Hurlers is actually a combination of three stone circles, which are close together on Bodmin Moor. These are supposed to be men turned to stone for hurling a ball on a Sunday. We walked on to the Hermit's cave, where a man had lived, isolated on the moor. The original dwelling had been moved but the stone on the roof was the original. I had read about the hermit studying the stars at night from the roof of his hut and decided to sit on the roof, which was carved with a series of squares joined together known as 'the Unsolved Problem'. I sat and linked to the stone when a strange thing happened. Like a computer in my forehead, I received a clear technicolour printout stroke by stroke of a flower with a stalk and leaves in a lovely shade of blue! Immediately I realised there was intelligence from somewhere in space or one of the planets, aligned with this area that was communicating with me. This was quite exciting even though I had no idea which planet, who or where the information came from. We walked around the Cheesewring and returned to the car.

The next stop was Trethevy Quoit. Trethevy Quoit is the most impressive 15-foot Quoit and had a Capstone with a hole in it. We must have arrived about midday on Easter Day. This was an enormous stone Quoit. We walked around it, impressed with the magnitude of this enormous relic of a pre-historic time. We both took photos and then went off to find a cafe and had lunch.

The following day we visited St. Michael's Mount and I had a feeling of completing a journey as we sat in the Chapel.

When my photos were developed and I saw the rainbow emanating from the base of Trethevy Quoit, I realised that the connection to the planets was the prime link these Quoits had and that they were built on natural magnetic earth energy within the Ley line system. Surely the knowledge and Pagan festivals were copied and adopted by religions. Originally the communication between planets and the earth was accepted and celebrated with feast and festival days, still prominent in many parts of the country. Obviously a greater spiritual link existed in ancient times and telepathic communication operated somewhat like the communications Native Aboriginees and the Tibetan Monks used, when sending messages to one another.

St Michaels Mount
16 April 1990
Showing a red path
up the Mount

A Dagger like object
over the well

The light leading up the hill on St. Michael's mount finishing with a dagger like shadow and various colours at the Well on St. Michael's Mount left me gob smacked! There was definitely something happening and I was, somehow involved as the instrument, which helped, these things show on photographic material even if they are unseen to the naked eye. Whereas Christian feast days, such as those still happening in Spain, torture animals as sacrifices to the Gods, the rainbow at St. Paul's Cathedral and now the one showing directly from Trethevy Quoit were part of my own journey to search for the truth of the matter which involved this blazing light connecting through me to the very earth itself. Recent research demonstrates that not only our planet but other planets within the solar system give evidence, through the placings of the vortexes, volcanoes and sacred sites, of the existence of underlying tetrahedral forces within the planetary structure.

Trethevy Quoit 12 noon 15 April
Easter Day 1990

The etheric body is our light body, which links us to the light body of the Earth. The Light body is not something which we have to create but that which already exists at higher levels of consciousness as our divine etheric imprint. Everyone of us has at some time felt and thought discordant thoughts, spoken negatively and brought disharmony into our own lives, all vibrating within the body and around it in the individual's aura. We create a vibratory resonance with this fact. We create a vibratory resonance with this imprint to which animals are extremely sensitive. If we are inwardly balanced then children and animals respond by drawing close. Through interdimensional communication this vibratory resonance links us through our individual Light body. Our divine matrix and coding is held in the light body, in the same way that the planets ability for sacredness is stored in the grid lines. The state of the light body reflects in our physical condition and any damages to our light body affect our ability to balance and handle light. By energizing, vitalising and healing the etheric body we create a clearer vehicle for light to pass through and literally step up our ability for Earth service. I seemed to be involved in healing the earth this way - as future journeys were to also prove. There are many tools available to enhance the vibrational alignment of the physical emotional and mental vehicles, which then, magnetically, attracts the Soul's Light to merge with the Personality's life. Through meditation and the proper use of sound, colour and geometric forms one can safely facilitate the alignment between the lower chakras and the upper chakras through the heart centre.

While passively meditating the 2nd ray of Love Wisdom and intuition is brought into action. The sacred geometric web, which entwines the Cosmos solar system and planets, as I had seen in the triangles around the world connecting the earth and planets at Findhorn, contains a precise geometric relationship based on the tetrahedron and the pyramid. The tetrahedron represents the Fire principle, which Pythagoras spoke of. The principle, which makes changes within all things. The dictionary says: - a solid figure enclosed by four equilateral triangles. This is the seed geometric pattern, which underlies all other patterns. Could this be the "Mustard Seed?" We are beginning to learn that apparently 2-dimensional structures such as crop circles are in fact two-dimensional reflections of hyper dimensional tetrahedral forms. The pyramids, which are built in precise geometric form, contain the angles of the Divine Proportion, which is the expression of Beauty in Nature. This proportion is integral to the planetary matrix and is reflected in ancient sacred sites such as the Great Pyramid. It has been shown to contain coded information such as the size of the Earth. Sun, moon and the birth dates, transition dates and reappearance of the Christ Spirit. Through using the pyramidal forms the vibrations of atomic and subatomic energy within the body stabilises to where the atomic level radiates and vibrates.

Obviously sitting under my pyramid daily for two hours had stimulated energy connecting me to the principle underlying the truth of this connection. I was enjoying the energies, photos and underlying truth of where these things were leading me within my daily life. Everyone who is aligned to dissolve their human creation will free themselves of the negative discord in their lives and become Master everywhere they move in the Universe. How many Masters are already out there? Over 32-recorded Saviour Gods have been worshipped around the World. They all 'Ascended' after dying and were seen after death, causing some form of worship instead of emanation. The Ascended Master is as far above a disembodied individual as Light is above darkness. They show themselves as Light without a form and are androgynous which is neither masculine nor feminine. In fact, as we build our own light within us and shine brightly, the Light dispels darkness and keeps the physical body harmonious for a long enough time for the cells and molecules to become a fine enough garment to allow the full Power of Light and Love to express and expand the perfection of the Soul, in order for it to ascend, which is the aim of all those who accumulate good in their lives.

In one of my experiences I felt the enormous power of a Light Being come so close to me that I was vibrating and intensely fragile to the point of being unable to hold the frequency more than a few seconds. This caused me to realize how much more developing was needed before I could ever be used as an instrument for this radiance. Normally the room fills with light or I become aware of blazing pillars of light at my side. At one time several other people noticed this presence and I believe I was instrumental in allowing someone that was helping them to show themselves. Sometimes a radiance of light is all around me and I know clairvoyants can see the presence too. It is a great storehouse of energy, which can be released into physical use, like a bank balance stored in other realms for the individual to use in times of need.

# CHAPTER 14

## ONLY TIME WILL TELL

W hen I visited Stansted in the Autumn, Gordon asked me how my Circles were going and I explained that they had once again fizzled out.

"What is wrong with people?" He exclaimed. Later he returned, after conversing with his guides and explained that the trouble was that most people, these days, are only interested in developing themselves and not willing to let Spirit do the Work, which is very sad. I agreed and wondered if there were any other people like myself who just enjoyed GIVING to Spirit and RECEIVING whatever rewards came as a result, without trying to develop anything. I loved what ever happened and was not in the slightest way interested in doing anything at all with myself.

The weeks at Stansted confirmed my own development. When Gordon asked me, about the circles, on my next visit to Stansted, I explained that they had all fizzled out again. It was strange that each visit I planned to go to Stansted seemed to happen as we reached a zenith in the Circles and many chose to leave at that time, then new ones seemed to be prepared to come in when I returned, as if each visit to Stansted was like an initiation on to the next stage of growth.

I had so many accuracy's in group situations. I thought that all the Mediums staying in the College were way ahead of me, until one day I was in a group where we were all asked to go in to the stillness and then when we received a picture - to put our hand up. I had no sooner closed my eyes than I saw clearly a man with a mohican hair cut. I put my hand up and remained that way until we were called back. I looked around and no one else had their hand up. What was going on - these were the developed Mediums on platforms around the Country? I was asked to go to the front, which I did. I was asked what I got and I described the man with a mohican hair cut and said he was not in the spirit world but on earth. I was then asked whom I was with. I looked over and was immediately drawn to a lady saying that this was a friend of her son's and didn't he have a mohican hair cut. She said yes and I carried on saying that I had her father telling me this. I described her father and said he went with all of his own hair - not one grey hair giving the actual year he died to which she agreed. I gave her his thoughts on the matter and his concern and finished. Now if I could do this and I was not even a platform medium why couldn't everyone else do it I puzzled?

At this time I visited Stansted every year with different people from my groups. We shared a room together most times. We all went to different groups to learn more and I usually missed the afternoon sessions and meditated in our room on my own, receiving remarkable experiences and a tremendous booster to the next level of my own development.

When in Nita's group we were asked if we had ever done colours and the ribbons. I said I hadn't as we had always gone direct to Spirit and missed out the games. I was asked to do this now and with a tremendous trembling inside and my knees shaking, I rose and went to where I was led by spirit. I immediately had to kneel down at the side of Nita's husband and did the colours and ribbons for him. At the end the whole room exploded in applause. I didn't know what I had said but I was told I was spot on and it was very accurate.

On another day I had a lovely message and a reading that could relate to many people.

28 3 88. Nita Saunders to me in a Group situation. "When a Medium walks a lonely path, unfortunately it is unavoidable because it requires a degree of concentration. It also builds around it sensitivity, so that the demands of the material world become quite intolerable and it is necessary for that Medium to escape. For those who cannot achieve that escape, life is quite intolerable. For yourself that lonely path can be augmented by the addition of good friends, who will not stay, and who will not adulterate the direction in which you go. If you cast your eye around you -if you cast your direction, you will see the vast majority of those who aim very high, whose work with spirit is on a high level, you will see with them, that their lives are very hard because of the sensitivity they bear. The hurts and jars go deep. Deep Trance does not, quite, have that effect. Deep Trance produces in most people the basin of Jess. *(Her control.)* As you progress. As you allow that condition to build, you will find you will make many enemies. *(I still puzzle over the reason for this truth owing to my wish to emanate the Ones who had taken this route before. Why were people jealous or envious when they, too, could emanate others rather than pull them to pieces?)* That makes your path even lonelier. Are you prepared to walk that path? If this is so, as you progress, you must ask yourself: 'what do I wish to do with this information? What do I wish to do with the Trance state? Where am I taking my body that those in Spirit can communicate and teach?'

You realise that many many years are necessary to produce Trance Mediumship. When that period of learning is complete, what will you do with that which you have achieved? If you can answer positively, all these questions, then you must make yourself acceptable and sitting quietly, asking those in spirit to come close to you and following their direction and instructions will acquire that. *(Which I was already doing and when the time was right I would be in the right place at the right time for whatever was to be.)*

Most certainly your body is acceptable to use because, already, you have the ability to help and accept. You are in control of your time. You are in control of your body. Once that fusion is achieved, then you have to decide you wish to give of your time. If you have, give of your very life. To work for spirit in such a manner, means turning away from that which you have accepted all your life. By turning your back on your home and your loved ones, which is a very, very great price to pay - more in keeping an open door. *(I had already given my life and this confirmed what I knew.)*

Have you noticed since time began, Seers, Psychics and Prophets were associated with Gypsies? Perhaps wise. They who had vision. They who had the communication between the Spirit and Material World did not have the weight of the material possessions. They had no holds that demanded time. They had the freedom to go where the spirit sent them. That is why they could hear and they could see. As we talk, you listen with your machine listen again and you will find I have given you your answer. *(Years later when I went through these readings I realised that I now had the time and was going with the flow, in the right place at the right time for happenings in my daily life and didn't need other people around me at all. The Pictures came objectively and subjectively, I heard in my mind and as an outside link and I became more sensitive and aware to being moved as well as with a physical feeling of Spirit people around me. I was also trained for the deep sleep state Trance by Spirit in Meditation and used a lighter state for private readings where loved ones came and showed themselves or spoke. It seemed to be for those who had a genuine need or requested for something, in prayer, rather than for everyone and surprised me.*

Privately Nita gave me a Reading, which I will share with you. "They are very happy with what you are achieving, with what you're working at. Take new hope, new vigour and go onto the next step. A door has just been opened to you. Has there not please? A door not just physical, not just material but very much on a spiritual level. Open that door and go on. There's a new start for you please carry on in that particular direction...Very much an Eastern influence. Have you done Yoga at any time? *(Yes)* Someone handed me a Lotus Blossom and it began to open out and I feel very much, this is what's happening with you. An opening and a beginning and that's why I have to give you this message, 'cause it's a way of saying; 'We've got you on to the right track but we'll get there,' but lady I've got to tell you, 5 years ago there was a terrible cock up to your life. Terrible like

186

your whole life was torn apart and I know you've gone through a very severe emotional period. *(This happened when I came back from America and lost my baby as well as when the first group left my circle and my trust in humanity was severely jolted.)* She says it was a distress and now you have come out of that. You didn't think you would but you have come out of it just saying, 'Now go on there's work for you to do.'

Do you know Inge? *(Yes Schwester Inge, she was the Sister in charge of the Children's Home in Switzerland, where I worked for 2 years.)* "Mountains. Tell her please. It's nice to come again.' She speaks precisely so English is not her first language. *(Correct and we all went to the mountains every year with the children too).*

I'm seeing the lawn here and the flowerbeds and I saw you walking on the lawn and I felt there were two spirits always with you, one on each side. It is as if you are walking together and they are walking with you and I feel very much that you have been brought here. This isn't your first time here is it? This is part of your development. Part of your own evolution because there is something here which builds you now and again. Which builds you up when you walk in here, as if something builds beside you and pushes you that little bit forward there. *(Quite true, confirming all I already thought myself. I always came at the end of a phase to be built up for the next stage.)* It's nice. It's a nice feeling, nice light, nice power. It's good that's going with you. I'm also very conscious of.... I see a lovely building, an old building, and, at the side of the building, there are lean to conservatories in which there is a lot of flowers, like hot houses, like greenhouses. *(This description reminded me of Harry Edwards Sanctuary where there was a lean to conservatory filled with hothouse plants, which I loved to visit.)* They are full of flowers and full of lush greenery. I can feel the warmth. I can smell the warm damp air and as I get that, my impression is that this is a way of saying; what you have, what ability you have is special. To say you're a hothouse plant makes you sound terribly exotic. I don't mean it that way but you never really toe the line with other people. You don't fit in to the common mould. There's something that's that little bit special with you in your own way for your own purpose and when I'm seeing that building and that lean to greenhouse situation and I'm also getting that this is a purely Spiritual level that I am on. A purely spiritual level and I feel very much that you are an old soul. Are you interested in Astrology? I don't mean just reading the Horoscope out of the papers. I feel a wee bit more because there is an Astrology thing with you. *(This confirmed my experience after visiting Glastonbury and Avebury, of an Ancient Parchment Astrology Chart that people were handing to me.)* I'm very conscious of that. It's a whole situation round about you. I feel there is a link with you here. Someone is building

187

with you, whose work was on an Astrological plane because there is... Are you born on the cusp of a month? *(Yes)* Because I'm getting very very much an old soul who is balancing, most beautifully, two signs at the one time. Only old souls can do that. They have to be able to balance those two signs. I would say to you also, now I would feel very much, that I am on a number nine please. You're not under the ninth sign are you? I want to bring in the number nine and I don't know exactly where you started but I would ask you to please understand that what I am getting at the present moment, with you, is the very, very strong influence of Astrological knowledge with you. That is coming from somebody in Spirit whose love that was. Whose work that was and it's also a way of saying to you, as far as you're concerned, you will experience, altogether, the twelve signs. Each time you re-incarnate under a different sign. Then, only then can you experience the problems that befall each influence. *(The ninth month, was when my baby died.)*

There is a gentleman coming in here. The English version would be Peter. It's not a Gypsy but it's a name like Pietro and this gentleman was holding his hands and as he held his hands forward, I saw his hands gold and what he was writing, what he was using his hands for, was well intentioned and he is handing these, sort of, gold hands to you to say that which she's putting.... Do you work with pens and pencils then please? *(I used to.)* Because I saw with your hands what you were putting. Yes well I feel you're going to pick this up again or something that has to do... That's strong, this Astrology thing is strong and there is something in your hands, something to do with pens and pencils that you know. It will come into your brain yes, but it's coming out of your hand more than your mouth. So I don't know if you do Inspirational writing or Automatic writing? Yes. It's your hands. This is where the knowledge is coming from. This is your tool, your hand. Whereas my tool is my voice and that's what I'm getting with you very, very strong and just as I got that somebody just beamed a big smile, you know and Jess said again, I bring... and he speaks sort of, not broken English, but um with an accent. 'Again we meet.' I feel I want to drop my voice down there and have a very deep voiced gentleman. There is a lovely man with you and he's saying to you, as he comes forward. He lifts his hand but I wanted as a salute, as he saluted. I'm getting a gentleman that has actually physically met you, at some time. Lady, have you always lived in the South please? Because I want.... Did you live abroad at one time please? *(Yes, Switzerland and America)* Because I'm going abroad and as I go, I have a gentleman coming in that has a foreign accent. Again I'm getting the letter P. Did you know a gentleman that was Polish? There is a gentleman showing me shelter, so whether you offered him shelter at anytime or sanctuary. He comes to offer shelter and sanctuary back. A way of protection and helping and saying: 'Favour given is a favour returned' and he brings this back....

I get a sharing of knowledge, a passing on of knowledge from yourself to someone else. You have a lot of knowledge because I am being told here, you have above average intelligence. I am not asking you to acknowledge anything other than the truth. Nothing to do with self pride or false pride. You do have more knowledge than many people and this is inside and this is two fold, because as I get that, I'm feeling that is from your own intelligence and education. It is also a Spiritual build that you have had with you. Does 1943 mean anything to you? I just got 43 written with you. I just got the number 43 and thought it was 1943. Was that a turning point in your life? *(I could take age 43, when I started groups in my own home or 1943 when I had many vivid experiences in dreams.)* I felt that that was important. There was a beginning there and that is now a course, a beginning of an age, you're associated with. Do you help run a Spiritualist Church in any way, a Sanctuary? *(My home has been called a Church, many times but it is a Sanctuary.)* Because I'm building around about you a Power. I see a Power building round about you and here I am watching you standing in the middle and it's, for all the world. Have you been sitting for Phenomena? I'm seeing you sitting and it's as if somebody has taken an icing bag and they are doing that round and round and roundabout you and it's that, I am seeing. White, so presumably it's an interpretation of ectoplasm because I am watching a white building around about you and it's as if you are in the middle and it's going to take a long time. If you have the patience, we have. I felt we were going to have to build, like a beehive around about you. You will be in here and this will build around about you and I have to say to you. Please you need patience, you need a great deal of patience. You need to allow your own material mind to take second place and to become dulled. In so doing it becomes absorbent and it absorbs even more information. I have to tell you. We are well aware of what you are doing. There is a very powerful religious influence. Material religious condition with this soul who is now working with you. *(A religious person often overshadows me. I have a psychic picture of both a Bishop, who was associated with the phenomena in churches before the changes, after Gregory 8th and the black Presbyterian Minister who both work with me.)* So you can be sure, in your mind, that all you do has a blessing and a protection. You have not to worry. Would you please, rather than have, at the present time, even a bulb. Would you please, for the present time, only work with a candle? Now I am seeing for all the world like a crystal vase or dish and the candle is being popped inside it and what is happening is, that I'm seeing reflected light; prisms of light coming off the candle. I have to

189

tell you to do that please. Now I don't know why but I have never seen anyone doing that so I have to tell you. 'Would you please do that.'? That is part of the next step. It is something to do with the prisms of light that they are going to use. You have a tumbler or vase. Something that is cut glass. Please put the candle inside so that the light is reflected. There will be a way. Something will be found. *(I put a candle in a crystal Brandy glass and we had some quite amazing results with beautiful energies lifting everyone's spirit and causing beautiful feelings.)*

Lady, please have you packed a suitcase? Are you moving to somewhere else? Is someone moving away from you? Because I see a suitcase. A large brown suitcase, either being brought to you or taken from you. I see it coming in and out of your life. A movement back and forward with a suitcase and it's for all the world the bit is - just a minute there are not clothes in it. It's books and papers and writings. Lady have you written articles for magazines? *(Yes)* I saw this and I have to say to you, good, I got this being read by many other people and I wanted to push this a little bit more...As far as you yourself are concerned there is still a journey that you must go. There is for you at the present time, a way ahead that seems dark and seems without, on many occasions, light and yet, it will unfold to you in time. You were brought into Spiritualism and into the higher teachings of Spiritualism only when you were ready to accept. As we look back over your life there was a period of time, where you were not quite as determined and as assertive as you are now. You had to alter your way of thinking and direction because of the way life had treated you and out of that, we found just how strong you were and what you were able to cope with. Everything that has happened to you, everything that will happen to you is part of a plan for your journey through this life. You have strength, a strength that enables you to cope with the demands that this belief will have on you, a beauty that will be worth digging for. At the present time, you continue to sit in the condition that you are creating and from that you will learn much. There will be on occasions, physical feelings of nausea. *(Constantly these feelings were to recur until I put them in the light and handled them.)* You will find this perhaps slightly distressing and yet to be coped with. You will find also, that your demeanour may well alter. As you respect that power which is in and around you, when it becomes very obvious, not only will that develop but also the senses within yourself. Your senses of perception, your senses that you have, at the present time, of being able to understand and to evaluate other people very rapidly. This is a perception and a gift, which many people would wish to deny you. *(So true, I seemed be seen as a threat without knowing of what or why this was happening.)* Do not lose patience with those who do not understand. They have not yet acquired the knowledge, which the suffering in your life has caused you to gain. You look back many years and you had many roads, many Avenues that were blocked to you. *(Seven proposals and I didn't marry!)* You have had three very serious and unpleasant kicks in your life and even yet there are those who will deny you, that, which you have achieved by your own determination. You chose a spiritual pathway. You chose to fight this life and the material conditions alone and in so doing, those souls walk alone. I think you are now well aware that there was a previous time, before this material life, that you have sojourned on to, where, again you have walked alone. You have always walked alone. You are what is commonly known as a loner. That is your way. That is right for you but you see, because you do not conform. There are many who do not understand. Always know that we are very, very strongly behind you. You are going the way that we wish you to go. That way which is right for you. Do not worry about your family. They are well able to take care of themselves, but even as I talk to you, there is a material condition, surrounding you, which is going to open up even further and which will bring you a degree of happiness, but at all times you will retain your individuality. We are well aware of the conditions that exist with you. We are well aware of the purposes that bring you here and as the next few days unfold around you; you will find the answers you seek. As I leave you, I would remind you that the beauty of the crystal, the solidity and the natural abilities are for those on a less spiritual level than yourself - you understand? Have I answered all your questions? Would you be very careful please - not to allow your physical body to become over tired? We are well aware there are quite decided dull patches which are over tiredness of the material body. You like to read, you like to absorb information. You make your brain work too hard".

During the week, I became aware that Betty W. was getting past watching out for some of the students, who needed watching, straightening out and teaching. I mentioned this and was told I was not the only one to have spoken about it.

In a psychic experience a few days later I had Gordon crying his eyes out on my shoulder saying; but I cannot work without Betty."

The words that came from me explaining the purpose of the College and training that was intended surprised me. What was this connection? It must be my higher self that was communicating.

Gordon did three Advanced weeks one year and Teaching and Lecturing too, so I managed to go to 3 weeks that year and learned a lot about running groups, lecturing and leading discussions etc. It was a really good experience until I had to do a demonstration. I tried to link in with spirit and was told that I was on my own for this one. Someone ran out of the room and I thought they have gone to tell Gordon I was linking with spirit. I was right because he came in to the room and stood behind me nodded and left. Although I have taken business meetings and groups without any bother in my daily life this was different in that my mouth completely dried up. I couldn't even finish my words properly and the whole thing became a huge effort. My lesson was learned. I knew for a fact that there was no way I was any good at anything without my link to the divine source. Another friend came up to me and said exactly the same thing about her performance and she also worked with spirit. So these lecturers did not have to be mediums to perform and I saw them in a new light after that although I preferred people of Gordon's calibre who were inspired to lecture under the influence of the spirit world and had a knack of talking personally to everyone, as individuals in the room. At the end of the week Gordon announced to everyone that we could now go back to the Churches and lead Discussion Groups, Lecture and do Teach-ins. There was a roar of laughter from the back of the hall. Gordon looked taken aback and asked what he had said to cause laughter. Then one by one everyone said the Churches would not have them and that Churches shunned them. I had thought I was the only one that couldn't work in the Churches and was surprised at the comments coming from everyone else. It seemed like Spirit were training more and more for work in their own homes and Centres away from the Spiritualist Churches and I was not the only one.

For once someone was able to tape Gordon's trance with Paddy, whereas normally this was not allowed with deep trance, and this is what was said to me: - "They call yer Cynth now - yes - eh? But your name is Cynthia - eh because there is someone here that's trying to get a contact with yer - *(thank you very much)*. Eh they're saying that when you go back you'll be going to see someone that's been in hospital - right? *(I don't understand)* eh you know someone that's been taken to hospital now? *(yes)* - and then you'll go to see them? *(That's right Paddy)* and you've been thinking about them - because you've been sending power and thoughts to them *(that's correct)* and they used to visit your house *(that's right Paddy.)* You told them to go and have what they are having done you said go and have it. It'll do you good. *(That's right Paddy)* You can remember saying it and I have to say that you were quite right because they are going to benefit by what they're giving to them now. *(Obviously something was happening to her whilst I was away, to help her keep the healing energies and stop her from giving them all away. I had suggested she went in to a private room at the side, as she was being drained of energy in the main ward.)* - Can you follow? *(I had said to myself, that I would not visit until she learnt that the energies were for herself and not for everyone else. This seemed to be confirming that what I had decided was good for her)*. So you'll be able to carry on here and I seem to go - as though you go some where and there's someone that comes to you; because you've got your own little place in your own house - *(that's correct)* in the back and not at the front *(that's right Paddy)* and you plant some flowers and when the gardens there, you like to take them out of the garden; because you feel they're better than the ones that are bought *(that's right Paddy)*. Some green in there that you cut from the garden yourself - are you following what I'm saying? I have to say that you've gone through a rough time because your house has seen many faces - that are going at the moment *(that's correct)*. That little place in the back and they've been saying all nice things to you - but once they close the door you don't hear from them at all *(that's true Paddy)*. You say to yourself; I don't know how this is supposed to be working, but if it's working, I don't mind at all - if it's just doing no good at all, why should I bother *(that's right Paddy.)* Are you following what I say? *(Paddy you're quite right)* I have to say you are going to see someone named Susan soon. *(Susan was the one in hospital.)* Can you follow - but it's not your Father but your Grandfather here; and he's brought his stick him. I say that some times by the end of the day, you feel that you want a stick yourself *(I do, yes.)* And you've got a little table in there but be careful about it because you see you weigh more than the table - are you following what I'm saying? *(Yes)* and so I've got to say to you just don't look back and just go on your way rejoicing. *(Thank-you very much.)* I have to say that you will go to a place with an owl in it *(I do Paddy)* - and when you do someone visits you there? *(Yes I do Paddy)* you get a feeling of peace - is that right now? *(Yes that's correct)* ah well they go with you and they're trying to bring peace. *(I actually live in Owlsmoor and this is where people visited me)*.

I know I'm going past my time, I'm working here I'll have three A's and a Plus. And I looked round the classroom and saw that I had a teacher here *(Linda Muir who was teaching the teachers to teach)* and I thought I'd better be on my best behaviour. In my day they had a cane and in your day you have looks. I've been trying to notice, what your face was like and I've just caught your eye as you came round the corner. I have to say good morning to yer and that is like saying good night; is it not now - its been nice to see you if some of you come across don't forget that I'm over here and don't forget to ask for me - and if you put in to your mind the most handsome man with lovely hair that you've ever seen before - you'll find myself - will yer remember what I'm saying tonight? Don't all send for me at once but if you get into trouble the best person that you can ask for is myself".

When I returned from Stansted, I did visit Susan in hospital and she had been moved to a little room on her own and now benefited from the healing. Susan had been visiting me in my home *(with the Sanctuary at the back and not the front of the house),* before she had her accident and ended up in hospital - so all that Gordon said was quite true.

One year I had to leave a day early to be at work. I had breakfast then went out to smoke a cigarette in an effort to ground myself in order to drive back. As I smoked and thought of the week my "Voice" said, "Go and give Gordon Higginson a big hug" "No way" I replied. "Who am I to go in and hug Gordon? I don't even know him that well". The "Voice" carried on stating that I was to go and give Gordon a big hug so much so that I jumped up and said, "All right I will go and give Gordon a big hug." I walked back in to the Dining Room and straight up to Gordon where I asked if I could give him a hug. He didn't look at me but slightly above me and opened his arms. As I hugged him I felt absolutely nothing at all and heard myself saying; "Thank you for all you are trying to do for us." Gordon then looked at me and said; "You are developing at a fantastic rate." I walked away thinking about this royal "We" who was it? Why didn't I say "Thank you for what you have done for me?" Who was this "We" and why didn't I feel a thing when I hugged Gordon?

That night, after a busy day at work, I was lying in bed reading "God Calling" when suddenly I was impressed to look at the wall and turned my head to see an enormous technicolour picture of Gordon with his chin on his hand looking at me. This was clever! How did he do it? I was impressed that he was thinking about me and what had happened that morning. What was it all about? The royal "We" was just like my writing - maybe the same source but why?

The following year I received the next instalment! I arrived at Stansted with a friend and was absolutely frozen in my bed. I asked my friend how she could sit in bed with short sleeves whilst it was so cold. She laughed and said she wasn't cold. I put my vest on under my nightie then added a cardigan, my dressing gown and slippers and was still frozen. I hunted for more blankets and piled them on the bed too and then managed to sleep.

This week Gordon had put me in his group, testing my so-called mediumship. I explained that I was not a platform medium and he said, "I know dear, you will be number 3 - up you go." We all had to do an inspired talk from a word that Gordon would utter as we passed him on the way to the Rostrum. We prepared before going up on to the Rostrum one by one as we were called. This was not my scene at all as I had no wish to be on a platform. I therefore had no interest in pleasing anyone and was quite nonchalant as I passed Gordon and he whispered, "Spirit" to me. I was astounded at the talk I gave about the word Spirit. It was just like I was at the side of myself as I spoke. My guides had certainly been listening to the Advanced Teaching and Lecturing week because all the things Linda Muir and Gordon had taught us, about throwing our voices to the back of the room and specifically looking at individuals to involve everyone in the room was happening, as I threw my voice without trying, looked at the ones at the back, held eyes of some and looked at the front in a 'not quite there' hazy day dreamy state. It was certainly not I and I was being used by someone in the world of spirit. Comments of how interesting my talk had been and of how I had inspired some to a different way of looking at things to do with spirit caused me to realise how clever the world of spirit was.

In another exercise we also had to pretend someone in the audience was a Psychic Artist and all link, one after the other to the same link. I didn't do this sort of thing and wondered what on earth would happen, as I wasn't even a Clairvoyant. I took my turn and went up as requested, mentally calling for Help from my guides. Immediately I had a clear technicolour picture of a man who had died in my forehead or third eye. "Give it to the first one", I mentally asked Spirit. He was waffling and getting nowhere but the picture remained with me and I wondered how on earth this would ever fit in with what was being said. The next one took over and brought the whole conversation around to the point of this man I was seeing and I was able to go on with a complete description of the picture I had been given, before handing over to the next one. This was very cleverly done by the spirit world and amazed me at how the links had been made. I also admired the way each had linked with the same link all connected to the one who sat in the audience as the proposed psychic artist. This was very interesting and enlightening as to how cleverly spirit used their channels and how each one of us had opened ourselves just as instruments for this to happen.

Another day Gordon told me I was to give private readings and said my first client was waiting for me and after that I was not to come out of the room as a second one would come and both would be taking notes. I went as requested and again asked for help with some pieces proving survival just flowing and the rest as part of some knowledge I was reminded of at that time.

Gordon suggested that if we were in a bedroom, with space, to sit with a friend.

On the Wednesday night I asked a friend if she was going to the service or would she like to sit with me. She chose to sit and we went in to a lovely state of meditation, no talking but quite an experience. Afterwards she said we had been in the centre of the earth and it was absolutely freezing although she would have thought it was quite hot there. That night, for the first time since I had arrived, I was throwing off covers and stripping down, as I was not cold anymore. Whatever the freezing cold was, had gone and the temperature was normal so I thought I had completed my work for the week.

On the Thursday, Gordon tested us for trance states saying that the best way was to test and try the spirit and for this we mentally talk to the guide before talking out loud. He asked us all to go in to the silence and as I did I suddenly found my head nodding causing me to wonder what Gordon had seen and what he was saying mentally to whoever it was that he was seeing. He then said "Thank you everyone . That will be all."

As we arrived for the evening I mentioned to Gordon that I had completed my work for the week and he looked at me with a smile saying; 'Really.' I told him what had happened the previous evening and he just smiled.

As the evening progressed, Gordon picked individuals to go to different rooms with different Tutors. I went to the Lounge with Judith. Here she said we were just going to sit in a Circle like we normally did and go in to a Meditation. I sat on the chaise longue and suddenly went in to a hold. Judith asked if I needed some support for my back as I sat bolt upright. As I could not move a muscle, I declined her offer saying I was O.K. After a time Judith brought us back, only I couldn't get back and knew I wasn't being released yet. Everyone began to talk about their own experiences and I would be the last one to speak - except I couldn't open my mouth either. I was in a hold and my mouth was glued tight shut. It came around to my turn and Judith asked if I had got anything to say, then suddenly said "Bless you friend, will you give us a name?" I was suddenly jolted to one side and heard myself saying;" We are a group. We come from the realms of Light and are attracted by the light you are sending out........ " I seemed to be right at the side of myself, like I had been slightly moved over to watch and listen. I felt my head moving, looking all around the room and heard myself saying: "We have met before ..." - but I hadn't and was anxious to see who they were talking to. I was astounded as this made sense and answered my question of who the "We" was that wrote with me and also explained the individual who had hugged Gordon last year saying; "Thank you for all you are trying to do for us." Gordon must have instigated this when he had us in trance states that morning and spoke with whoever he did mentally, causing my head to nod. So now I understood his secret smile, when I said that I had done my work for the week. After I had finished talking and yawned myself back to full consciousness Judith said I must have been doing this for a long time and added that it was better than

196

most. I said I didn't do this sort of thing and this was the first time. I came out of the Lounge bewildered and sat down to think about what had just happened, only to look up and see Gordon come out of the Library giving me a cheeky grin. He had instigated this and knew what had happened without being told!

The following year culminated with Gordon bringing out a picture that had been done in a physical Circle where they all sat in pitch darkness. He explained that before sitting they placed a blank canvas on the floor with paints at the side of the canvas. After the Circle finished and they turned on the lights; they found a completed picture of the Body of Light. I took a photo of this as it seemed relevant to me in working with this group of Light Beings from the realms of Light.

It was after Gordon died that I read the book about his work and found out that his main guide that only spoke once a year was known as LIGHT. It all began to make sense. I wonder what would come next, only time will tell.

197

Cynthia Bradshaw was born with clairaudience and gifts of the spirit. She has trained and learned various disciplines, since 1972, including:- Mediumship, Auras, Energy Fields, Shamaniusm, Transpersonal Psychology, Psychosynthesis, Aromatherapy, Tai Chi, Yoga, Shiatsu and Healing. She is a Member of the NFSH and has worked in a private Practice, a Relaxation Centre and for T.V.B.P. as a Healer as well as at her own home.

Cynthia has been facilitating Personal Spiritual Development, Healing appointments, Groups and Workshops since 1982. Cynthia is a Unique, Amazing Catalyst for change, with an enormous ability to attune as a Conduit for the Universal Divine Healing Source, to Heal pain, wounds and traumas spiritually. Her presence is soothing, calming and relaxing. The Spiritual Dimensions are encountered, then explored with simplicity and ease, enabling even children to understand themselves, with simple truths.

We all have a responsibility to create our own destiny and manifest our desires on the physical plane, without interfering with the destinies of other people. Cynthia uses the Power of Healing for Transformation and Regeneration, empowering each person to tap in to their own creative resources, and heal themselves, as well as sharing her personal knowledge of the workings of the Universe, when a spiritual awareness emerges which causes a profound effect of wholeness and wonder to touch Individual lives.